Freedom Flights

Freedom Flights

Cuban Refugees Talk about Life under Castro and How They Fled His Regime

Lorrin Philipson
and Rafael Llerena

Random House New York

Grateful acknowledgment is made to the following for permission to reprint previously published material: Viking Penguin, Inc.: Excerpt from *On Revolution* by Hannah Arendt. Copyright © 1963, 1965 by Hannah Arendt. Reprinted by permission of Viking Penguin, Inc.

Library of Congress Cataloging in Publication Data
Philipson, Lorrin.
Freedom flights.
1. Cuba—History—1959– 2. Refugees, Political—
Cuba—Biography. 3. Refugees, Political—United
States—Biography. I. Llerena, Rafael—joint author.
II. Title.
F1788.P486   972.91′064′0922   79–3882
ISBN 0–394–51105–0

Manufactured in the United States of America
2 4 6 8 9 7 5 3
First Edition

To all Cubans who have fought for freedom

Los derechos se toman, no se piden;
se arrancan, no se mendigan.

José Marti

Under the concerted assault of the modern debunking "sciences," psychology and sociology, nothing indeed has seemed to be more safely buried than the concept of freedom. Even the revolutionists, whom one might have assumed to be safely and even inexorably anchored in a tradition that could hardly be told, let alone made sense of, without the notion of freedom, would much rather degrade freedom to the rank of a lower-middle-class prejudice than admit that the aim of revolution was, and always has been, freedom.

Hannah Arendt,
On Revolution

With grateful acknowledgments to

Roberto Fernandez Fuentes
and
Cecelia Sandoval Strausz

With thanks also to Raúl Chibas, Juan M. Clark, Tomás Regalado, members of the International Rescue Committee in New York and Miami, members of the Cuban Refugee Program, Marie Antonia Mier and members of the Agrupación de Ex-Presas y Ex-Presos Políticos de Cuba, Elena Mederos, Frank Calzón, Humberto Medrano and Kenneth J. Rosenbaum

Contents

Introduction

There is an unforgettable passage in the history of our War of Independence, narrated by General Miro Argenter, Chief of Antonio Maceo's General Staff . . .

"Untrained men under the command of Pedro Delgado, most of them equipped only with machetes, were virtually annihilated as they threw themselves on the solid rank of Spaniards. It is not an exaggeration to assert that of every fifty men, 25 were killed. Some even attacked the Spaniards with their bare fists, without machetes, without even knives . . . These men, following their daring chief, Lieutenant Colonel Pedro Delgado, had earned heroes' laurels: they had thrown themselves against bayonets with bare hands, the clash of metal which was heard around them was the sound of their drinking cups banging against the saddlehorn. Maceo was deeply moved. This man so used to seeing death in all its forms murmured this praise: 'I had never seen anything like this, untrained and unarmed men attacking the Spaniards with only drinking cups for weapons. And I called it impedimenta!' "

This is how people fight when they want to win their freedom; they throw stones at airplanes and overturn tanks!

Fidel Castro,
"History Will Absolve Me"

THE UNIQUENESS of the Cuban Revolution was that it had vast support from the people. A small vanguard of intellectuals did not have to transform the thinking and aspirations of the whole country. Rather, Cubans from all social strata—the 26th of July Movement of workers and students, the Directorio Revolucionario members of the middle class, particularly those in the Movimiento Resistencia Cívica (Civic Resistance Movement), and peasants who joined the Rebel Army—struggled against Batista.

During Castro's first few months in power, in 1959, a survey conducted by Raúl Gutiérrez, whose firm was respected for the reliability of its polls, found that over 90 percent of the Cuban people favored the new regime. Their euphoria sprang from the fact that the flagrant greed, corruption and repression of Batista's dictatorship were over. Most Cubans were unified in their desire for honest government, free elections, an end to police brutality and corruption, agrarian reform to be accomplished by the redistribution of land among small farmers, and guarantees of steady jobs for the many victims of seasonal unemployment caused by Cuba's single-crop economy. Castro himself promised that the new order would bring "freedom and bread without terror." The new leaders were going to create a nation free from dependency on the United States or any other country. The Revolution was going to be "as green as the palm trees," establishing Cuba for Cubans, and realizing the centuries-old dream of freedom embodied by José Marti, the famous Cuban poet and patriot, in his struggle against Spanish domination in the 1890s.

Several accomplishments during the first years of the Revolution were auspicious. Public work programs were begun to combat un-employment. Though Cuba had never suffered the crushing, wide-spread poverty of other Latin American countries, the distribution of wealth had been extremely uneven—workers in the cities, for example, enjoyed a much higher standard of living than *campesinos* (farmers). To combat this inequity, one of the Revolution's first major programs was the Literacy Campaign. In 1961, volunteer brigades traveled deep into the countryside to teach peasants to read and write. Young, energetic, self-sacrificing *brigadistas* almost completely eradicated illiteracy in Cuba in only one year. Cubans who had previously been barred from learning received the first stages of formal education, and, as a result, were able to advance from menial work to better jobs. In addition, farmers living in remote rural areas received medical care, for the first time. With these practical achievements came the sense of a people shaping its own destiny, joining in a historical, heroic mission.

Since it seemed that Castro had steadily improved the life of the average Cuban citizen—by constructing hospitals, schools, state farms, cattle-breeding centers, and by expanding recreational facilities—I was shocked to learn, while working for the International Rescue Committee in 1976, of Cubans fleeing their country in the most improbable ways. They had not left legally by ship or regularly scheduled flights. Instead, their passport to freedom had been remarkable courage and ingenuity. With little chance to prepare or to take even meager provisions, they had crossed the Florida Straits, clandestinely, in small boats or on rafts hastily improvised from inner tubes wrapped in canvas.

Curious, I began to delve into files and newspaper articles on the exodus from Cuba. I came upon dozens of accounts of Cubans resorting to all kinds of daring measures in order to escape: hijacking fishing vessels, stowing away on commercial ships, traveling a hazardous route to Guantánamo Naval Base. Many who put out to sea were caught and imprisoned or shot by Cuban patrols. Some were attacked by sharks, and others drowned or died from hunger or dehydration.

The risks taken by these fugitives—numbering more than 16,000 from the beginning of the Revolution to 1979—argued such desperation that I decided to explore further. Departures by *Batistianos* or members of the upper class were understandable. But it was precisely those who were supposedly benefiting most from the Revolution—young people, workers, blacks and students—who were defecting.

From 1976 to 1980, with Rafael Llerena, a photographer from Havana who had left Cuba in 1961, I interviewed several hundred Cubans in the exile communities of New York, New Jersey and Miami. We selected only those Cubans who had fought for the Revolution, participated in the new government, or sympathized with it, and young people who were born under it.

The Cubans whose voices are heard in this book are not a random sample. They represent the whole range of Cuban society and were chosen for their articulacy in recounting their experiences under the present regime. Their beliefs, feelings, and reasons for escape typify those of the Cubans I spoke to: guerrillas from the Sierra Maestra days, university students, shopkeepers, truckdrivers, stevedores, mechanics, electricians, engineers, mothers, teachers, farmers, fishermen, factory workers and former political prisoners. They come from the various provinces of Cuba—from cities and rural areas—and range in age from twenty to seventy. The ways in which they fled exemplify the most dramatic forms of escape.

What the Cuban émigrés decry, above all else, is the system's domination of every facet of their lives, which they blame on the one man who runs the machinery—Fidel Castro. Cubans see him as a *caudillo*, a traditional Latin American boss who rules Cuba as if it were his private estate. For the masses, the oligarchy consisting of the Castro brothers and a group of loyal Fidelistas belies the Revolution's claims of egalitarianism and democracy. Fidel Castro is himself Commander-in-Chief of the Armed Forces, First Secretary of the Politburo of the PCC (Cuban Communist Party), First Secretary of the Secretariat of the PCC, member of the Central Committee of the PCC, deputy for the National Assembly of Popular Power for the Municipality of Santiago, president of the Council of State, president of the Council of Ministers (responsible for the Ministry of Culture; the Ministry of the Armed Forces (MINFAR); the Ministry of the Interior (MINIT); Central Planning Board (JUCEPLAN); State Committee of Finances; State Committee of Prisoners; State Committee of Statistics (CEE); State Committee of Technical and Material Assistance (CEATM); Cuban Institute of Hydrography).

Raúl Castro is a general of the army; Second Secretary of the Secretariat of the PCC; member of the Central Committee of the PCC; deputy for the Assembly of National People's Power for the Municipality of the Second Front; First Vice-President of the Council of State; First Vice-President of the Council of Ministers, aiding the President, Fidel Castro; Minister of the Revolutionary Armed Forces; President of the Commission of Patriotic Military Education. His wife, Vilma Espin, heads the Cuban Women's Federation, and Fidel's other brother, Ramón Castro, runs extensive agricultural projects.

The Communist Party numbers 200,000, or 2 percent of the population, and of the one hundred members of the Politburo, Secretariat and Central Committee of the PCC, there are only seven blacks.

Outside observers are often mesmerized by Castro. His indefatigable energy, intelligence, charm, and *machismo* make him an imposing figure. In the absence of anyone else to match his political virtuosity and charisma, Castro filled the power vacuum when

Batista fled. Throughout his career Castro has shown a knack for seizing the right moment to act, an ability to convert failure into psychological gain and a facility for using the media to further his ends. In the days of the Sierra Maestra campaign he duped the visiting *New York Times* correspondent Herbert Matthews into believing that the number of rebel soldiers was many times greater than it was. This kind of clever manipulation of the press earned the guerrillas international recognition.

Castro has awed listeners with deft legal arguments, dazzling expertise on the intricacies of various projects, and paeans to freedom and social equality. He has convinced visitors touring the island that they are seeing the realization of "socialism with a human face." The beard, the gun, the cigar, the uniform and boots, and the jeep ignite the imagination of intellectuals who harbor secret longings to be on the barricades. Physiognomy determines revolution: El Ché with the face of a poet; Camilo Cienfuegos with the look of Christ; Alicia Alonso, the ballerina of enduring style and stamina, and Fidel, the eternal guerrilla.

Castro's dynamism has undoubtedly imparted color and drama to the lives of Cubans who admire him. His oratorical skill has stirred them to risk and sacrifice and work still harder. For many Cubans, however, galloping socialism under *el caballo* (the stallion) has more panache than practical result. They are appalled by the style of his leadership. Instead of listening to advisers or to the people themselves who are conversant with agricultural or technical matters, or setting realistic goals, he has rushed precipitately from one ruinous enthusiasm to another, insisting on grandiose accomplishments that fail to happen.

The tragedy for Cubans is that a leader of inordinate gifts has brought terror instead of liberation. Cubans cite organizations and institutions begun in the early sixties that intrude on privacy, coerce people into absolute acceptance of state policy, and suppress dissent of any kind. Among the mechanisms for maintaining conformity and docility are the CDR's (Committees to Defend the Revolution) —deplored even by former members. Vigilance groups composed of citizens from every block, they inform against possible enemies of the Revolution. Although they have been credited with performing useful services such as cleanup campaigns and blood-donation and immunization drives, their function of surveillance produces a sense of continued harassment.

A grievance frequently expressed is that one feels constantly spied upon by one's neighbors as well as by the police. (The possibility of imprisonment for some unintentional infraction is ever-present.) Cubans remark that instead of uniting the country, the government sets Cuban against Cuban by using its institutions to engender hatred and divisiveness. The climate of fear has introduced a style of living particularly repugnant to Cubans, who value close family ties. They feel that the fabric of their society has been sundered by the government's methods, which divide loyalties, alienate parents and children from one another, and undermine and destroy friendships for political reasons. Older Cubans point out that in previous eras, friends and members of a family could have widely divergent views without ideology breaking the bonds between them. In an atmosphere where friendship is now shrouded in suspicion, the striking feature of the groups of younger refugees is their closeness and camaraderie, which arise from secretly shared ideas and the common purpose of supporting one another while evading the strictures placed upon their lives.

Cubans cite the Seguridad del Estado (G-2, or State Security) as a brutal agency for persecuting alleged opponents of the regime. The despair felt is all the keener because one of the situations Castro rightfully denounced in his famous speech, "History Will Absolve Me," and which had rallied the country against Batista, was his officers' ruthless murder and barbaric punishment of the revolutionaries. By contrast, during the insurrection, the Rebel Army won admiration for its humane behavior toward captured soldiers. But today when Cubans are apprehended, they find themselves completely at the mercy of the government's whims rather than subject to lawful procedures during arrest, trial and imprisonment. Former revolutionaries explain that their disillusionment with Castro's regime began in the early sixties, when large numbers of people were arbitrarily arrested for opposition to the government and when many were summarily executed at the *paredón* (firing-squad wall). Cuban refugees describe intimidation and torture during interrogation, denial of proper legal counsel, detention incommunicado, and the government's failure to present evidence at the trial. In prison they experience extreme overcrowding; lack of sanitary facilities, so that prisoners were often forced to eat, sleep and defecate in the same confined space; inadequate or inedible food resulting in severe malnutrition and other illnesses; denial of medical assistance; the presence of rats, lice, bedbugs and other insects; solitary confinement for extended periods of time; incarceration in special punishment cells that were totally dark, without ventilation for the heat or insulation from the cold; refusal to grant visiting rights, and confiscation of correspondence to and from the prisoner; the mixing of political prisoners with *communes* (common prisoners); re-sentencing upon completion of one term if a prisoner refused to participate in the rehabilitation program; and forced labor for political prisoners in numerous *granjas* (concentration camps) throughout the island.

Ex-political prisoners condemn the punishment of women political prisoners, particularly those among the *plantados* (the stubborn ones), who reject Marxist indoctrination and re-education programs that would allow them to live a little better or be released. Far from being accorded a minimum of respect as women, they have been victims of vengeance for their refusal to renounce their religious and political beliefs. They have been insulted and abused by sadistic guards, mixed with common prisoners, who assaulted them, and shut inside *tapiadas* (dark, totally walled-in cells), where they are forced to sleep naked on the floor regardless of ill health or old age.

Castro's authoritarian rule has ramifications in many other areas of life. Freedom of thought, expression and movement is severely curtailed in a variety of ways. Cubans feel that they are constantly lied to and kept in ignorance about the rest of the world because of constant propaganda, the abolition of a free press, which occurred in May 1960, and stringent censorship of books, film and art. The requirement of having to carry an ID pass and working papers which frequently have to be presented on demand, is considered demeaning. These records list whether a person has ever been a political prisoner, a status which often prevents an applicant for a job from being hired, and which usually bars his relatives from employment in all but the least desirable jobs. Prohibitions against visiting other countries, traveling freely within Cuba or changing one's place of residence without government approval are regarded as undue encroachments on freedom.

Religious repression is often mentioned as a cause of animosity toward the regime. The point emphasized is that religious affiliation reduces one's chance of attending universities or being promoted. In the beginning of the Revolution, the Church protested the adoption of a Communist system. Castro then disbanded the Catholic and Protestant schools, and expelled several hundred priests, and prevented the Church from holding services. Later a number of clergymen, together with homosexuals and others labeled by the government as social parasites, were sentenced to concentration camps, UMAP's (Units to Aid Production). Eventually these punitive measures ceased and churches were permitted to hold services. In the seventies, however, there was a major confrontation between the government and the Jehovah's Witnesses. The sect was banned and its churches were closed on July 1, 1974. The Witnesses do not actively oppose the government, but wish to remain impartial in political matters. One thousand have been imprisoned because their children would not salute the flag, and several hundred young men have been jailed for refusing military service.

In general, Cubans are excluded from policy making. They are not consulted about government decisions, which are issued from above, and at the risk of being persecuted as enemies of the Revolution, they are obliged to accept whatever is decreed. The government declares that the constitution of 1976 and the new penal code are nearly unanimous expressions of the will of the people. When asked about the new legislation, however, Cubans are unable to discuss the particulars because they were not involved in formulating the laws, and were called on only to vote their approval. Lately the laws have become stricter and prison sentences longer. Merely speaking against the government or not demonstrating a sufficiently revolutionary attitude are punishable offenses under a vague statute known as La Ley de Pelegrosidad (Law of Danger to the State).

The Poder Popular (People's Power), termed by Castro "*los abogados del pueblo*" (lawyers of the people), are groups that meet to discuss local issues and elect delegates to the National Assembly. Supposedly a bridge between the people and the government, the

Poder Popular is viewed by Cubans as a sham, offering the people merely the illusion of power. Ultimate authority rests with Castro, of course, and his ministers. Because of a lumbering bureaucracy that causes delays, solutions to problems and materials requested are not forthcoming. Consequently, people cease attending meetings.

Progress made in education, one of the Revolution's top priorities is hampered by the totalitarian nature of the system. Cubans regard education as another means of ensuring compliance with the government through Marxist indoctrination. The notion of free education is deceptive because students are forced to work for the state. Children above the sixth grade work in agriculture for various periods, and the secondary-school system is being transferred to the countryside, where pupils work in the fields for half a day. Isolation from one's family and familiar surroundings, burdensome labor that interrupts studies, and a monotonous existence with few recreations or amusements cause a negative response to this form of schooling. A spirited, outgoing people, Cubans find such regimentation intolerable.

Higher education is reserved for those whose loyalty to the regime is unquestionable. If a person is not "integrated into the Revolution" by belonging to mass organizations like the CDR's, the Women's Federation or voluntary work brigades, a university education is impossible. For many who do receive training for a particular occupation, there are no jobs available in their field. Studying one trade and being compelled to work at a different one is not only a frustrating waste of time and energy but also a source of economic inefficiency because people are doing work for which they are unqualified.

In response to the growing discontentment of young people over the question of work and the large numbers of people who refused arbitrary placement in jobs, the government passed the Anti-Vagrancy Law in the spring of 1971. It states that all men from seventeen to sixty who are mentally and physically must be productively employed. Earlier the government had reportedly recruited 100,000 idle men into the labor force. Toward the end of 1970 the rate of absenteeism was 20 percent. Thereafter, in May 1972, work quotas were re-established with each worker assigned a specific output to be produced on a given schedule. In August 1975 the government specified persons for which it could find no employment as Fuerza de Trabajo Excedente (Work Force of the Temporarily Unemployed). In mid-1978 their designation was changed to Fuerza de Trabajo Disponible (Force for Available Work), which included university graduates. Unable to find jobs for them, the government sent some to Africa and other countries.

It should come as no surprise that many Cubans are uncertain about the higher social good they are supposed to uphold. Promises of a better future abound, but economic deprivation increases. *"No hay nada"* (There is nothing) and *"Hay hambre y mucha miseria en Cuba ahora"* (There is hunger and much misery in Cuba now) are phrases reiterated by refugees. Instead of advancing, the country is regressing, and there are greater shortages of all kinds. Most Cubans attribute economic backwardness not to the U.S. embargo, but to the government's mismanagement of the economy and to corruption, and to the lack of incentives for work. Issues of political and social rights are inseparable from economic problems. The picture that emerges is of the system defeating itself. The use of force and terror and the subjection of the people to daily indignities and scarcities produce apathy, negligence and sabotage. These retard production further, and in turn dissatisfaction grows and repression increases.

Older émigrés explain that the government itself hindered Cuba's progress at the start. Harassment of members of the middle class, who had actually helped bring about the Revolution, meant the exodus of many professionals and skilled workers. In August 1972 Vice-President Carlos Rafael Rodríguez regretted "the loss of valuable technicians who fled at the beginning of the Revolution due to excessive radicalism and other errors of leadership." Thus, it has been a continuing struggle for Cubans to counteract this mistake, and professionals are still fleeing. Although they enjoyed a better standard of living than the rest of the people, infringements on their freedom, a stifling atmosphere and insufficient reward for their labor impelled them to leave.

To compensate for these departures and to maximize productivity, the government has relied on voluntary labor, a misnomer because the work is required. At the beginning volunteers went off willingly to cut cane, but over the years enthusiasm has waned for several reasons. When the spirit of the Revolution was high and when they were not going under duress but by choice, people responded eagerly. Then, as the government's tactics became oppressive and indicated a lack of trust in the people their fervor subsided. With regular work becoming more demanding and with projected goals unattained, Cubans began to reject the idea of volunteer work. They no longer felt inspired.

After the failure of the Harvest of Ten Million in 1970, it became apparent that shifting people around to do voluntary agri- cultural work with which they were unfamiliar did not yield satis- factory results and detracted from progress in other areas. The number of professional cane-cutters had declined from 350,000 in 1958 to fewer than 73,000 in 1971. Urban workers could not make up for this loss because of limited experience and therefore low productivity. Since the use of urban manpower for the Harvest of 1970 greatly damaged industry, fewer volunteers have been "sum- moned" for subsequent harvests. For the one in 1970–72 the participation of university students was drastically cut because their time was deemed more usefully spent in studying. Often the cost of food, transportation, and electrical power for mobilization of volun- teers exceeded the value of what they produced.

One of the strongest indictments of the system comes from *campesinos* who fled. They consider the abrogation of the Agrarian Reform Laws of the early sixties to be an act of treason against the ideals of the Revolution they fought for. After dividing up the *latifundios* (large estates) among the farmers, the government later appropriated most of the land and organized it into state farms. The experience of Cubans suggests that this is the kind of arrange- ment devised by theoreticians who are not in touch with the people, who perceive every farmer with a plot of land, however small, as a budding capitalist ready to exploit his neighbor as soon as possible. The major fact unaccounted for in the agricultural programs that replaced the original reforms is that a peasant—no matter of what nationality or century—wants his piece of earth, with which he can feel an affinity. He wants to be a farmer, not a hired laborer of the state. Castro himself spoke passionately in "History Will Absolve Me" of "*the one hundred thousand* small farmers who live and die

working land that is not theirs, looking at it with the sadness of
Moses gazing at the promised land, to die without ever owning it,
who like feudal serfs have to pay for the use of their parcel of land
by giving up a portion of its produce, who cannot love it, improve
it, beautify it nor plant a cedar or an orange tree on it because they
never know when a sheriff will come with the rural guard to evict
them from it . . ." No understanding of the Cuban mentality is
possible without acknowledging this universal sentiment and other
specifically national characteristics. Cubans are a people who are
at once strongly individualistic and extremely generous and gre-
garious. Even in the most reduced circumstances, hospitality is
accorded to one's countrymen and to complete strangers—usually
with a jaunty half-of-what-I-have-is-yours attitude. Thus, older
Cubans often say that as bad as conditions were under previous
regimes, people in the country could somehow scratch together
some food and share it or trade it for other things. Today, this kind
of barter still goes on, although it is proscribed, and it has become
increasingly difficult for farmers to provide food for people in cities
in order to supplement the small rationed amounts. Some of the
most poignant moments in conversations with Cubans came when
they spoke of the impossibility of feeding their families. It was a
subject they had difficulty discussing because the blow to their pride
was insupportable. The fact was stated simply. The injury and
remorse were expressed eloquently in their eyes and gestures. To
see one's family without enough food was a cruel reminder of one's
own helplessness. For this reason many escaped with their families
and others, who left alone, try to bring their wives and children
over later.

Farmers emphasize that the government's refusal to consult them
on agricultural questions about which they are knowledgeable con-
tributes to Cuba's economic stagnation. By ignoring their expertise
the government makes mistakes in planning, which only intensify
discontentment. An unending cycle of error, waste and hostility
ensues. The government's approach does not allow for the fact that
agricultural production increased in 1958–61, when most of the
land was still privately owned. By the end of 1975, private farm
owners numbered 162,126, holding 20 percent of the arable land.
In 1977 Castro stated that Cuba had the highest percentage of state

ownership of land of any country in the world. He did not mention that one fifth of the land in private hands produced 80 percent of the total tobacco and coffee, 60 percent of the vegetables, 50 percent of tubers and fruits, 33 percent of the cattle and 18 percent of the sugar cane. Recently farmers have been permitted to sell surplus products, but previously, buying food from a farmer was an "economic crime." Like the farmers who were dispossessed, many shopowners have fled, especially after 1968, when the government took over the rest of the small businesses—even street stands and kiosks.

When medium-sized farms were incorporated into official plans, 10,000 farmers were abruptly expropriated. In response, farmers engaged in seven years of armed opposition, especially in the Escambray. An estimated 3,591 *campesinos* were killed in the struggle. A plan was then instituted whereby thousands of *campesinos* were sent to prisons and work camps, and their wives and children to re-education centers. Farmers were transferred to other provinces and were prohibited from returning to their villages.

Cubans describe the problem of rationing as one of several symptoms of the worsening economy. Begun in May 1962, rationing has grown more stringent. The hardships are twofold: meager quantities and lack of diversity, and the considerable time consumed waiting in line to purchase essentials. Consequently, a black market has developed. In discussing it, the escapees express a sense of debasement at having to resort to illegal ways just to find sufficient food for their families. They were forced to become criminals subject to stiff penalties if caught for behavior that did not arise from venal motives but desperation. For others, wages are too low to afford contraband goods to supplement the inadequate quotas allotted. One of the gravest consequences of the prevailing economic chaos is increasing theft and prostitution just to obtain food or clothing. In order to acquire simple appliances, it is necessary to participate in a highly competitive system. If one wins enough points from membership in the mass organizations and for doing many extra hours of voluntary work, one's name may reach the top of a list of exemplary workers. Then there is a chance to buy an item like a small refrigerator, which costs about 600 pesos, the minimum monthly salary being 95 pesos.

A serious housing shortage has driven many Cubans to flee. According to an article on February 16, 1979, in *Bohemia,* a government magazine, only 16,500 residences were built in the previous year, while 25,000 are destroyed annually for lack of repairs. Although willing and able to salvage existing buildings, Cubans cannot secure the materials. Apartments are crowded, with as many as nine people living in one room. Couples often cannot get married because they have no place to live, or they must remain with their families. Others marry, but each spouse must continue living with relatives. As a result of these conditions the number of divorces has risen.

Life has become mere subsistence, work for the sake of working. Older Cubans say that few of the dreams they fought for have been realized and that existence becomes harsher all the time. The younger ones say that the glorious days of the Sierra Maestra are history to them, part of the propaganda that inundates their lives while their world is grim and mechanical, requiring either lip service to slogans and posing as a good revolutionary, or rebellion that means imprisonment. Thus, a Western record, a cassette, a stylish shirt takes on outsize importance to them. These become symbols, "objective correlatives" of freedom. Having these things is a way to gratify the innate urge to make choices in small, personal daily matters.

While the average Cuban receives little for his sacrifices, a new class has arisen which benefits from the repression suffered by the masses. Those in high positions—*"mayimbes"* or *"pinchos,"* as they are called in slang—enjoy all sorts of privileges. They drive the latest cars and live in the best new housing or in villas formerly occupied by the wealthy. They can avoid rationing by shopping at special stores reserved for foreign technicians. As members of the elite they do not have to wait in line at recreational centers or medical facilities, and their children receive the finest education available.

Cubans feel betrayed not only by the emergence of a bourgeoisie but by the imposition of an alien culture on their country. After centuries of colonialism, national sovereignty was the overriding concern. Hence the alliance with the Soviet Union is regarded as anathema. Cuban antipathy to the USSR has roots in the early days of the Revolution. The Communist Party, the PSP (Popular Socialist Party), had a long and devious history. Its members had cooperated with Batista and until the rebels' success was nearly certain, had condemned the revolutionaries' tactics as "putschist." Thus, Cubans who turned away from the Revolution explain that they did so because they had fought for a democracy and were unwilling to accept a Communist system. They soon found that although they were the ones who had brought about the triumph of the Revolution, they were being shunted aside while the Communists, who had contributed the least to the struggle, were being rewarded with appointments to important government positions.

The affair of Major Huber Matos was a critical event in provoking the disaffection of revolutionaries who fled. Matos, the military chief of Camagüey province, was sentenced to twenty years in prison for the crime of disagreeing with the path the Revolution was taking. Matos had brought the necessary weapons in the spring of 1957 to the survivors of the 1956 *Granma* landing who were hiding in the mountains. Later he arrived in the Sierra Maestra from Costa Rica with a planeload of badly needed arms. Rather than oppose Castro on the issue of placing Communists in key posts, Matos, who wanted to return to teaching, offered his resignation. Nevertheless, he was accused of slandering the Revolution by calling it Communist, a charge later changed to treason.

The fact that the shift toward a Communist system was made without popular dialogue or choice alienated many Cubans. After the Bay of Pigs, Castro announced the Marxist nature of the Revolution, and the elections that had been promised were indefinitely postponed. Without public agreement about the leadership, a new party was introduced in 1961 as a merger of the 26th of July, the Directorio Revolucionario and the PSP, which became the new Communist Party of Cuba (PCC) in 1965.

With their institutions, economy and military forces modeled according to Soviet plans, and with the presence of Russian troops and personnel, Cubans feel they are living in an occupied country. On a personal level, they have no rapport with the Russians, who remain aloof in separate communities or appear egregious in their role as managers and technicians. The comments of Cubans reveal a hopeless clash between their candid, joking, tropical temperament and the Russians' dour style. Cubans are still in the humiliating predicament of dependency. Their situation is doubly ironic because Cuba relies more on the Soviet Union than it did, under Batista, on the United States. Furthermore, the justifiable accusation against capitalism is that it forces underdeveloped countries to depend on only one crop. In 1963, sugar again became the basis of Cuba's economy and concentration on it surpasses what it was before Castro came to power.

As a result of the 1973 trade agreements, Cuba receives an estimated $10 million per day in economic assistance from Russia. Cuba's accumulated trade deficit with the USSR exceeds $3 billion, and total Cuban indebtedness has been calculated at $5 billion. Soviet military weapons and equipment, valued at between $2 billion and $3 billion make the Cuban armed forces among the strongest in Latin America and more powerful than those of the East European satellites, except for Poland, whose population is four times Cuba's. Cuba has 190,000 regular troops, 90,000 army reserves, 10,000 state security troops, 3,000 border guards, and 100,000 in the militia.* The economic advantages are receiving most of it oil, machinery, grain and fertilizers from the Soviets, as well as being able to sell sugar above the world market price to its Soviet allies. When you mention the payment from Russia, Cubans express surprise. They say that it is not used for providing their daily necessities. Rather, they mention the reduction of the coffee ration and the scarcity of cement because these products are shipped to Angola. While their own diet is minimal and unvaried, they are aware of seafood, oranges and other fresh fruits and vegetables being exported. Subservience to Russia has meant not only the depletion of materials resources but the death of Cubans fighting for Soviet hegemony in Africa.

In a system that controls life so completely, no resistance movement has survived. Unable to protest openly or alter the situation, Cubans have been defying the government for the past two decades as political prisoners or fugitives without benefit of an underground network—and while the world scarcely noticed. It took the defection of 10,000 Cubans swarming into the Peruvian embassy in

* See Hugh Thomas, "Castro plus 20," *Encounter* (October 1978).

Havana, in April 1980, and the subsequent arrival in the United States of 120,000 refugees to focus international attention on Cuba. A just appraisal of the Revolution must account for the sheer numbers of those who fled the moment the right occasion occurred and the extreme measures taken by Cubans escaping on their own for the past twenty years. Their stories are of special significance at a time when Castro has become the spokesman for the Non-Aligned Nations and offers Cuba as a model for the Third World.

Lorrin Philipson
October 1980

Freedom Flights

To Plant Again

While I was in prison on the Isle of Pines, the guards came to my cell one day and brought me to a special air-conditioned room. A Cuban writer arrived and explained that he was not with the government and wanted to interview me for a book he was writing about the *campesinos* in the Escambray who were opposed to the government. While I talked to him I told him that they had taken twenty-three of my buddies and shot them, *a seco* [just like that]. Shot in the back—those were my words. And I said, "If you write that in the book, by God, I would die for you." Well, when the book came out, nothing of what I told him was published. Absolutely nothing.

Alvaro
Interviewed October 1979
Miami, Florida

The man first seen tramping across the thick living-room rug, then sitting at a marble-topped coffee table, is dressed in a white T-shirt, blue jeans and tan work boots. He wears other weather—a long way from here; different terrain rolls beneath his feet. A farmer from Las Villas province, Alvaro gives an impression of healthy round-ness—in his face, his wide-awake brown eyes, his mellow voice and his muscular, rotund body. Dark hair falls haphazardly across his forehead as if ruffled by a fresh, unseen breeze. He is clearly not in his natural element here, among china figurines and plastic-covered upholstery, but he is cheerful about his surroundings and the present conditions of his life. Someday, he hopes, he will live again in the open air. Until then, even his laughter has a round, glad sound.

As Alvaro recalls details of his escape there is a sense of mischief, of being pleased with himself and savoring all the elements of in-trigue. He has the typical Cuban flair for superb casualness, even in the most dangerous circumstances. Theirs is not a sardonic, gallows humor, but rather an irrepressible capriciousness—of wanting to extract merriment from any moment of life.

I WAS a *campesino* from the north, in the Escambray. I was opposed to Batista's government and at the beginning I cooperated with the revolution. The Escambray is completely different from other areas where rebellion began against Castro's regime. The people there had either fought in the Revolution as members of the Second Front in the Escambray Mountains or belonged to the Partido Directorio Revolucionario. Now all the people from the Second Front have been executed or are in prison or exile. Yet they had had great popularity with the *campesinos*. The revolutionaries from the Second Front had spent a lot of time with the *guajiros* [farmers] and were themselves from those parts. The greatest cause of their discontent was the government's *estafa* [cheating] of the people.

The propaganda said that there were no more classes in Cuba, which was not true. And although the agrarian reform was supposed to have distributed land to the farmers, all they did was turn everything into cooperatives. These belong to the government and the *guajiros* who had owned land lost it and are now employees of the government. So, 90 percent of the *guajiros* were upset, in a fit! They are a practical people—intelligent. You cannot tell them stories that "All is for you," when they can see perfectly well that they own nothing. They did not want to lose their land.

What the newspapers said was a swindle. Almost no one got land, not even a deed. Those groups who received titles for so many acres have to give up a third of what is produced and they are charged X number of pesos for rent. The government helps the small farmers by giving them equipment so that they will produce. But the state owns most of the land and the majority of those poor *infelices* who work there. There is really just one boss—Fidel Castro. The farmer gets paid very little and when he goes to the store, there is *na-a-da* to buy! In the little towns where there used to be five or six stores, only one is left. That store gets merchandise once a month and in two days all of it is gone. Then the store closes, since there is no more to sell. There is nowhere else to go look for what you need because it does not exist. When I was in Cuba most of what was grown went to Russia, to Spain, to France. My brother has a piece of land, but he cannot sell one iota to anybody. The farmers are also frustrated because they are led by people who know nothing about agriculture, that is, Communist administrators who were put in everywhere.

Until 1969, the year I left Cuba, the main thing that Castro had built in the Escambray was highways. The motive was to be able to launch an offensive whenever necessary. The *guajiro* in Cuba is in the same position as the peasants under Stalin. In 1964 the *campesinos* who were left in the Escambray were accused of fomenting trouble in a railroad station. They loaded hundreds of cars with *guajiros* and took them to Pinar del Río province. It was the same kind of thing Stalin did in the Soviet Union. The farmers were ordered to be there at a certain time and they all arrived on foot, horseback or by car. The farmers did not know what was happening. They were told nothing. They were just taken away and were not allowed to return. They were put in houses, where many of the children died of diphtheria and other diseases. This was criminal. The families living in the area now were brought in trucks from other provinces, while the *campesinos* from the Escambray were spread throughout the whole island. They cannot go back to their land, to their homes, to their families, to the place where they were born and raised! There are parents who still don't know where their children are, and vice versa. They work in the fields as if they were prisoners, since they aren't permitted to leave—they don't have the proper papers. In Cuba you have to have identification in order to move. So the rest of the country is closed to them.

In May 1959 I began to have trouble with the Communists. One day in the mountains there was an ambush by soldiers in the Ejercito Rebelde [Rebel Army] who shot some people, although they did not have the order to fire. Some truckdrivers were going to pick up rice on the coast. But it just so happened that at the same time the government was moving the minister's guard of Batista. Well, the other people arrived first and were attacked by accident. I picked up a wounded man and while I was taking him to a hospital in San Juan de los Remedios, in Las Villas, I ran into some troops. The captain asked me what had happened and I said that I had a kid who was wounded. The captain told me to kill the boy and I had an argument with him. I told him that I did not kill in cold blood. So they began to fire at us. What an utter disdain for human life, but that is the Communists' way.

Later, on June 22, my two brothers and I were taken prisoner. I stayed in the house of a captain for forty-eight hours, paid bail and was released. Since my brothers were caught near the meeting place of the Communist Party in the town of Venegas, they were charged with sabotage. The three of us went to see the commander of the province. An argument followed and the military police arrested us. Once more I paid bail after two days and was set free. One of my brothers got three months, and with pull I managed to get the other one out. Then I left for the mountains.

In July 1959 they searched my house, found arms, bullets and things left from the Revolution. They caught me and took me to Santa Clara, where I was a prisoner for seven days. I was able to use influence and was set free. By the beginning of 1960 the rebellion had begun. I became chief of a group of guerrillas, and in December of 1960 there was a big offensive of military rebels who rose against the government. There were about a thousand of us. The fighting went on for about eight months and was heaviest in January, February and March.

The government sent in a great many troops to look for us, and in March 1961 I was wounded and taken prisoner in Topes de Collantes. During the time of the Bay of Pigs, they told us we would all die, and so some of us tried to escape, but we were betrayed. As a result, we had to spend three months without visits or contacts with our families. In 1962 we staged a hunger strike. Their response was to tie our arms and legs like pigs and load us into buses to take us to Cienfuegos. There we were put on a warship and transported to the Isle of Pines, where we stayed until 1964. In that year they separated some of us from the other prisoners and we were told that we were going to be exchanged as political prisoners and sent to the United States. For a while they treated us very nicely. It was the only time we were not abused, not beaten with bayonets, and we got rice, meat and vitamins for a change. But then they said that there were problems with the money that was supposed to come from the United States and we were not freed. Instead, they took all of us who had been in the hunger strike and separated us from the others. Since we all did not fit on the same plane they had sent, some went on a different one. Twenty-five went to Las Villas and twenty-five of us went to La Cabaña Prison in Havana. Only two people survived from the first group. The rest were machine-gunned.

We were held incommunicado for seven days, sleeping on the floor. One morning they woke us up, pushed us at bayonet point and put us on trucks to go to Columbia Airport. We were returned to the Isle of Pines. The head of the Central Committee there told us we were lucky to be back alive because all the others had been shot.

In 1967 I left with the last group from the Isle of Pines. Four hundred were taken elsewhere. Ordinarily the prisoners were sent to Sagua, but there were too many of us to fit, so we went to Remedios, waiting there three months while they made arrangements in the prison. Finally we went to Manacas in Las Villas, where we had to do forced labor as we had done on the Isle of Pines. They called it a farm, but it was a concentration camp with four barracks and surrounded by double barbed-wire fences twenty feet high. It was all sealed off. The first day I was taken there, I fled. I was able to get out because they trusted in the fact that the camp was well protected, with the fences and the guards. While the guard was calling roll in the group to which I had been assigned, I stood behind him. When he came to my name, I pretended to be someone else and said, "Sick." The guard checked off my name. Of course, he did not know me, since it was my first day. Then, without being noticed, I walked over to the side where the men whose names had been called were. They were a group of seventeen who were sup-posed to go to work outside the fence. Instead of seventeen, we were eighteen.

Nothing happened. The trucks arrived. It was well organized. First came the chief of that particular zone, and then the G-2 (State Security) officers, who counted again. I managed to switch lines so that they got a total of seventeen. When we boarded the truck I quickly sat in one of the seats. We went out to a field, which was clean, broad and even. They were putting up stakes for growing tomatoes and there was no place for me to go. At first I did not know how I could possibly escape in the middle of an open place like that. Then I realized what I could do. My plan was to bury myself in one of the irrigation ditches.

We had arrived at seven in the morning and we worked straight until two in the afternoon. Since we had not brought lunch, we were to be taken back to the prison to eat. At two o'clock, when they called out, "Work is over," I told the guys in my group that I was an extra and was staying behind. I explained that I was going to bury myself and they agreed to help. I jumped into a ditch and they covered it with twigs, dirt and leaves. They also threw down some sacks. Of course the guards did not notice anything irregular because they were at a distance and I was surrounded by seventeen men. The fellow who was supposed to be my bunkmate had replaced a guy who had fled two months before and had been caught. The man was taken to the jail in Santa Clara and given nine months in solitary. Well, the one who took his place helped me in another way.

Generally, they use dogs—bloodhounds—in these fields but there were none at this particular time. The guy agreed that when I was gone and the police came with dogs, he would give them something of that other guy's to sniff so that the dogs could not trace my smell. I stayed buried in the ditch from two until six in the evening. Then I climbed out and began walking toward the highway. The central highway. I had kept a close watch to make sure there were no guards around. You know from the other prisoners the routine of the guards. It was December, dark and it was *un frío de madre* [bitter cold]! I stopped along the road until I ran into a *guajiro* from Cienfuegos. He had come to look for his son. I told him that I, too, was looking for a relative—my brother—because my father-in-law was sick. All lies, of course! So I told him that I needed to go early. We walked along together and it was nice having someone to talk to. Also, it offered protection.

I remember that the man had a rope with him. One of those you tie up cattle with—oxen, that is. As you know, there is nothing in Cuba. You cannot even buy rope. The man told me that at the place where he had bought the rope, they sold beer and one ration of *croquetas* [fritters]. He said to me, "Come on. My treat." I said, "Fine. You can invite me, but I will pay." I had money. I had saved it for a long, long time. I will never forget the cold of that day. The beer made me even colder. I could hardly stand up. We continued talking and went back to the highway. He needed to take a bus to Santa Clara.

An interprovince bus stopped because the people on it knew that in this place they could get something to eat. They were friends of the fellow who worked there. I dared not talk because I was an outsider. A real outsider. I did not belong. I did not know anything, so I let the *guajiro* speak. They complained about the usual troubles of being a driver. The guy driving the bus said, "Someone gets on and wants to get off only a few blocks away." They said that they had come from La Habana province and were going to Oriente. "Listen, friend," I said to that guy, "I've come to get my brother in Sagua because my father-in-law is dying." Then followed some small talk about Sagua. I continued to speak of my urgency to go. "O.K.," he finally agreed, "but don't ask to get off in Santa Clara, because I will not let you. You are just like all the others who want a little ride!" He was just kidding, but I sat there wanting desperately to get out of that area. After all, they knew my face and the guards had probably discovered that someone was missing.

I got out in Santa Clara and went to a relative's house, where I spent the night. Then I took a bus to Caibarién. I was not wearing prison clothes. What I had was a white sweater and khaki pants. On top I wore a pullover from prison from which I had been able to remove the *P* with gasoline. It took me over two weeks to get it absolutely clean! In Caibarién I made contact with a friend to come to the United States. This is the way I finally got to my escape point. Through my friend I made the acquaintance with an official of the G-2 who took money for helping escapees. Since I had nothing to lose—just a twenty-year sentence as one of the *plantados*—I played for all I had. It was a big gamble, but life was worthless, anyway. In Cuba a man's life is worth nothing.

Well, I went to a place where I was known and where I could get help. If they know that you are a pretty open sort of guy, they lend you a hand. Meanwhile, I had been able to borrow money. In Caibarién someone picked me up where I was hiding. He told me, "Follow me and walk for two blocks. Then you will see a couple walking. Follow them. Be sure not to be too close to them in case you are caught so that they won't have any problems. When they get near a house, walk after them, and when they enter it, you go inside, too. Be sure to go through the same door. Someone will be waiting for you."

I did as he said and arrived at about eight in the evening. There I found myself among other people who were escaping with me. There were seven of us. The next morning we left before dawn—at about four o'clock. Two fishermen came to pick us up. They took us in a small rowboat and brought us to a larger boat, which was about nineteen feet long. We were scattered throughout the boat and covered with a drop cloth. Two of the men were placed very close to the motor. I was near them and realized that they had been poisoned by carbon monoxide. The captain tried to wake them up but could not. I came out from hiding and gave them artificial respiration. I was able to bring them back to life. Thank God they did not die.

I did not know the people I escaped with, nor how much they paid the captain. I, myself, paid 2,000 pesos for the trip. The captain had planned to let us off and go on his way. He expected to do this in one day, but it took four days and five nights because the weather was absolutely awful. I have great respect for that man. He has guts—*un valor del diablo*! If it had not been for him, we would not have made it. We had left Cuba with a small Russian motor, but after two hours it broke down. We had to continue with an auxiliary sail that we rigged up. Finally we were picked up by a boat about ten miles from Miami.

When I left I was married but had no children. My wife, who was also in prison, could not leave. I made every possible effort to get her out of Cuba, but they told me to come and get her. If the system changed, I would most certainly return. I have a butcher shop now and I live well here, as you can see. But I belong to the country. I love the countryside, the fields, the peace. I would like to go back to my own land, to plant again.

Rum and Thunder

In the factories of Cuba, workers do not work with zest. They have no enthusiasm, because they are going through great misery. The majority of them are bitter, since life has become only work for the sake of working—without reward or even the simplest necessities.

Agustín
Interviewed October 1979
Miami, Florida

An elfin man in navy-blue shorts and red rubber sandals opens the door. Eyes of Pierrot and a body like a Giacometti sculpture. Ribs stick through his skin as sharply as the staves of a paper fan. His face is slightly lopsided, with the flesh hollowed out unevenly and deep creases along the mouth. Most of his teeth are missing. But as Agustín talks, the energy thrumming through him becomes more compelling than his emaciated appearance. He is in constant motion. His hand sweeps through his thick, wavy dark hair. He snaps his fingers to stress a point. He rubs one palm briskly over the other in a gesture of rejection. He aims his index finger at an imaginary distant point, re-enacting a moment during his escape. Feisty, laughing, he is a silhouette of strength. Here in this man are the bare bones of courage.

AM thirty-six years old, born in Isabela de Sagua, in Las Villas province. I went to school only through the fourth grade because necessity forced me to support myself. At fifteen I began working in a bakery and continued in that occupation until my escape. I left Cuba because of the needs of my children. I have a daughter who is seventeen and a son who is fourteen. The problem was that we were very short of food. These last months hunger has increased to an unbearable degree. My children used to return home from school saying, "Daddy, I'm hungry," and many times I had no food to give them. In the primary schools some meals are provided, but not in the secondary schools, where my children were.

After the Revolution my salary was 80 pesos a month. Then it went to 105, and 118, and finally 160 pesos a month in the last five years. I received that raise when an old man left and I took his place. They gave me an intensive course to qualify for that job, but I did not really learn anything because after years of experience I already knew what they were teaching about baking. Other workers, like stevedores, make better salaries—killing themselves by working twelve to fifteen hours a day. Practically speaking, the money you earn is more than enough if you buy according to your quota. But the money does not bring you what you need because, for example, five pounds of rice—which is the main food you get—does not last for a month. Therefore, since the state does not provide sufficient amounts, you have to get the rest on the black market and for that the police persecute you. If you are caught, they take the food and you go before a tribunal. They can fine you 100–300 pesos or put you in jail.

Life in Cuba consists of a constant scramble to take care of your family. There are very few diversions. For instance, workers have one month of vacation a year. If you want to go to the beach, you have to be in the workers' vanguard—that is, in the CDR's [Committees to Defend the Revolution, or block associations], patrol guards, or weekend groups cutting cane. I can tell you, though, that the average worker in Cuba spends his vacation at home, usually fixing it—trying to paint it if he can. You have to be "integrated" and go to INIT [the National Institute of the Tourist Industry] in order to make reservations in advance for the good beaches like Varadero or Guanabo. Only a minority go there. If you do extra hours of volunteer work and accumulate a certain number of points, then you can apply for those beaches. I, myself, never went to one —not because I didn't want to, but because I couldn't. In Isabela de Sagua, they have a beach for the people but you have to bring your own food. What they sell is too expensive for a poor worker. And transportation is terrible. The buses and trains that go there are forever breaking down. When this happens they are just set aside, useless and wasted. The machinery comes from the Soviet Union, but they don't sell the spare parts.

The attitude in the factories is that if you do not have a job to do at a particular time, or if the machine breaks down, you don't care because there is no incentive to work. Often when you tell the boss your machine is broken and they change it, the replacement is worse! We lived on beans, half a pound of grease to fry them, rice, and meat every nine days. Finally I asked my relatives, "What are we waiting for—for them to kill us here? *Irnos para el carajo de aquí!* [Let's get the hell out of here!]" Then we started to plan.

The CDR's were responsible for watching everyone. The control was so strong—*ahí, ahí, ahí* [here, here, here], that we could not move. And of course, they were always checking to see that we weren't buying or selling on the black market. If you go to look for food for your children, they let you. But when you come back, they arrest you, take your food and put you in jail. So the family loses the food and the man.

In effect, the only way we could get news of the outside world was by radio. The government tries to jam the broadcasts, but Cubans are clever about inventing ways to get around that—making an antenna or something else. So once I bought a Russian radio for 80 pesos. Excuse me, but what shit! I had to spend 50 more pesos to fix it. That thing cost me more than a *hijo bobo* [retarded child]! I finally had to throw it out. The same thing with a Russian watch I bought. I really needed it, but such shit; it broke on my wrist.

In the beginning I was sympathetic to the Revolution, thinking that there would be a change in the system of life. I was an *integrado* for four years, doing voluntary work and serving in the militia. But then I began to withdraw as I saw that the government was not solving the problems of the people. Take something like the Literacy Campaign. It was a good idea but not the success it might have been, because they did not go about it in the right way. You have an illiterate and a teacher comes to him, teaching fast: "Hurry, look at this; look at that!" Well, afterward the person does not know what the teacher said. Some of the teachers did not know how to deal with the people, and others knew less than the people. In many cases *campesinos* just learned to write their name or a letter sent to Fidel to thank him. It got some people started, but not the majority. In my opinion it was an elementary form of instruction, not a profound education, and I think it served mainly to propagandize people. They had books for the alphabet with *F* for Fidel, *R* for Raúl [his brother], or military words like *F* for *fusil* [gun].

You have a similar situation with the Poder Popular [People's Power, i.e., local groups that elect delegates to the national assembly], which is supposed to help the ordinary person. I did not want to attend the meetings because I was so busy working and looking for food for my family that I did not have time. When I went they would say, "We're going to do this and this and this," and I would be saying to myself, "Yes, keep telling me this shit." They promise so many things, but they don't do anything. As an example, the ceiling over my bed was leaking badly. Whenever it rained, we had to cover the bed with plastic. So I went to the Poder Popular for two rolls of tar paper to repair the roof. They sent me all over the place and I came back with nothing. I tried to forget it because I did not want to create problems. At the time, I was living with the six other members of my family in a house that had once been a bakery. When the owner went to Spain, we moved in. It looked less like a bakery than a place to raise pigs and I had to work a long time cleaning and fixing it up!

It is possible that if there was a change of government in Cuba, I would go back. Probably, though, if Fidel was out of power, the system would be worse because Raúl is even more of an animal. In reality, Cuba today is one big army. The majority of the people are in some branch of the armed forces, and the minority are civilians. You can be sure that if the government allowed anyone to leave who wanted to, there would be nearly no one left except Fidel and his little group because Cubans feel humiliated in so many ways. I know many people want to leave but don't have the chance. Life is such a pretense that even people who are "integrated" really are not and would leave if they could.

Eighteen of us escaped—including my granddaughter, who is a year and a half old—on a thirty-five-foot fishing boat. The other men and I had been exchanging ideas, but when our first plan didn't work, we had to come up with another one. Originally, we were going to take a young man who was in the military service for a year in Havana. The signal for him to come to Isabela de Sagua was that we were going to celebrate a birthday—which meant our trip. But after we sent him a telegram, we saw there would be trouble. It was too late to do anything, so he came, anyway.

One problem was that there was too much vigilance. The other obstacle was that we could not wait for another time and have the boy come back again from Havana, because we had called him home once before. The boy was afraid that since they had given him trouble the other time, they would be angry and put him in jail if he asked to leave again. We had to make a plan fast, take a risk and save him. I decided to hide him in my house. Later my wife and I moved in with my sister-in-law and the boy remained in our house, which we had locked up to make it look as if no one was there. For five days I sneaked back to bring him food in a shopping bag.

My brother-in-law, Silvio, was the leader. As an employee in Maritime Security he was a mechanic on the *prácticos* [small boats that guide ships into port]. We had to choose one of those boats that would be big enough for all of us. The one we picked was tied up near the office of the Ministry of the Interior. Silvio asked his boss to lend him the boat to fish and the man gave it to him because he trusted him. Silvio explained that he wanted to take his father, who was coming from Havana, out fishing. Afterward he came to my house and told me he had gotten the boat. Then came the next stage of our plan. We went to the pier and bought two bottles of Aguardiente Carta de Cano rum, which were $9.60 each, with the idea of getting the captain of the boat drunk—we knew he liked to drink. We planned that once he was drunk, we would get him off the boat. We met him at the pier and the three of us took the boat out. We were on the Sagua la Grande River and traveled to the point where it enters the ocean. From there we went to the place where the fishermen gather the lobsters they catch. The state then ships them outside the country. In Cuba we didn't get lobsters; they are only for export.

I had talked with one of the members of my family who arranged to bring everyone else to a certain meeting place. The fellow watched for our boat to pass by and stop at the area where the lobsters were. Then he made sure everyone else was present. The signal for us was that if two people were standing on the side of the pier, everyone had arrived. If only one person was standing, it meant that some of the group were missing. Meanwhile we were out on the boat getting the captain more and more drunk. Looking back on it now, I know that it didn't take us too long. But while we were out there joking, telling stories and pouring the rum, I thought the time would never pass. As I smiled and filled his cup, I kept thinking, Drink now. Drink some more and hurry up and get drunk. Soon your mind will be fuzzy and we can get rid of you and go! I felt the small knife in my pocket, hoping I would not have to use it. If we had to take him with us, we were going to use it to cut some rope and tie him up. No, old man, I thought, we will have to be stuck with you. We will never throw you overboard. We could not treat a human being that way.

Finally I looked up and saw two people standing. I whispered to my brother-in-law, "O.K. We're ready." We headed the boat back to where it had been moored and helped the captain off. Fortunately he was feeling sick and told us we would go fishing together another time. We said good night and he went home. I was so relieved and eager to start that I cannot remember clearly my last glimpse of him. Since the boat was already prepared with water aboard, the only other thing we had to do was put more gasoline in the tank. We left again and by then it was getting dark. It was about seven o'clock. Then the strangest coincidence happened! As the rest of the group was boarding the boat, there was a blackout in town. These happen often all over the island. In Isabela the problem is a shortage of electrical power, but I couldn't help thinking that maybe God sent us that piece of luck at the right moment!

With everyone finally on board we started the motor. Then we turned on the boat's light. It consists of a white light on top and a red one in the middle. When the two lights are on, it means the boat is in service as a *práctico*. We left without any problem. Since we had checked the area beforehand, we knew there would not be any coast guard around at that time. We had been watching their movements for twenty days. As we went through one of the channels I checked with Silvio, who was at the tiller, to see if everything was O.K. He was used to that kind of boat, and another man with us was an old fisherman. The direction we chose was north. Later, however, we got off course and we were lost.

When we left the shore, a storm started up. I got excited and shouted, "Silvio, *coño*! The elements are with us," because in weather like that there wouldn't be any other patrols around. From where we were, all we could see were the lighthouses and then the lights of the town, which had come on again. Finally Silvio said, "O.K. We're going to turn the lights off." I told him that just to be safe we should wait till we were farther out. Even though all was going well, I didn't want to take any chances. Except for the knife, we didn't have any weapons to defend ourselves if we were discovered. Five miles later we extinguished the lights and continued on. Then, far ahead we saw *una trompa marina* [whirlwind]. That was the moment I felt the most afraid during the trip. The old man and the rest of us are believers. He said a special prayer and the whirlwind disappeared. It is very common for fishermen to do that.

We spent the rest of that Saturday night fairly well. Then the sea began to get very rough. All we had taken were two *compotas* [jars of baby food], a can of powdered milk, and a little coffee. There was a small stove, where we heated some milk and gave it to the baby with a bit of sugar and water. When we were about fifty miles from Cuba, many of the others began vomiting—green—from the boat's plunging up and down on the swells. I exclaimed, "What have you been eating? Grass!" Then my little granddaughter started saying, "*Papi*, give me some milk." It hurt me to hear that and I told her, "Sweetheart, don't make me desperate!" I asked her mother to give her something to go to sleep. I was trying to save the *compotas* in case we needed them for her later. Finally I had to give her one and we made some coffee for everyone else. All we had from our quota was seven ounces. The rest of the time we used the same coffee grounds over and over.

On Sunday at about three-thirty in the afternoon we could not find our way. I was feeling crazy and began punching my head with my fists, saying, "Oh God, why are you doing this to me? Why don't you help me? *Carajo!* [Hell!]" Then I saw two ships far away. I grabbed the binoculars and yelled to the others, "It's two fishing boats. Make a signal to them!" I was about to remove my underwear, which was the only white clothing we had, but we found an old white shirt which we had covered our knife with so that it wouldn't make reflections. We started waving the shirt like crazy.

The ships came closer and we saw that they were from the United States. One, called *Popeye*, had a Cuban crew. It came toward us and the second one went around us. I shouted to the near boat, "Please give me food for my children. I don't want anything else, only food." One of the guys asked where we were from and when I told him Cuba, a fellow from the *Popeye* called back, "We are Cubans too." They got close to us and I began crying from all the emotions I felt. I had to go off by myself, hiding my tears from the women. Shortly thereafter I explained more quietly that we had just fled from Cuba. "Look how many children we have here," I told him. Another member of the crew shouted, "*Cojones*," and started throwing a lot of food into our boat—juice, *compotas*, crackers, candy, cans of spaghetti. Then I asked, "*Chico*, where's Miami?" He said, "Forget about it. You'll go with us. It's enough that you are Cubans." I was so excited and happy I began hitting the boat. Until that moment we had been lost, without anything for the children. As they towed our boat I turned my face toward the children, watching them eating.

I told the crew of the other boat to let us use our gas because we had five more gallons. We did not want to strain their boat and they did not have much gas. When ours was finished, we signaled them, but they said they had arranged for the other boat to bring more. During this time it was very windy and the sea was turbulent. Since the other boat did not have binoculars, they asked me to tell them if we saw a lighthouse.

I saw a little point in the distance, which turned out finally to be a lighthouse, and we headed for it. By the time we arrived, we were out of gas. One of the men came from the other boat and asked if the adults had eaten. I said no, that we had given all the food to the children. Another guy called out, "We have plenty of fish here," and they started throwing fish, and fish, and fish into our boat! After we cleaned it, we fried the fish and ate our first meal.

A helicopter flew over us and the other boat signaled it. In a little while a green light began flashing at us. I asked what it was, because I was afraid. They explained it was a ship from the Coast

Guard and I relaxed. The people on the other boat told the Coast Guard about us and they towed both boats. By then it was eleven o'clock at night and we were about six miles from Key West. We had been on the sea for twenty-four hours. When we arrived in Key West we received wonderful attention. I never imagined we would have such a welcome. We were surprised at our reception here because the Cuban government had deceived us. They told us Cubans in the States were living in terrible conditions and starving to death. I was so overwhelmed by the way we were treated here that I walked away from everybody for a while and wept.

Silvio, who planned the trip, is a thin, soft-spoken, diffident man with shiny, straight brown hair and a nose that juts clifflike from his narrow face. He seems enclosed in an invisible cage, his body drawn in on itself, his footsteps charted. Caution and the habit of conserving energy seem so ingrained in him that there are no random gestures or excess motions. He is self-contained, with eyes thoughtful and alert, and lips pursed around frequent cigarettes. He exhales weariness that is not a sense of defeat, but rather resignation, as if he were saying, "Yes, I have known hopes that didn't flower and I have seen terrible things. Still, we go on as we can, but with our dreams diminished."

COME from Las Villas and am forty-two years old. I used to work in a fishing cooperative, and at the time I left I was a ship's mechanic. Before the Revolution came I worked for the cause in clandestine activities against Batista. I was then seventeen years old. The group I belonged to were young Orthodox Party members, who supported Eddy Chibas.* Because I was distributing propaganda, I

* Objecting to the corruption of the *auténticos* [Authentic Revolutionary Movement], to which he belonged, Eduardo Chibas, a senator from the province of Havana, founded the *ortodoxos* in 1957 and was a presidential candidate. Castro, who greatly admired Chibas, joined the *ortodoxos*, and as a member ran for Congress from the province of Havana.

was taken prisoner for two years and tortured. By 1960 the Revolution started to change. Now the government tries to show the world that we have freedom and benefits for the people, but in Cuba what really exists is a system of psychological terror. Everyone lives in fear all the time. If, for instance, a friend says the government does good things for the people, you feel obliged to agree because you are afraid not to. Perhaps that person does not really believe what he is saying, but he is afraid of you, too. Even within families, people are afraid to discuss their political beliefs sincerely.

The world tightens around you so much that you feel hemmed in, guilty of crimes you have not committed. You are watched, pursued, told what to think and what to do, and constantly restricted as if you were not a human being. When I was a fisherman, we were mistreated in many ways because they thought so little of us. All of the fish we caught had to go to the government. If you gave some to anyone, you went to jail. Then they put up signs and fences, limiting the physical space where we worked, as if we were cattle to be herded into a corral. It was a crime even to look at a warehouse, because they suspected you of sabotage. This was just one more proof to us that the government has no confidence in the people. Yet remember, at the beginning of the Revolution Fidel said, "*Armas para qué?*" [Arms, for what?] But very soon he started to collect guns from everyone and at the same time he began buying weapons.

I was a *responsable* [the official in charge] who received the fish that was caught. At the beginning we froze it and sent it to different zones in Cuba. Now they export most of it. If they see a citizen with a lobster, they put him in jail. It used to be that your salary was determined by the amount of fish you caught. But now fishermen must work for a very low salary, depending on how good they are. I made four dollars a day. The government has done the same thing in the country. They have small-farmer associations, which are controlled by the state.

In Cuba we worked without hope. Here the young people study and have a chance. In Cuba it is work, work, work, and then the salary is not enough. The government has not even been intelligent about winning favor among young people in the military service.

Their labor is hard and they are constantly hungry. Consequently, the majority feels exploited and resentful. Take the case of my son, which is typical. His job in the army was to remove ammunition from *rastras* [large trucks usually used for interprovince transportation] and load it into warehouses. The food he got was insufficient, especially for that kind of heavy work, and with the 7 pesos a month he earned, he could not afford the fare home when he was on leave! This treatment is not only a great injustice but a serious mistake on the part of the government to alienate its own army.

The quotas of food allowed are a great abuse. The *pinchos* [members of the new, privileged class who collaborate with the government] have no problems, but the majority of the population does not have enough to live. They have to buy necessities on the black market at very high prices, which they often cannot afford. Another feeling that drags you down is that little gets accomplished because of the bureaucracy. If you go to an office to solve a problem, *es un peloteo* [delaying the game by passing the ball from one player to another without trying to score]. The thing you ask about could be taken care of in half an hour, but they keep sending you from one person to the next and it ends up taking three days! Or you need a bus to go to another town—it can take you a day to get there because the bus breaks down or they have to wait to find oil or gas. You want a cold refreshment, and they don't have it. Then, at meetings the people are told to do voluntary work and the government declares a Red Sunday for doing it. When this idea was presented to our work center, no one said anything. Then one person raised his hand to accept the plan and everyone else followed and approved because they were afraid to say no. It was not because they wanted to cooperate.

Naturally, all of these things make the people very bitter. So now they have the Poder Popular to assuage discontentment. It is rarely any help at all, it is mainly decorative. When the people were angry, they used to send a member of the Poder Popular—some poor guy who wasn't to blame—to tell them to go to a meeting at night. The people usually were not in the mood. What was on their minds was going home after work or the fact that there might not be any food in the house. But the people had to go to the meeting, anyway, and

give an account of the work they had done that day. They went out
of fear, but I did not, because by that time I did not care anymore.
I knew that the only thing for me to do was to leave.

*Salvador, the oldest member of the group, is a hardy, rough-hewn
fisherman with skin the color of baked clay. His face, smitten by
sunlight, is a map of ocean and earth. You can read in it the wind-
drawn veins of the sea, furrows in the soil, the sun hatched from
behind clouds at dawn, and rain like a moving mesh of silver that
has tinted his thick hair gray. He has reached that balance point of
old age when all seasons turn in his bones. He is a plain-spoken,
direct man. As he talks you can feel the relish he took in working
well and his pride in the fruits of that labor.*

I AM sixty-nine years old, from Las Villas, also. In Batista's time
I was a *bracero* [stevedore] and I have been a fisherman for
many years. In the last nine years I was the supervisor in a
warehouse at a fishing terminal. In my case the main difference between the present government and this one is that we were short of
work under Batista. But in those times, if you wanted to make
extra money, people like me could easily do it. The important thing
for me was that you had enough to take care of your household and
there were no scarcities. People did not have to look all over as
they do now for necessities. Although today you can earn a good
salary—I was making more than 200 pesos a month in Cuba—the
difficulty is that the food quotas they give you are very small. Therefore, you have to buy on the black market and pay high prices. Even
so, most of the time I could not get the food I needed because the
campesinos cannot always bring extra food for the people. Being
alone, I was not worried about myself, but my children and grandchildren lacked the things they needed. Sometimes I took them to
a restaurant, but I could not afford to do that too often, since there
were seven of us.

I was never very involved in politics, but I started to gain interest before the Revolution. I thought that if I helped in it, we would have a change in the situation of my country, but it was not like that. I belonged to the militia, in a special infantry company formed to protect the people against infiltrators, counterrevolutionaries or any aggression from outside. I was in it for about four years, but afterward they took me out because of my age. At that time I was fifty. I also belonged to the Committees to Defend the Revolution. You have to join organizations over there. Otherwise they look at you as if you are not with the Revolution.

My own situation was not bad. I retired in 1973 and they gave me 120 pesos per month. For myself it was enough. But I was worried about my children and grandchildren. I began to be dissatisfied with the system because the situation of my family was very hard. Originally I thought the Revolution was going to be good for the whole country, but on the contrary, only some people—*los jefes* [the bosses]—live well. They have no hardships, but the poor people have a bad time. The promise was that it was a revolution for the workers, but that is not what it is. The economy now is the worst.

I recognize that they have done some good things. They have built factories, schools, and many hospitals and polyclinics, which in my experience gave good medical care. They have built homes for the *campesinos* and provided them with things like refrigerators and television sets. The problem, though, is that the farmers have to live in a way that is not what they wanted. Many dislike the apartment houses constructed for them and call them *"palomares"* because they feel as if they are stuck in little pigeonholes. The other objectionable condition for them is that they have to work for the government. First the land was taken from large landowners and given to the *campesinos*. When they got it they felt as if they were in heaven because many of them had never owned any land but had worked for other farmers. However, with the new laws, the land was then given to the state, in cooperatives. But the farmers prefer to have their own land and work it in their own way. The farmer who has lived all his life working the land does not need studies and technicians! He knows which land is good for which particular crops and the time needed to grow them. All he needs is a tractor, or two bulls pulling a plow, in order to cultivate the land! The *campesino* working his own land does double the work when he can benefit from it himself and when his family and other people can. I am sure the cooperatives produce, but I do not know where most of the products go.

Before the Revolution I was working on a sugar plantation in Camagüey province from 1943 to 1948. There I really learned how to grow cane. The methods of raising sugar cane then and now are different. Then the farmer grew cane in the proper place. The plants were placed about three feet apart, because like all crops they need air and space to grow. Today they have other methods. I did a lot of volunteer work in the country and I used to say to myself, I don't understand this kind of planting. It seemed to me that it did not produce a good yield. They put the seeds too close together. That meant that the first year there was a good harvest. But after you cut it twice, the stalks did not get thick the way they were supposed to, because there was not enough space for the plants to expand.

Today more land is cultivated for sugar cane than before, but the methods are inefficient. The Harvest of Ten Million was not done by the farmers or the *macheteros*, who ordinarily cut the cane, but by all the people. Many of the *campesinos* had moved to the cities or were in the army and there was a shortage of them. Since the people from the cities did not know how to work, they ruined the cane. I thought to myself that it was a shame the way they lost so much cane. The proper way to cut it is close to the ground. If you do it too high, the next plant that grows from that stalk is weak. I said this to one of the *responsables*, who got very mad at me, answering sarcastically, "You look like you know a lot about sugar cane." I did! I had worked in the past planting cane for a total of twelve years. Another reason they lost cane was that when the part that is used was cut off, the workers didn't pile it in the right place and it got covered up by the part you discard.

One of the main problems in Cuba is that they try to produce more than the figures they give. Also, on the Isle of Youth, for example, they grow a lot of citrus fruit and large melons, which go to other countries. I know this because one of my sons is the captain of a refrigerator ship that carries grapefruit to Holland. In my opinion, Cuba exports more than it should. Obviously, a country has to export certain things, because you produce more of some things than the people consume, but a country should export according to its economy and not sacrifice the needs of the people by exporting too much. For instance, in Santa Clara there is a textile factory with Japanese machines that produces a large quantity of cloth each year. All of it is exported, with the idea that the money it earns will benefit the Cuban people. We did not know, however, how that money was being spent. We never saw what became of it.

You must understand that fundamentally most Cubans are not a political people. They are a working people. Therefore, it is a question of individual pride—to work and then be able to provide for your needs and those of your family. I always tried to fulfill all my responsibilities at work. But seeing my children and grandchildren hungry made me sick. That was the main motive for my escape.

Explosion

When the government arrests a small group or even one man, it is common for them to send so many militiamen and so much equipment that it looks as if they were coming to fight a war. Any enemy, no matter how small, seems big to them.

Gerardo
Interviewed January 1978
Miami, Florida

Gerardo, now the owner of a furniture store in Miami, is a genial man with a no-nonsense style and a pleasant appearance—tall and sturdy, with chestnut hair and pale-green eyes. He is immensely likable, for the mild, intermittent sarcasm of his remarks, the determination that made him gamble on escape three times, and his reasonableness—a sense of what's fair in life and what isn't, without ambivalence or rationalization. In his early forties, he's a man who started on a simple course, whose only ambition was to be allowed to continue.

I N CUBA I sold secondhand electrical appliances and wanted to go on with that because it was what I knew how to do. But after the Revolution there was constant surveillance over all private businesses. I was always being watched by the Committees to Defend the Revolution. Since I had a license from before and my business was small, they didn't care so much at first. By 1963, however, the situation was getting worse. I was kept under stricter observation because the government knew that anyone with his own business was not in favor of their prohibiting free enterprise. But the propaganda made no sense to me! How did owning a small store, where I worked hard to provide for the needs of myself and my family, mean that I was "exploiting people"? It was my means of survival. Daily life was a struggle for everyone. You had to wait hours in line for food and clothes, and many times they ran out of what you needed. If you have any pride in yourself, you cannot accept being told what to do with your life, and how to think. And if you love your homeland, as I do, you cannot stand to see another country—Russia—so foreign to yours, planting its system on your soil.

One day a militiaman came to check on what I was selling. It happened to be used televisions. I got into an argument with him and told him he could not come into my store without papers from the government. His answer was, "I'm from the Revolution and we don't need any papers." We had a fistfight and then a patrol car came to take me to a detention center. They kept me there seventeen months without giving any reason.

At the trial they went through all sorts of theatrics. The lawyer, who showed up in a green uniform, like the judge and the prosecutor, lectured me on the Revolution, the progress it was making and the fact that free enterprise is not for poor people. But the only opportunity for getting another job is if you are "integrated" into the Revolution. If you are not, they send you to do farm work— picking tomatoes, cutting cane, etc.

They took me to La Cabaña but decided I was not a political case and transferred me to Príncipe, where they put me in a cell that was not for political or common prisoners. At the end of my term they told me I had to be integrated into the Revolution. I said I wanted to leave and asked what I could do. Their answer was that someone in the United States had to sponsor me. Even though my brother did so, time passed and nothing happened. Meanwhile, in 1966 I met some other people who were against the government. I cooperated with them by taking medicine to the Escambray to help the anti-Castro guerrillas there. When the government caught one of the guys in my group they made him talk and he gave my name. When I found out I had been denounced I decided I had to leave the country any way I could.

I prepared a raft with some friends, but before we reached the ocean they caught us. I was arrested and sentenced to ten years in prison. The evening set for our escape we had driven in an ice truck to a prearranged spot on the coast of Matanzas. But we couldn't hide the truck anywhere because the ground was too wet and there were too many bushes to go through. So we parked on the side of the road. As we were getting ready to leave, a gasoline truck passed. The people who drive them usually belong to the G-2. Sometimes they stop and ask if they can help, but these men did not say anything to us. As soon as they left, however, the driver called the local police on his radio. Very quickly *ten* army trucks arrived. It was like an invasion! This is, of course, their psychology, to try to terrify everyone. If someone reports just one person, they send half a fortress. The first thing they did when they came for us was to turn on the Bengal lights on a special truck that lit up everything so brightly that it looked like daytime. When they saw our truck they immediately opened fire as if they were in combat, and there we were without any guns. Theirs is a tremendous terrorism.

Before I finally escaped, I was shifted in and out of various jails and concentration camps for the next several years. I started out in Taco-Taco and was sent to Guanajay, which used to be for women. Now it is for the men who are the most opposed to the Revolution. They took some of the women to Bauta and to the camp there, Nueva Amanacer [New Dawn].

One morning at four, while we were in Taco-Taco, two other prisoners and I put on our *enguatadas* [heavy T-shirts] inside out so that the *P* on the back (for "Prisoner") would not show. On top we wore a shirt right side out, and we did the same thing with our pants. I had instructed my friends to do this. The guards did not pay attention to the fact that we were wearing two uniforms because at that hour it is cold. Later, when we arrived at the fields to work, the guards did not bother with the usual procedure of checking prisoners by having us remove our clothes. The soldiers were in a hurry and wanted to get as much done as possible.

We were careful to pick this day for our escape because there had just been a *requisa* [an inspection] and it was unlikely that there was going to be another right away. That particular day seemed a good time for another reason. The man in charge was not as strict as the other guards. The prisoners and the guards were playing a watching game the whole time. The guards watched the prisoners, but we were watching them in return, always waiting for any chance to escape.

My friends and I were bouncing over the rough dirt roads in an open truck. We were scanning the countryside carefully and had memorized every detail of it. We knew exactly where there were dense clumps of bushes to hide in, the spot where the truck had to stop because of a big hole, and the river, where the dogs would lose our scent when we made our jump. I remember glancing around at the twenty-five other prisoners and studying the four soldiers with rifles positioned in each corner. Frankly, I was more worried about the reaction of the other prisoners, who might interfere as we were escaping, than of the guards. I had learned that in any group of prisoners there are always some who are more indoctrinated than others, or who are in jail for some slight mistake, not because they are at odds with the system. There are also the dangerous ones who are *chivatos* [informers]. Often they are guilty of only a minor offense, but to deceive the other prisoners, in order to extract information, they brag about having committed major crimes. I knew how to detect that type.

The second the truck stopped at the hole, we leaped over the side and ran off into the early-morning darkness. The soldiers immediately forced the others out and made them lie face down on the ground. Then they alerted the guards in the area to start searching for us. Meanwhile we ran without stopping. It was hard to go fast because of the tree branches lashing against us, but we kept going until we reached the main road. When we arrived, we paused long enough to stop panting and until our legs were not shaking anymore. Then we hailed a truck and boarded it in the hope of embarking on the second stage of our flight from Cuba. Instead, the truck stopped at the police station, and the G-2 arrived to question us about why we escaped and who helped us. But we had already prepared our answers and denied having plotted together. We said we did not know each other and that jumping was a spur-of-the-moment act. Nevertheless, we were put in jail for ten months incommunicado and my original sentence of ten years had no possibility of being reduced. On our records they drew a red line to indicate that we were the kind of prisoners who try to escape. Even though this was my second attempt, they did not shoot me; if they had shot *me*, then they would have had to kill half the population—that's how many people try to escape.

We were taken to another concentration camp with greater security and no chance of escape. There you had to work inside the prison grounds, breaking rocks in a quarry. Then we were sent to Fajardo in Pinar del Río. The prison was surrounded by houses of *campesinos*, which encouraged some prisoners to try escaping. Thereafter they moved us to Taco-Taco again. Then they decided to bring all the men there who had escaped from military service. One night without warning we were all told to gather up our belongings. Ten *rastras* arrived full of military deserters—three thousand of them. They were put in our cells, and a thousand of us were sent to La Cabaña, another thousand somewhere else, and the rest of us to El Morro, where conditions were very bad. This is a fortress built in colonial times and used by the Spanish as a prison. In the beginning of the Revolution it was for people in the Havana area who evaded military service and for Communists who had problems with the government. Everything is completely closed. You can't see outside at all. There are about ten *galeras* [long cells], originally built for twenty people each, but now they hold eighty to a hundred. Each one has bunk beds, along the walls. These accommodate only some of the prisoners. The rest have to sleep on the floor. It was so wet inside that water collected in the corners and moss grew all over the walls. We were plagued by all kinds of insects, bedbugs, crabs, etc. Our food was mainly spaghetti and by the time they brought it from La Cabaña it smelled so rotten you could hardly eat it. This caused many stomach ailments among the prisoners but we were not allowed any medical attention and we could not even receive food from outside because no visitors were permitted.

The overcrowding resulted in so many protests by the prisoners that even the guards realized that too many were there. At times it got so bad we used to bang on our cell bars with whatever we had, screaming and insulting the officials. Finally the authorities decided to send us to La Cabaña. Life there was even worse, although the prison was a little better organized and the garrison was bigger. Some men were in wheelchairs, and many of the old prisoners died for lack of medical care. Others were killed by firing squads in the yard. In the place where I was, some people committed suicide. I remember one cutting his wrists and another hanging himself.

My stay there ended because there was a lot to be done in the sugar-cane fields, and since they don't have enough people to do the work, they send the prisoners. One day they loaded us like cattle onto four large trucks in which we stood completely closed in for three hours, although the trip usually takes about an hour and a half. Then we arrived at a sugar mill, ironically called Por Fuerza—we certainly were there "by force"! What greeted us was an abandoned camp like the ghost towns of the Old West. In one week they had to put together a concentration camp. To do this they pick the prisoners who are more indoctrinated to build it, and they send the G-2 to organize it. Only the *galeras* were completely closed and roofed, and finally they at least sent us some mattresses filled with straw.

One day while I was working in the field the pain in my back was so sharp that I lay down. I had told the guards that I was having a bad problem with my spine but they didn't believe me. Stretched out on the ground, I was watching the guards standing with their rifles poised. (They stay at a distance so that none of the prisoners can attack them with a machete.) One of the guards started shouting, "Come on, hurry up, keep working." Then the re-educator came by and tried a softer approach to encourage the prisoners to work, saying, "Listen, we have to cut a certain amount of cane. Don't look for trouble, just do the work, because it's for your own good." While all of that was going on, one of my friends came over and asked very quietly what had happened. I whispered to him not to worry and that during the break for water I had spoken to Pepito about escaping. Later, inside the *galera*, I finished talking with my friend. Pepito, who was twenty-eight, had come to me one day, saying, "I've known you for a long time and I know I can talk to you. There's a young guy here who tried to escape from Guantánamo Bay, so he's had the experience and could help us try the same thing. But he's young, twenty-one. Do you think we should go with him?" I told him we should definitely give it a try. In the meantime, every day two or three prisoners escaped from our *central* [sugar mill]. The

guards would come back saying they'd caught the prisoners, but
we didn't see them again because they never brought them back to
the same place.

One Sunday in December 1973 Jesús, the young man, came to
tell me that the escape was set for the next day. I showed him and
Pepito how to disguise their prison clothes by wearing another pair
underneath on the reverse side. When we arrived at the cane field
that day we waited for noon, when the soldiers were eating. We
chose that time because they were as hungry as we were and looked
intently at their food instead of watching the prisoners. This was
only one of many details to consider in deciding when and where
to make our run. For example, most of the time the guards counted
the prisoners after lunch. But they needed so badly to get the cane
cut that they did not want to waste time counting. We knew this
and also realized that the guards were inexperienced. For two days
they had not bothered with roll call and had said they wanted to
finish the day's work quickly and leave by five o'clock. And that day
they happened to be short of guards. Another important part of our
plan was figuring out which part of the field we could escape from
most easily. Then we requested to work at that place, and the
guards let us go there.

The tricky part of our escape was that three of us had to get out
in rapid succession. There were two soldiers mounted on horses.
We had to pass between them right at the moment when they were
looking down at their food, and run into the bushes beyond. It was
to our advantage that they remained stationed in one place to
oversee the area where they are. If they see prisoners trying to
escape they shoot or blow a whistle to alert the other guards that
someone's running away. Then the soldiers all mobilize to search.
Since the guards were not expecting anything like what we did, they
were not paying attention to us. The first one in our group got out
without any problem. Now we had to watch for the instant the next
one could leave. This depended very much on luck. The guards
could not hear any noise, for they were a considerable distance
away, and when we ran we bent low so that there was less chance
of their seeing us. The second one made it through, and then the
third, without being noticed.

Once out, we crossed the fields and kept going for what seemed like an endless trip. And now we had a new danger to worry about. We knew that if any *campesino* saw us, it would be all over. In such a prisoners' zone, the first thing the militia does is ask at the house closest to the prison whether anyone saw an escaping inmate. Now the *campesino* is trapped. If he says he has not seen anyone, but he has seen you and they catch you, the soldiers apply clever psychology. They ask if the *campesino* saw or helped you. Probably you say, "Yes, he saw me, but I didn't talk to him." Then they arrest the *campesino* because he said he did not see you and you said he did. This serves as a powerful example to the rest. In the next *bohío* [hut] they know their neighbor has been arrested, so that family and all the others around take it as a warning. They all decide to tell the militia if they see a prisoner escaping. The *campesinos* are afraid and therefore they cooperate with the government, even if they are burning inside against it.

Naturally, after going by three or four sugar mills, we saw a farmer passing in his cart. We flattened ourselves against the ground and stayed like that until he was gone. I tell you, we were more afraid of that man than of the chief of the garrison! Finally we came to a town, but even there we could not take a bus because three men together in prisoners' uniforms, even reversed, look suspicious. So we kept walking until three in the afternoon, when we arrived at the entrance to the town of Colón. There we had a lucky break—a truck with an open back passed by. Before it appeared, we had noticed a young couple with a suitcase on the other side of the road. We went over to them and struck up a conversation so that we would not be complete strangers, because when they hitched a ride we planned to get on with them. When the truck stopped for them we jumped inside too. After going through three towns, we had to get out—the driver's trip was over. Since we had to continue our journey, we took a terrible chance: we thumbed a ride on a truck driven by a soldier. The whole way we were hoping desperately that he wouldn't head for the police station, as the other soldier had during my previous escape attempt. Fortunately he took us as far as the quarry where he had to stop and we parted company without further incident.

The first stage in an escape like ours is a successful getaway. Afterward it is just as important to be able to travel to a specific destination inside the country in accordance with a prearranged plan. If you don't have a definite place in mind and a way to get there, particularly when you have had to break out of jail first, sooner or later you will be caught. The various types of transportation have to be anticipated. Bear in mind that if you take a bus from one province to another, you need an ID card showing where you work in order to buy the ticket. Usually you have to make the purchase in advance. In prison we prepared for the possibility of escape by keeping money hidden. Once we were out and had gotten some rides, we had enough money to take a taxi and then a milk train—a very old one in bad condition! For that trip we paid the fare by using someone else in the station to buy the ticket for us. At nine that night we reached Havana. Seeing the city again after such a long time was a shock. It looked dilapidated and dark, since not many of the streetlights were turned on.

I went to my mother's house immediately and she was very scared and asked if I had escaped again. I told her no, that they had given me a pass and I was on my way to work in another place. It was a tremendous relief finally to be able to take off my boots and change to civilian clothes so that I had a better chance of escaping. The three of us had agreed to meet the next day and one of my friends was in contact with someone who helped us. Three tickets on the train to Guantánamo were bought for us. Then we took all kinds of precautions to avoid being conspicuous. I tried to look like a musician by carrying a musical score. I sat in my seat pretending to study the notes. One of my friends deliberately sat next to a pregnant woman who was by herself so that he appeared to be her husband, and the other fellow sat near a window and spent his time looking out at the scenery.

When the train arrived in Guantánamo it stopped at the border-police station. I put on my *campesino* hat, stepped off the train and strolled over to a stand to buy a beer. The whole way over there one of my friends was whispering nervously to me, "We're really in trouble now. Do you see how many guards there are!" Without moving my lips, I answered in a low voice, "Never mind, don't worry about it. Calm down because we have to go by them." Since cigarettes were scarce, I counted on using some as bait to get out. I walked over to a soldier and said, "Excuse me, *compañero*, do you have a match?" He answered just as I expected, "Yes, if you give me a cigarette." I obliged him and we passed by without a hitch.

When we got out of the station we walked in the direction of the woods, where my friend Jesus showed us the place to enter toward the U.S. naval base, since he knew the spot from past experience. It started raining, but we could see far in the distance a little house with lights. It looked like a painting, but as we got closer we discovered it belonged to the border patrol and was the main guardhouse. Nevertheless, we had to continue crossing the fences on that property because we were already inside. As we came nearer we could see the guards changing, soldiers with rifles, and a jeep. We waited until they passed and then we walked to the back of the house, where we discovered a road. Despite Jesus' acquaintance with the area, we realized we were lost. In a few paces we came across a sign saying DANGER, MILITARY ZONE. Guided by the reflectors shining from the American side of the base we kept going anyway, past another sign, announcing CUBA, FREE TERRITORY OF AMERICA. Then we couldn't see anything else because we had to climb a hill. Once we reached the top we saw down below us the Cuban guards, lights and trucks. We walked back down to where we had been and decided to cross the first fence.*

Electrical connections run along the top of the fence. When you touch them, Bengal lights illuminate the whole area. To avoid contact with this wiring we chose to make our way through the fence by pulling out the nonelectrified wires close to the ground. This was hard to do because the wires are very strong. When we managed to tear a hole in the fence, I was the first to pass through. I stopped and waited for Pepito and Jesús to join me. Another danger we had to worry about was the minefields. Someone had explained to me how they work. The mines are actually a network of thin wires connected to explosives, but we had no idea where they were. Therefore, we crawled along the ground very carefully, our hands extended to feel for the wire. We proceeded in this way to

---

* In 1966 Castro spent between $6 million and $15 million to make a no man's land and military zone out of a wide strip of terrain adjoining the Guantánamo base. An elaborate system of obstacles and fortifications was constructed around the fence separating Cuban territory from the base.

the second fence, and this time someone else went first. We passed through without any problems and groped our way toward the third fence.

At this point we felt very emotional because we were so close to freedom. Can you imagine, after all the waiting, planning, tension and traveling, what that felt like? The young kids were so excited they rushed forward to cross the last fence. I told them to stop and calm down and go carefully because the mines might be there. In their eagerness they did not listen to me and ran ahead. The next thing I knew, there was a loud explosion and one of my fingers was cut by flying metal. At that moment I was still standing at the second fence. In my confusion I ran to one side as a reflex, even though I could have gone straight ahead because the mine had already exploded. When I got to the third fence I yanked out the wires and went through. After I reached the other side I heard someone calling out, "Pepito, Pepito," and a voice answering, "Be quiet." Then a militiaman shouted, "Don't worry, we'll catch them. Anybody trying to cross is never going to make it." Obviously they say things like that to intimidate you. Suddenly I heard Jesús saying, "Go ahead, we'll follow you. Use that green light in the distance as a guide—it's on the American side." When I heard him I relaxed a little, thinking there was no problem, after all, and I discounted the possibility that anything serious had happened.

I was in neutral territory now and it was like a menacing jungle. All you find are trees and holes in the earth. Scattered along the ground and heaped up in places there was barbed wire. Three hours passed and I began losing hope and getting anxious at the thought that maybe one of the boys was dead. I felt discouraged but continued. As I was walking on, I nearly got killed by something I had not expected at all. I fell into a trap like the ones used in Vietnam. I saw a spike flash past me, but luckily I did not fall on it and avoided getting hurt. I climbed out of the ditch, which was covered lightly with earth so that the unsuspecting person would not realize there was a hole underneath. I continued walking until I saw signs saying DANGER U.S. ARMY. I thought to myself, What kind of danger can there be now, after what I've just come through!

I tried to scale the American fence by grabbing the wires, but I could not make it because I had no more strength left. Then I noticed a tree nearby, which I decided to climb. At first it was much easier doing that, but suddenly one of the branches broke and I fell to the ground. By that time I was so weary and my body was aching so much that I could not feel any more pain. After a little while I managed to stand up and tried to climb the fence again. I finally hauled myself to the top, where there was barbed wire in a V pattern. I crawled through one of these Vs and got to the other side without a scratch. Now, at last, I was actually walking along the American territory and you can't picture the happiness I felt, how many things I was thinking! When I reached the guardhouse they flashed a light, aimed their rifles at me and said a lot of things in English I could not understand. All I could answer was "Please, please." Then I figured out that they were ordering me to lie face down on the ground. They continued talking and I could not follow what they were saying. Finally, in my nervousness I asked for a cigarette and they threw me one. Then they said, "O.K., sit down." Everything was being spoken from above in the guardhouse. A soldier told me to remove my jacket and he called a truck, which arrived full of soldiers in olive-green uniforms. I was terrified, wondering what was going to happen. They took out their guns and came close to me, but then I realized I was safe. They put me on the truck and wrapped me in a blanket because I was so cold I was shivering.

When we came into a coffee shop it was incredible to see all that food I had not seen in a long time. They gave me a lot to eat, but I was not really hungry then. Afterward someone took me in a little bus to a special place where they bring everyone who arrives at the base. I was overjoyed when I saw Pepito sitting there. Right away I asked, "Where's Jesús? Is he all right?" Pepito, who was very sad, said they had taken Jesús to the hospital. The soldier responsible for that area said in very bad Spanish, "No talking." They separated us and interviewed each of us individually. Later Pepito told me that after the explosion Jesús, who was bleeding very badly, said, "Let me stay here and you go ahead because I'm almost dead." But Pepito carried him, anyway, pulling him under the fence and crossing through the part where I had broken the wires of the third fence. I could not figure out how the two of them had been able to arrive before me.

After interrogating us, the soldiers put us in what is called Freedom House, with a coffee shop where we could eat whatever we wanted. As a result I got sick to my stomach, because after you go so long without eating and then see a lot of food, you overdo it. In the meantime, Jesús had been put on a plane and flown to the United States the moment he arrived at the base. Later, when we saw him in a Miami hospital we found him very ill, with a fragment of the mine in his brain. The doctor did not want to operate on him if someone did not give permission, and since Jesús had no relatives in America, they waited for his condition to improve a little bit so that he could sign the form himself. Eventually he recovered. Oh, something I forgot to mention—while we were at the base the Americans told us how surprised they were that we had made it through, because it is so dangerous that no one else had ever escaped from the place we chose.

Hijack

I decided to escape by the simplest means. To accomplish something with the least amount of resources possible is a revolutionary principle. And what were the minimum resources? A pistol, my intelligence and my physical capacity.

Octavio
Interviewed January 1978
Miami, Florida

Octavio, a mulatto, is a forceful man in appearance and speech—broad-chested, with powerful arms, and a resonant voice that issues from deep within him, giving full play to his passion. His hands trace arabesques in the air as he re-enacts his experience. Meanwhile, a highly analytical mind is at work. The description of the situation. Then "Resultado!," like a pistol crack.

I WAS born in Santiago de Cuba, the capital of Oriente province, in 1936. After graduation from a private school I went to the University of Havana to study electrical engineering. My father worked for the government as a labor inspector and my mother was a housewife. For a while I worked as a surveyor and would have liked to continue my studies, but they were interrupted by the political problems of my country.

I was greatly influenced by a friend who was a revolutionary, and I began working in various clandestine activities against the government of Batista. I did not belong to any political parties then, but became secretary of the Federation of University Students in the School of Electrical and Civil Engineering at the University of Havana. My feeling at that time was that only a civil war would

eliminate the dictatorship in Cuba and I was not convinced by any
of the revolutionary parties, including the Directorio Revolucionario, that they would accomplish one.

AT THE MOMENT of Castro's *Granma* landing* I began my political
activities outside the university. I returned to Santiago de Cuba and
started working with members of the 26th of July Movement,†
which is where I met the woman I married a short time later. After
the Revolution I became a provincial commissioner in Santiago de
Cuba in January 1959. With members of the 26th of July Movement I worked out of the government building housing the CMCK
radio station, over which I used to broadcast. We established a direct
line to the people. After we organized the city within twenty-four
hours, the first thing I did was give the people access to us. My idea
was to communicate with anyone who needed to talk to us. Unfortunately, some members of the Rebel Army opposed my methods
and started a conspiracy against me. Two months later I gave up
my position as commissioner. What began to disturb me very much
was that I did not see the democratic procedures I had been hoping
for.

I became discouraged when I came across any number of political intrigues, jealousy toward those from the universities on the
part of some of the people directing the Revolution, and growing
domination by the Communist Party of different organizations. I

* On December 2, 1956, Castro and eighty-one guerrillas aboard a fifty-
eight-foot yacht, the *Granma*, arrived from Mexico at the Playa de los
Colorados, near Belic. A few days earlier, guerrillas led by Frank Pais had
fomented an uprising in Santiago de Cuba intended to culminate in a general
strike throughout the island. Failing in their efforts to rendezvous with the
rebel group, under Crescencio Pérez, Castro and his men proceeded to the
Sierra Maestra.

† On July 26, 1953, Castro and a group of one hundred and sixty followers, including a few women, attacked the Moncada and Bayamo Military
Barracks in Oriente. On October 16, Castro defended himself in his famous
speech "History Will Absolve Me" and was sentenced to fifteen years in
jail. He was amnestied eighteen months later.

Before leaving for Mexico to train guerrilla troops, Castro had a meeting
on July 19 for his supporters, which is considered the beginning of the
26th of July Movement, commemorating the Moncada Attack.

returned to the university to continue my studies, but left shortly thereafter. I remained a leader of the 26th of July Movement and for a while worked in Venezuela on behalf of the Revolution. Then I traveled around Cuba trying to stop the encroachments of the Communists. I worked with others for a fair election of the student president of the University of Havana. The 26th of July Movement chose Pedro Luis Boitel, an electrical engineering student, as its representative. But Rolando Cubelas was called back from his post in Spain, and at the insistence of Raúl Castro, Ché Guevara and others, was put forward as the candidate. I strongly objected to the government's imposing its choice on us without assemblies for discussion or genuine congresses of delegates. After the election, in which Cubelas won, many left the university.

At this time I was twenty-three years old and very romantic and idealistic. For me the university had always been a symbol of freedom. So it was a shock to see it changing. Youths from the Communist Party were taking over. I recall distinctly one assembly, attended by Fidel. I was outraged when the people present asked for the *paredón* [death by firing squad] for a group from the Directorio Estudiantil who were in jail. This was the first time such a thing had happened at the university. Well, by this time it was clear that I was not wanted there, and soon the government put me under heavy surveillance.

Finally, I was arrested on December 31, 1960, and on January 4, 1961, a law established the death penalty for those caught with arms or explosives. Although none had been found in my possession, I was sentenced to die for being friends with some people arrested for having weapons. I remember hearing Pardo Llada, the radio commentator, announce my death; he did not know that a friend of mine in the Ministerio del Estado had saved me from the *paredón*. Eventually I was given thirty years, later changed to twenty. After ten years of imprisonment in La Cabaña, the Isle of Pines, La Cabaña again for ninety days in 1967, and the *granjas* [forced-labor camps] of Taco-Taco, Melena del Sur II and Melena I, I was released.

What I want you to understand are the patterns I observed in prison. It is impossible for me to tell you how the prisons in Cuba are right now, because I left the country in 1972. But what is interesting and important to know is that the Communists like those I saw in Cuba never use the same methods twice. By this I mean that they act as it suits them and no one knows what will come next. The prisoners certainly never knew what would happen in the future because if they had known what to expect, they would have known how to react, and the idea was to keep us off balance. I repeat, the Communists never use the same approach. At this moment, the situation of the prisoners might be the best in the world.

Let me give you an illustration of how they switch their tactics to manipulate people. In 1967 we had been under great terror on the Isle of Pines for ninety days. I had lost so much weight that I was down to 117 pounds; ordinarily I weigh about 175 pounds. We had been suffering from diarrhea because at that time our families could bring food now and then, but since we had so little to eat the rest of the time, this change in our diet created intestinal problems. Well, they suddenly gave us a delicious meal of shrimp, shellfish and chili, with better rice than my wife makes, and fried bananas— I thought I was in heaven! Then the next day they tried to force us to change our uniforms, from the yellow ones, those of Batista's soldiers, to the blue ones worn by common prisoners. The guards took us one by one through a door and each prisoner came out with the new uniform tied to him. You can see the psychology. So what do you think the reaction was? One part of the group took the blue uniform, and the others stayed in their underwear, refusing the new clothes despite the good meal. Changing your clothes at that moment was supposed to mean a change of attitude, because for us the yellow uniform had become a symbol of rebellion.

At this point the prison was in an unorganized state, one of complete pandemonium, and we were without beds or furniture, sleeping on the floor. I believe they had deliberately mixed workers, students, professionals with common prisoners in order to create confusion. There were speeches constantly, prisoners preaching different things. Some said, "I'm going to change my clothes," and some said, "No, I'm not going to change." Others said, "I'm going crazy." I united some of my friends and told them I was going to change, but they said they wouldn't. After three days of being in my underwear I put on the blue uniform because by then I no longer thought it made sense to maintain a rebellious attitude. When I changed, they transferred me to the concentration camp of Taco-Taco and later to the *granjas* of Melena.

To give you another example of how they operated, I remember our situation early on in the Isle of Pines. In 1963–1964 the majority of us had an average of two million red blood cells. I had about a million and a half and had to go to the hospital, where I stayed nearly a month till my count went up to four million. For two years I had had anemia, and there were many men like that. Because of malnutrition some used to fall down when they had to stand for only half an hour. Well, then the administrators improved our meals and gave us chicken and eggs once a week. Soon the red-blood-cell count went up. And immediately they went back to the forced-labor plan. This was their method. Working in the sun was exercise. So when our families came to see us after two and a half years without visits, packages or letters, what did they find? Men tanned and healthy, and no malnutrition! So naturally they thought, These people don't suffer at all. Who could understand our situation? Even our own families could not.

One of my first observations in La Cabaña was that, for no reason, they would put a *campesino*, or a worker, or a professional, or a member of the military before a firing squad. In the beginning I did not see any sense in these executions. Then I realized that what the administration wanted to do was introduce terror by this kind of random killing. And they succeeded. Inside prison we felt terror. We were right there under the executioners and we were in a state of deep depression because we saw people being put up against the wall and we were powerless to do anything. The only weapon some prisoners had was prayer. I remember one old man from the Cuban navy who carried a prayer book all the time, believing he could save people with it. The attitude of others was to wait for whatever they believed God wanted, since at any time they could be summoned to the *paredón*. In this atmosphere the visits we had during the first months of 1960 were pathetic. But, in my opinion, many people outside lived in a worse state of fear than we did. They were afraid of the unknown—of being sent to jail; we were already inside.

My feeling was that Cuba itself was a prison, that the govern-

ment practiced its methods of terror inside the prisons in order to
use them on the rest of the people. It seemed to me that they put
thousands of people in jail for no reason, but especially at the beginning because they wanted to induce fear in everyone. Then, once
they had a great volume of people locked up, they could experiment
with them and apply that experience to the Cubans outside. This
method became apparent to me during one *requisa* on the Isle of
Pines when two people were killed. There was a character dressed
in civilian clothes in the guardhouse writing notes on everything
that happened. I saw him with my own eyes. Like him, I was watching the reactions and they were typical of what frequently happened: prayers for peace; the national hymn sung to show we were
ready for combat; noise, silenced by a few shots; protests. The
officials wanted to know how we would respond, and when your
response was different from the others, they removed you from
the group. They isolate you so you won't influence others, and then
they try to make you change your mind.

The case of one brigade of about fifty students is instructive. They
took the group to the fields to work. As a form of protest the students talked to one another and worked slowly. Consequently, they
were taken out of circulation. The guards put them in a special
section on the sixth floor, segregated from everything—even sending up their food and not taking them out to work. Meanwhile there
were rumors of an exchange of prisoners between Cuba and the
United States. Prisoners thought that these students would be part
of it. At that point the students made a serious mistake. They
criticized the *campesinos* who went out to work. Their behavior unfortunately created animosity toward the *campesinos*, who then lost
respect for the students. After sixty days the students were taken
to an empty house near the main building, where the administrative
offices were. This move strengthened the students' belief that they
were going to be exchanged soon. But one day you heard the news
that the soldiers took them to do forced labor and that some were
wounded because of a rebellion. Their resistance continued for a
few months. *Resultado?* Either you keep up a continuous resistance,
risking injury or death, or you change your attitude.

I thought constantly about what twenty years in prison meant.
Twenty years of being away from my family. Twenty years of being

unable to use my abilities. Well, you can keep resisting. You can give in. Or you can try to escape. My decision evolved slowly. What I was confronting in prison was an anarchic situation. So my response was to draw back and observe the workings of the system. The only reason I survived was that I studied what was going on. My hobby in prison became psychology, which I learned from some psychiatrists who were there.

I managed to get out of prison before my term was up by turning their own methods against them. I entered the rehabilitation plan and did the work so that they could not fault me for my behavior. But I never renounced my principles and signed a statement that I was not a Marxist. When I got my first pass to leave jail I asked for nine days to visit my parents in Santiago de Cuba.

Upon arriving, I removed the pistol I had hidden and took it to my wife's house in Havana. I never considered leaving then, or breaking out, because I thought it would be too hard to escape from two places. Even if I'd made it out of jail, they could have caught me on the street. But if I was already free, I was sure I could get off the island somehow.

When I got out of jail I withdrew from everyone. I turned inward and proceeded to plot my escape without distractions. My wife was tolerant of my attitude. Occasionally we went to the movies, but that was about all. I was thinking twenty-four hours a day about getting away. An individual who thinks in this way is capable of anything. Such a person can hide without eating, he can withstand hunger and walk miles. It does not matter. He can do the impossible. I deliberately adopted a hostile attitude. That does not mean that I saw enemies all around me, but I put in my mind that I could not live in Cuba anymore. Someone who is integrated into the Revolution may be in disagreement with it, but he adopts an attitude and maintains it. Or you can create a sense of determination through a decision that will mean your freedom. In jail you are isolated. But once I was on the streets I retained that same sense of isolation and made my plans. I analyzed and studied everything.

I came to the conclusion that it was fundamental not to count on anyone. I needed to choose the simplest way. In the insurrection at the beginning of the Revolution I had learned that everything is possible with the least resources if your mind is so disposed. You also have to take into account the enemy's resources. And he has all of them—like boats for possible escape. If I had started to build a boat on the beach, I probably would have been captured. Many who tried to do so were taken to prison. There is always some imprudent action or noise. Or someone sees something moving where you are, or a person notices your returning to the same place. So I decided I would have to leave on a fishing boat.

At first I tried to get some members of my family to go with me, like my wife's brother, who had been with me in jail. But he did not want to leave Cuba. He told my wife that he did not have anyone but that he could understand me, since I had daughters in the United States. It is true. They were a powerful incentive for my leaving. I was concerned about them because of letters I received from their aunt—my sister-in-law. I did not want them to be sent to boarding school or to live in a dangerous area. Despite the fact that my wife's sister was doing all she could for them to live as well as possible, I was worried. I hardly knew my daughters. When they were three and four we sent them to the United States because we did not want them to be educated under a Communist system. The little one I saw once when I was in prison on the Isle of Pines. The older one I saw for the last time in Cuba when she was ten months old.

There was no point, however, in trying to get permission to leave because that would just have been announcing that I did not want to live in Cuba. Someone with my background would never have been allowed to go. In fact, when I was in the rehabilitation plan, the head of prisons, sent by the Minister of the Interior, came to see me one day. He said, "Well, now that you're in the plan, it's possible you'll get your freedom. We'd like to know if you're going to bring your daughters from the United States. We could have them here in seventy-two hours." I answered, "Revolution is inevitable because man has a tendency to be a revolutionary. But that is not enough for me to decide the fate of my daughters. I've been out of their lives for ten years and have no moral means of judging them or making a decision for them." The man was insulted, but I could neither agree to his bringing my daughters back nor compromise myself by saying, "Yes, they're returning." I was trying to figure out what the psychology of the government would be. If I succeeded in escaping, there could be a reaction against my wife. They could hold her and prohibit her from leaving. But there was another principle involved. Cuba and the United States had agreed to keep nuclear families together. It seemed to me that if the majority of the family was outside, the situation would prompt the government's release of the remaining members. And, clearly, if the two of us stayed in Cuba, the government would pressure us to bring our children back. So I counted on getting out and then being able to bring my family over. A few years after I escaped, my wife was allowed to join me in the United States.

Before the forced-labor plan the prisoners gave classes not only in English, French, German and Italian but also in air and marine navigation. Knowledge of the latter proved valuable once I was out. While checking the coast to find the most feasible place for my departure, I used what I had learned in jail. You cannot ask anyone for that kind of information or you will give yourself away. So, after eight hours a day working as a mechanical draftsman, I walked and traveled around to investigate. I decided to leave from the place where the least number of people knew me. The problem was that I was known inside revolutionary circles and too many people knew me in Oriente, more than in Havana or Pinar del Río. One day I visited the beach of Santa Fé, on the north coast, but decided that would not have been a good choice. I had too many friends there and no boats were around. I also checked Santa Cruz del Norte as a possibility. A friend there was a doctor whom I had known at the university. He wanted to escape with his family. Ultimately I decided not to take a chance with him. I did not mind if there was just another man going, but I did not want to risk the lives of women and children. After all that had happened in prison, I did not intend to surrender if they caught me. I planned to fight until I killed them or they got me.

In the end the best location seemed to be on the north coast of Pinar del Río province. I came to this conclusion when I went to lunch one day in a restaurant there, where I found a tourist center and a fishermen's cooperative. It was a good place to leave from because there was a bar, which gave me a reason to be there, and not many military personnel around. Pretending we were vacationing, my wife and I stayed in the hotel for a little while in order to study the situation. We walked along the shore and the man in the guardhouse gave us permission to look around. I thought it would be a good place, but I needed to know more. What were the weather conditions? Which was the best time of year to go? How would I get there? Who were the people using the boats? How would I enter the boat? What kind of general movement was going on around there? Answering these questions meant making many trips back at different times.

Since I knew I would have to talk to people, I devised the strategy of posing as an inspector checking the restaurants used by tourists. I would enter a place and ask for the bathroom, as if I were there to evaluate the sanitary conditions! Then, before leaving I would open the kitchen door, poke my head in and peer around. I would comment authoritatively, saying that it looked nice and clean. People naturally concluded I was an inspector or an officer in the army. I even invented an outfit for myself to carry out this pretense! I had a gray uniform which had been given to me during the Harvest of Ten Million, when, under the plan, I was out on parole. I had a pair of boots that had been provided in jail, and a blue beret lent by a friend. I didn't wear the beret when I left my house. I kept it in my pocket and put it on just when I arrived at the bus station to go to Pinar del Río. This will sound funny, but when I was in La Cabaña in 1967 I was imagining a new army being created to confront the situation in Cuba. Ironically, I had thought of those soldiers wearing blue berets, gray uniforms and black boots. My getup confused the people of the town because they could not tell if I belonged to the army, the Ministry of the Interior or the Ministry for the Harvest—since there were some sugar mills in that zone. I never considered carrying a gun until the moment I was ready to go, because it's too hard to do so with being noticed.

Then came the moments of doubt. You start asking yourself, "When am I going to leave? When am I going to capture a boat? What can I do?" Sometimes I was all set to go, but then I had to check the weather. I would walk along the Malecón [coastal highway in Havana] to look at the coast. I remember going to Oriente one day during the Carnival when I had a vacation for fifteen days. At that time I got a letter from my wife's sister saying that they were going to put my daughters in boarding school. That was the end for me and I told my wife to stay there. I went to Havana, where I lived in my brother-in-law's house. I was by myself and felt very lonely. I think the action of leaving my wife held me back, not wanting to go. I tried to rest and read, but I could not and I started feeling claustrophobic. I took my pistol, left the house and walked to the Malecón to see how the weather was.

I happened to eat lunch at a table with the cook from the restaurant in Pinar del Río. As luck would have it, a fellow in the coast guard who was the boyfriend of the cook's daughter was with us. He mentioned to the girl the time he went off duty and in this way I discovered the hour they changed the guards—from three to three-thirty in the morning. While in prison on the Isle of Pines, I had discovered that the guards leaving their posts were sleepy and the ones arriving were also tired. In fact, for about a half-hour to an hour after the new guards took their posts, they would be asleep. So my plan was to pass close to the guardhouse at the time they were changing, and then board a boat.

At midnight I arrived in Pinar del Río from the place where I would escape. After getting off the bus, I left the main road and entered the woods on the side, where I sat under a tree to wait. When I saw it was close to the time I should be leaving, I returned to the main road leading to the coast. As I was walking along, one of my boots started creaking. That had never happened before, but of course, it had to at this crucial time! I had no sooner pulled it off than I heard a dog barking. I remembered someone telling a story about escaping from the quarries on the Isle of Pines. He had said that that kind of dog cannot smell you unless you are walking in the direction of the wind carrying your scent. Otherwise, the dog will bark only when he hears you. With these thoughts in mind I walked to the other side, which was lower than the main part of the road, so that I was out of the wind. Right away the dog stopped barking. At that point I did not feel afraid anymore. I had the impulse to go to the coast and jump in the water. I was ready! I chose a boat—called *Cuba Libre*—from among three docked in the harbor, went inside and hid in a shallow hole used for storing ice. There are usually two, and this one was empty.

I had to crawl into such a small space that my knees pressed against my chest. The top of this little compartment was covered by a sliding wooden lid. While climbing down, I thought I made a noise. Then, through a crack, where the door did not fit the frame, I could see the light of a reflector, as if it were searching for something. It appeared to be about two hundred meters away. All I did was get my pistol ready, a Colt .45. In a little while I started to hear a lot of voices and singing. Then people arrived on the boat. I thought it was impossible that they were fishermen because I expected the boat to leave at five or six in the morning. I kept still and waited. The people were inside the boat now, talking and singing! I was sweating the whole time, not knowing what was going to happen to me. With boots and an *enguatada* [heavy T-shirt] I was sweating so much that I was getting dehydrated. When they finally left, I took off my shirt.

At about five in the morning another group came on the boat. They were talking the way people do who are starting to wake up. Then I could smell the coffee they were making. Half an hour later they started the motor and I could no longer hear the conversation. All I could see through the crack was day breaking. I had to guess at the time because I had no watch. I decided to stay put until the boat was far from the coast. I would have to wait for two or three more hours. The decision to reveal myself was difficult because I had no idea what to expect. What would I say? How would I impress the people? Where would the men be? From the voices, I thought there were three men. But there could have been more, since some people don't like to talk when they just wake up.

When I figured two hours had passed, I decided to show myself. I recall deciding not to swear at them, but to speak firmly instead. Although many people think you can frighten a person just by having a gun in your hand, I was thinking that it might have the opposite effect and scare them into attacking me. All these thoughts ran through my mind in a few seconds. I grasped the board above me and let it drop. Then I braced my body against the framework of the hole. My plan was to stay where I was in order to remain in command of myself and of the others. I did not want to move from that spot because then they might have been able to overpower me or throw me overboard.

The three men were surprised, and that's the moment you

have to act. I cocked my pistol to scare them and observed their reactions. I ordered the old man, the captain, to tie up the youngest one, who at first looked as if he might try something violent. The other one, who was about twenty-five years old, remained very quiet. Now, I felt in command because if the old man had been in charge before and now obeyed me, it meant that I had taken over. I could not afford to make any mistakes in the orders I gave. I did not want to kill anyone, so I acted in this way to prevent violence. I told them my situation and said I had to go to a Florida key or to the U.S. Coast Guard and that they were to take the direction I chose. They complied and said that if I found a key, I should stay on it. I told them I would make that decision myself. I felt very strange at that moment, with the awful responsibility of killing any of these men if they rebelled. I worried, too, that they could turn the boat quickly and throw me over. I knew I had to keep control of the situation from where I was.

At night when I saw a light, my idea was to turn toward the Gulf of Mexico, to the north, until we hit the commercial lines going from New Orleans to Panama. I learned that in prison because the fellow who escaped from the Isle of Pines had done the same thing and I had seen a map of the area. I did not want to try going all the way to the United States because I knew boats like the one I was in, a simple twenty-foot fishing craft, weren't meant for such a trip. I just wanted to reach those lines, but I did not tell the crew what I was thinking.

The light I saw was a boat and I told them to go in that direction. But then the weather changed and we could not even see the light clearly anymore. It looked as if it was going to rain. The waves rose up and I did not know what to do. Nevertheless, I insisted that the old man continue on the same route. He was getting anxious and said, "Look, I'm only going to ask you two things: let me untie this guy and don't make us go on this way, because if we do, we'll sink. I beg you to let me direct the boat. You don't look as if you know exactly what you're doing, and if not, we're going to be in trouble." He explained that we had to go against the wind. I answered, "All right, but when I see the first stars I'll take over again." He asked me to let the others sleep while he took the wheel,

and I agreed, telling him that he would be responsible if I had to
kill the other two. He was wearing a cap with a button on it saying
26TH OF JULY. I told him to forget that he had been awarded that
button and that I had escaped from the island, and just concentrate
on getting us on the right course. He understood and we continued
the trip.

I did not eat anything or sleep at all. Although he offered me
some bread, water and coffee, I did not accept. I figured that one of
the things I had to show him was that I was stronger than they were.
I noted that we had been navigating for about seventeen hours
altogether, and had made a semicircle to the south toward Cuba,
and could have returned there at some point. My decision was
to go straight to the north for four hours now, because that was
about the length of time we had lost going south. Then I thought
we should go west and that we would arrive at the point where we
had been when the weather changed. The crew obeyed and I think
they assumed I had had good experience at sea.

By this time the sun was very strong. In the brightness I could
see an enormous ship on the horizon, and then another one. It was
as if ghosts had suddenly appeared in the middle of the ocean. I
told the captain to go straight ahead. I thought it was just what
I was looking for—a commercial ship. About half an hour later I
saw a few more ships ahead, and a small white square far away. One
of the crew thought it was a building and that we were near Miami. I
thought we might be near Grand Cayman. The white building
turned out to be a big white ship with a red lifeboat on the side.
Then I saw an American flag in the stern. Someone with a mega-
phone asked if anyone spoke English. I was not fluent in the
language but I had studied it at the university. Surprising myself, I
answered them very clearly in English. Soon I was climbing aboard
with my pistol in hand. Before I got to the top of the ladder, I
removed the bullets, but the last one stuck. I did not know if the
gun had rusted, but I thought to myself, What if I had had to
shoot those men and the pistol didn't work? When I was finally all
the way up and looking down, I saw the little piece of junk I had
been traveling in for the last thirty-five hours. I could not imagine
how we had crossed the gulf in it.

They treated me well on the ship. It was like coming from one world to another. Simple things surprised me—the rice, and Coke that came from a can. And while I was in Miami, my daughters were there, by coincidence, on vacation from Brooklyn. The day after I arrived I saw both of them, but of course, they did not recognize me. It was as if we were seeing one another for the first time.

Chanson de Geste

When the anti-Castro guerrillas were in the Escambray Mountains, Fidel's forces took prisoners from among them. With their legs tied they were hanged from helicopters. The pilots flew with them like this over the zone to terrorize the others. From 1960 to 1962 they did things like this to clear the area of guerrillas. But there are still people there conspiring against the government.

Rolando
Interviewed January 1977
Miami, Florida

Rolando is a tall, robust man in his forties, with dark eyes, black wavy hair and a handsome, ruddy face. His experiences in Cuban jails are emblazoned on his soul and he has no wish to forget them for the sake of peace of mind or safety. He is less concerned with his own escape than with what other political prisoners have gone through. For many hours he describes individual tragedies, particularly of political prisoners for whose release he is still working. Few people can talk as he does, when he introduces himself, without sounding foolhardy at best or pretentious at worst. But there's no tinny ring of vanity. The words reflect his convictions. As a guerrilla, as a prisoner for eleven years and as partner in an audacious escape, he has earned the right to speak this way.

I AM in a position to demonstrate to the world the violation of human rights in Cuba. I am willing to talk to anyone, from any part of the world, about the situation of political prisoners there. I don't care if someone kills me for this—whether it's tomorrow on some street corner or by an agent sent by Fidel.

I came originally from Santa Clara and later moved to Havana.

I joined the fight against Batista as a revolutionary. Cuba had a constitution then, stating that a person could oppose any government that violated an individual's rights. So we went to the mountains to fight. I was with Camilo Cienfuegos in Yaguajay in Las Villas province. At the end of the Revolution I worked as a public-works policeman and continued in the Rebel Army for two months in the city after we had won. But in 1960 I left the army, became a bartender in Havana and began conspiring against the government. We understood that we had fought for something else—not what followed.

Our aim had been to establish a democracy, but the government was becoming a dictatorship, making decisions without the consent of the people. We were seeing leaders like Huber Matos, who had committed no crime, sentenced to twenty years in prison and others who had fought against Batista arrested and convicted without evidence by the *tribunales revolucionarios*. We were seeing Communists, not our fellow revolutionaries, being given power everywhere. And the elections that were promised never took place. Instead of truth, we had propaganda. Instead of justice, we had the secret police. Instead of liberty, we had terror. Since I was being persecuted, along with others, I went to Camagüey for a while and then returned to Havana, where the G-2 took me prisoner on October 30, 1961. They caught a lot of people who were plotting with me and gave us all thirty years, later reduced to twelve.

I was brought to G-2 headquarters, where I stayed totally incommunicado for two months. I had no rights—not even the right to see any of my relatives. I was humiliated and tortured and witnessed a Dantesque scene. José Pujals Mederos, who is still in prison, was tortured brutally. He could not move his legs after a long stretch in a *bartolina,* a cell so small that he could only stand up. He described to me how he had been given electric shocks in his knees, how the guards kicked him until he fell on the floor and then how they made him stand up so they could start all over again. This was done in a room where he was completely naked and where the temperature was drastically changed from extreme heat to extreme cold. After all these agonies he was kept in isolation for a few months and then transferred to La Cabaña.

At G-2 headquarters I shared a cell with Aldo Cabrera, a mulatto from Matanzas. He was of humble origins and worked as a candy-maker. During Batista's time he had been a union leader fighting against social injustices. When the Revolution succeeded he thought the problems of Cuba were over. But the same abuses began again and he started to plot against the government. On October 30, 1961, he was arrested at his work center. They went to his house and searched, but found nothing. They insulted his wife and daughter and shouted at them. "You who are black, you of all people, are supposed to be for the government." Cabrera was taken to what we called the *cabañitas* at G-2 headquarters in Havana. There he was tortured morally, mentally and physically to make him confess, to turn in those he knew, the conspirators. But they got nothing from him. At five feet eleven, he went in weighing 220 pounds. After two months, when he came out, he weighed 180 pounds. His feet and legs were damaged from having to stand for hours. He was sentenced to twenty years and in 1962 was put in solitary confinement. Thereafter he was sent to the Isle of Pines.

Cabrera was harassed constantly because he was black. But I remember him always with his faith and his smile. He said that until the Revolution he had not known racial discrimination. He had always worked, lived and shared with whites and blacks, and he had never been judged because of the color of his skin. He was in many other jails with us and was put in with the common prisoners. When they tried to force him to wear the blue uniform of the *communes* [ordinary convicts] he refused. Lieutenant Emilio González Alios took him out and beat and tortured him so badly that he lost his eyesight. *Este señorito* [this gentleman, i.e., the lieutenant] would put prisoners up against a wall and stick lit cigarettes in their faces. When a prisoner tried to turn away, his head was slammed against the wall. Some became blind from the burns and blows on their heads. Cabrera, Inofre Pérez, a group of peasants, and Mario Chávez, a comrade in arms of Castro's at the Moncada Attack and the *Granma* landing, were taken to Boniato Prison. There they were kept in solitary confinement for long periods, naked and without food or water, until 1976. By then Cabrera weighed 120 pounds. Thereafter he was taken to Combinado del Este Prison in Havana, where he was put in a special cell, closed up like a hermit, without visitors, correspondence or any contact with the outside world. His wife was able to leave and is in the United States, but she has had no news of him for years.

I can tell you of another man, Sergio, who was like a brother to me. A former member of the Rebel Army, he fought, while still a minor, in Oriente province, where he was from. He was taken prisoner in 1960 and sentenced to fifteen years. During that time he was transferred to many different prisons—the Isle of Pines, Boniato, La Cabaña, the concentration camp of Melena. Because of his recalcitrant attitude in not renouncing his beliefs, he was confined so often in solitary, without light, that he developed allergies. When he was finally released, the doctor's diagnosis was that he ought to live in a cold climate because of the extreme sensitivity of his skin to the sun. Since his wife and three children are still in Cuba, he has not been allowed to emigrate, the government policy being to permit Cubans to join their families in exile rather than let individuals go if they still have relatives in Cuba.

Another of my cellmates at G-2 headquarters was Alfredo Izaguirre Rivas, who lost so much weight from the questioning and torture that he looked like a skeleton of scarcely more than 100 pounds. He was beaten so terribly for two days, with intervals to revive him, that his whole body was black and blue. Among the others were Octavio Barroso and Lieutenant Muino, an ex-officer of the Rebel Army. Both were tortured and then executed. While I was at La Cabaña I saw more than a hundred men led out to be executed. Among them I recall: Hugo Rodríguez Sorio, Tony Chao Flores, Captain Isaias, Elizarbo Necolarde Rojas and Captain Bermúdez.

Alfredo was born in Havana and at the time of his arrest he was the youngest journalist in Latin America. When they instituted the forced-labor plan on the Isle of Pines he said that he refused to have anything to do with it, period, much less for a Communist, even if they were to kill him. So at nine o'clock one night, when the prisoners were already in bed and were supposed to be asleep, we heard the iron bars open. Our nerves and hair were standing on end. We wondered who was going to be taken out to be shot, along with those who had not had a trial—not an uncommon occurrence. The prisoners would be told that they were going to trial, but actually they were brought out at night to be executed at the *paredón*. Then we saw that a prisoner was being brought back to our *galeras*. No one knew why, how it was possible that someone condemned to death was returning. We were frozen. We waited for the door to open. There in La Cabaña there were about 250–300 men, where only 100 could fit. We were sprawled on the beds, on the floor, everywhere. We had to walk over one another to go to the bathroom. We were careful not to hurt anyone, but it was difficult, since there was only a small light in the back. Alfredo appeared and we asked him what had happened. He could not speak. He was choking. There was such pain inside him. There was so much rebellion in him. He had asked the guards to kill him—since he had no children and was not married—instead of Octavio Barroso. After a long while he was able to tell us that the decision had been reversed, and that his death sentence had been commuted to thirty years.

We found out later that it was a diplomatic gesture that had accomplished this. The Mexican government had intervened and some were spared. Imagine the shock of the others who were saved when Octavio was taken out and they heard the shots. In order to torture them more, the guards waited the whole night and then thirteen more nights, letting them wonder if they were going to be killed too. On the morning of the fourteenth day the prisoners were taken out and told that their sentence had been changed to thirty years, and of course, nothing was said about the role of the Mexican government.

In 1962 in La Cabaña they had *requisas* [inspections] conducted after midnight. We were made to walk in the yard no matter if it was a cold winter night. All of us—including the old, the sick, the crippled—were forced to leave our bunks at gun and bayonet point. The guards used to enter the *galera,* striking us with their bayonets. In order to get to the very end of the *galera,* they walked on top of the prisoners who fell down, and they started all over again, kicking us with their boots and hitting us with their bayonets. When all of us were outside, they began to search the cells, pouring water over the thin mattresses, throwing our belongings all over the floor, and taking with them whatever they wanted. Many times our few possessions were just thrown out. This was done only to harass us and to prevent us from having anything. What we called *recuento* [counting the prisoners] took place twice a day, and during this procedure they kicked us too. We tried to rebel against this mistreatment, but whenever we did, the result was always many of us hurt and wounded.

When my trial came up I was given twelve years. I would like to make clear at this point that there was no evidence against me. You are sentenced, without having been caught at a clandestine meeting, without possessing arms, explosives or even propaganda material. It is enough for them to say you are not in favor of the Revolution. Period. The witnesses are only from the government—from the Ministry of State Security. The man who is supposed to defend you asks you questions beforehand and tells you to confess. Then this same man lists the charges against you when you go before the judge!

After the trial I was transferred to the Isle of Pines Prison, of which I have the most horrible memories a human being can imagine. The number of prisoners there started at 23,000 and went up to 38,000. Approximately 15,000 political prisoners were there at one time or another from 1959 until 1967, when the government evacuated the jail and moved us to other prisons all over the island. The prison consisted of four *circulares* [circular buildings of cells]. In the time of Batista each *circular* had a capacity for 400 men; under Fidel there were 1,200 men in each one. During the *requisas* the prisoners had to leave the *circulares* and march between two rows of guards standing there with bayonets, and then enter the *corral* [fenced-in field] where guards were stationed behind mounted machine guns pointed toward the *corral*. The *requisas* happened daily, weekly, every fifteen days, or monthly, depending on what the guards felt like doing. They took us all out at four or five in the morning and kept us under the sun until about six in the evening without letting us eat anything or drink water. At other times they would take us out in only our underwear at one or two in the morning. They were looking for any information we might have had from the outside or over a radio. We had built one from bits of metal and other odds and ends, but we always disassembled it and hid it, so that they never found it. Our communication was restricted to one letter every month from our family, sometimes only one every three or six months. One time I went for two years without receiving a letter or a telegram and without seeing my family.

The regime was expecting an invasion in 1961. After the Bay of Pigs Crisis, dynamite was placed inside the prison and they said that if another invasion came, they would blow up the prisoners. The estimated amount of TNT put in each building was 2,300 pounds. They drilled into the basement of the buildings all around and stored the dynamite in holes. Then they connected it. Soldiers came every day or so and went through an underground tunnel to check the dynamite. The detonator was about two miles away. A technician in explosives who was there said that if they set off the dynamite, the Isle of Pines would disappear into the sea. When I was in cell 19 on the first floor of Circular #4, we dug a hole and saw the dynamite. A few days later during a *requisa* the guards discovered what we had done and I was confined for four months in one of the punishment cells. At night the guards poured water on the floor so that we could not sleep. Since there were no bunks, we were sleeping on the floor. Running water was controlled by the guards, who let us have some, once or twice a day for only a few minutes.

After the 1962 Missile Crisis they made a major *requisa* which we called La Pacífica because the soldiers told us that it would be a peaceful one, that they did not want to kill anybody. But what they did was bring in different kinds of tanks and cannon, and several hundred more guards with bayonets inside each building. They told us to come down in our underwear. They kept us inside, and forced us to face the wall with bayonets at our backs. Then they began throwing everything out of our cells—books, brushes, clothes, shoes, spoons, everything. They left every cell empty. At this time we staged our first hunger strike. We asked for our mail and for better living conditions. Since we didn't have any mattresses, we had woven our clothes together to make hammocks, but during the *requisas* they threw even those away. The result of our protest was more prisoners wounded and those of us on the hunger strike were sent to solitary confinement.

In 1962 the government began a re-education plan on the national level. They tried to put prisoners with short sentences—only

two or three years—into it. In the beginning they gave indoctrination classes. Then they applied the plan to prisoners serving longer
terms. As part of the re-education in the Escambray region in
the provinces of Matanzas and Santa Clara to make the farmers
accept the plan for collectivization of the land, the government set
up a trial in the middle of the town, sentenced people, then had
them shot by a firing squad so that everyone could see and be too
terrorized to help or join the guerrillas in the mountains. In 1972
after they caught all those fighting in the area they took five thousand *campesinos* from there and sent half to Pinar del Río and the
other half to Camagüey. The women had to stay behind. The men
were taken to minimum-security *granjas* [forced-labor camps] to
construct housing. Called "antisocial elements" because they had
been against the government, they were told to forget the province
of their birth and were warned that if they returned to see their
family or even went outside the *granja*, they would be killed. In this
way the government broke the contacts between anti-Castro groups.

    In 1964 there was a plan started for forced labor by prisoners.
We were told, "You are prisoners, so you have to work." We answered them by saying, "We are not supposed to work, because we
are political prisoners. In accordance with the United Nations
Resolution on Human Rights, we are not required to work. But if
you want us to work, you will have to force us to." We said this so
that they would know we were not obliged to work and would go
only because they made us. The plan was begun with a pilot program
with political prisoners who were *campesinos* from the Escambray.
They put about 300–400 men in punishment cells. Then they took
them out every morning, without shoes and at bayonet point, and
brought them back at six in the evening, after beating them until
they could not take it anymore. They continued in this way for
three months. Then the prisoners agreed to work, but on the condition that it be known that they were working only because they had
to. Afterward came the Camilo Plan, named after Camilo Cienfuegos, under which all the political prisoners on the Isle of Pines
were compelled to work. The prisoners were organized into blocs of
four brigades, each composed of 80–100 men. For each bloc they
had four heads, one per brigade. In addition, there was a sergeant
for each brigade, and the regular *cordón* [line] of guards with

bayonets. They took the prisoners out in trucks and forced them to work in the fields, raising citrus fruits, mangoes and pangola [grass for grazing cattle], and building fences. The prisoners also worked in the quarries breaking and carrying rocks.

On the first day of the Camilo Plan, Enrique Díaz Madrugas was killed with a bayonet. When Alfredo's brigade is brought out, he calls the warden and says he will not work. The warden calls Lieutenant Morejón, who says, "So he doesn't want to work. Take him to a punishment cell and we will see if he works or not." The next day Alfredo is taken out at six in the morning. The warden and a guard from Oriente, Luis García, and other escorts tell him they want to see if he is going to work or not. They bring him over to a tree and give him a machete but he does not take it. He says he is a political prisoner and will not work, that there is an agreement with the UN that political prisoners do not work. They begin beating him and after they have hit him many times, Alfredo loses consciousness. They drag him to a jeep and put him in solitary. They throw water on him, revive him, and the next day the same thing happens again. This continues for four days. He cannot eat the food they give us. On the fourth day, seeing that he is still refusing and is black from blows, with wounds all over his body, they take Alfredo to the hospital to treat his injuries. Two weeks later they return him to solitary. They do not take him out anymore, but they beat him daily and throw water from above so that he cannot lie down on the floor. It is made of porous cement and full of little grains that penetrate even into your soul. But the human body and the tenacity of men like Alfredo resist all of this. He remains there for two years, from 1964 to 1966. Then he is taken to Combinado del Este, where there are 5,000 prisoners.

In December 1966, Roberto López Chávez died. His death was a nightmare for all of us. He was transferred to a punishment cell because he had announced he was on hunger strike to protest the forced-labor plan. He was denied water because of his belligerent attitude and died of *thirst*. One day some guards came into Francisco Nogales Menéndez' cell and provoked him, yelling all kinds of insults and obscenities. After a few minutes they left, letting the door stay open. Francisco ran after them. One of the guards was waiting for him, rifle at the ready, and killed him with two shots. And there was Antonio Llerena Andrades. One day while he was out working under the forced-labor program he got into an argument with one of the guards. Antonio was beaten so brutally all over, including his head, that he died in the evening of the same day. I remember that by the time we were transferred from the Isle of Pines, we left behind about twenty-five prisoners dead from the *requisas*. And as a result of the brutality of the forced labor, twenty-three prisoners were killed between 1964 and 1967. Because they were working under duress and were resisting, about 450 prisoners were injured by bayonets, or lost fingers or arms. All the fruits and the trees of the Isle of Pines have been grown with our blood and they bear the stamp of our wounded and dead.

Those of us who had been isolated from the other prisoners and another group of 178 men were taken to La Cabaña. They took the rest from the Isle of Pines, some 6,000, to concentration camps all over Cuba. They tried to make them wear the blue uniforms of the ordinary convicts so that the political prisoners could not be distinguished from criminals. There began once more the problems, the blows, the bayonets, the dead. There were the wounded, the madmen, the people without legs or arms. And there were doctors and psychiatrists studying the behavior of the prisoners and giving orders about what should be done.

Our group here [in America], la Agrupación de Ex-Presas y Ex-Presos Políticos de Cuba [Organization of Ex-Political Prisoners of Cuba] is trying to obtain the freedom of our sisters and brothers who remain behind in Cuba's jails. From former political prisoners and from the relatives of the ones still in prison we receive news about the conditions over there. Prisoners who witnessed it, informed us about one of the recent atrocities, the Boniato Massacre of 1975. When Laureano Váldez Gallardo was denied dental treatment he extracted his aching tooth with a spoon because he could not stand the pain and developed tetanus. The other inmates began to scream in protest so that their buddy would be given medical aid. Lieutenant Raúl Pérez de la Rosa, the Assistant to the Director of Prisons, put a machine gun in front of the cells. In the first firing the protestant minister, Gerardo González Alvarez, fell as he was saying, "Forgive them, Lord, they know not what they do." With him fell our *compañero* Enrique Rios Corea, who tried to hold him back. Twenty-seven were wounded, eight of them seriously. And still, those who visit Cuba insist that the Revolution is good.*

In 1972 I got out on parole, before finishing the last year of my term. I applied for an interview with the Minister of the Interior of Cuba [where passports are obtained]. He refused to see me. The secretary asked me to write explaining why I wanted to see the minister. I wrote saying I did not want to stay in Cuba anymore, that I had been in jail eleven years, was not a Communist and never would be, and what did I have to do to leave? I never saw the minister and no one ever answered my letter.

Since I could not get out legally, I planned to escape with three friends by swimming to the Guantánamo base. I was thirty-five, and the others were in their twenties. One was an engineering student, another a sailor with the merchant marine, and the third a factory

---

* During the eleven years of my term I was in the following prisons: La Cabaña; the Isle of Pines; Melena II; Jaruco 1; El Príncipe; Manuel Fajardo Farm; Taco-Taco; Sandino 1–2 and 3; and Remate de Guanes.

These are the political prisoners they killed under the Camilo Plan on the Isle of Pines: Don Tomas Aquino, from Guines, Havana, died of the cold, Circular #4, October 1962; Ernesto Díaz Madrugas, September 8, 1964; Luis Nieves Cruz, September 21, 1964; José Guerra Pascual, September 21, 1964; José Alfonso Olarama, September 21, 1964; Gerónimo Godínez, January 8, 1966; Julio Tang Texier, March 9, 1966; Roberto López Chávez, December 11, 1966; Eddy Alvarez Molina, December 9, 1966; Diosdado Aquit Manrique, December 16, 1966; Francisco Nogales Menéndez, January 28, 1967; Danny Regino Crespo García, December 24, 1966.

During 1967: José Pereda; Tomás Aguirre; Ramón Quesada; Julio Hernández; Feliberto Polledo; Gastón Vidal; Manuel Cuevas.

Those who died in other prisons include: Luis Alvarez Rios, on hunger strike in El Príncipe; Rafael Domínguez Socorro, February 14, 1968, La Cabaña; Francisco Balbuena Calzadilla, August 1968, died insane from the torture he was subjected to in the *gavetas* [lockers] of San Ramón, Oriente; Eddy Molina, April 1968, Las Villas; Alfredo Carrion Obeso, murdered by the guards in Melena II, April 1968; Carmelo Cuadra, April 1968, in El Príncipe, on hunger strike; Estevan Ramos Kessel, April 2, 1972, Oriente; Ibrain Torres Martínez, January 27, 1972, Oriente; Olegario Charlot Pilela, January, 1973, Oriente; Rene A. Bueno, Melena II; José Acosta García, August 5, 1971, Centro Seguridad #4, Las Villas; Lázaro San Martin, Jaruca 2, Pinar del Río, December, 1972; Diosdado Camejo, Morón Prison; Oscar Morales Pascual, Centro Seguridad #4.

worker. We knew a group of people who had escaped that way and we were waiting to hear from them. A month went by without news. More time passed and still no word. We do not know what their fate was. They may have been eaten by sharks, or rather, the guards may have shot them and thrown their bodies to the sharks, which is what they frequently did. If they catch you jumping the fence at Guantánamo, and they kill you, they bury you in the cemetery close to the base.

When I got out of jail I worked in construction. My friends and I had to get identification papers like everyone else: from the Census Bureau, from our place of work, and from the military service. Without these you cannot travel in Cuba; if you do, you are sent to prison. The first thing we did was get out of Havana. On December 20 we boarded the train for Oriente province, then changed to another one going to Guantánamo. Our plan was to walk from the town to the base. We had deliberately chosen this time of year because, believe it or not, people still had the Christmas spirit. (Fidel changed the celebration of Christmas to July 26.) Families were gathering and receiving visitors, and the vigilance was less strict. Ordinarily if anyone saw you were not from the town, they would immediately ask for identification. If you did not belong there or produce a convincing reason for being there, you would be sent to jail.

We carried enough milk, sugar and water for two days, thinking that was how long it would take to reach the base. We started walking through the woods, peering through our binoculars to spot any danger in the distance. We were wearing dark clothes—dyed khaki pants and T-shirts, and straw hats like the ones *campesinos* wear. As a special precaution we had smeared our bodies all over with car oil, particularly under our arms so that the watchdogs would not smell us. The guardhouses scattered around the base have searchlights and dogs. Sometimes soldiers walk along the fence with these dogs, particularly at the places people have escaped from. All along Cuba there are guards constantly patrolling the coast. They start at six in the evening and finish at six in the morning, and they, too, have dogs with them. The soldiers shoot to kill escapees from Guantánamo, and if the bullets miss, they use the dogs to finish you off. It is only the remote places around the base

that are not watched. During the day, airplanes patrol Cuba. If
they see people escaping from a certain area by sea, the pilots
signal the position to a torpedo boat, dispatched to capture the
escapees.

We never dreamed it would take us eleven days to reach the base,
by which time we were starving. We rationed what little we had
and only twice a day took a few sips of water. We would walk at
night and rest during the day, or if we saw no danger, we walked in
the daytime as well. It took us so long because we had to cross
mountains and the ground was very rocky. Finally, on the eleventh
day we arrived at the first fence of the base. At that time on the
Cuban side there were three barbed-wire fences, about fifty meters
apart, with sentry posts all around. A road, where guards are
stationed, encircles the base. Then comes a fence where there are
minefields, then a space of about a thousand meters, and three more
Cuban fences. After those three you have a stretch of land and
then the American fence.

We waited all afternoon at the first fence, hiding and watching
the movements around us. I can still remember the cold. With our
binoculars we observed the passing of the guards. There was no
moon that night and by eleven we began to cross the first fence. It
had about five inches between the horizontal wires. It appeared to
be approximately fourteen meters high. Looking upward, we
noted that the higher you went, the more space there was between
these wires, but never more than six inches of separation. We
knew, however, that it would be fatal to try climbing the fence.
The pressure of our feet on the wires would have been heard far
away. Furthermore, in certain places the wires are electrified. It
took us five hours to get through all of them.

It is important for you to realize that the metal of the fences
expands during the day because of the heat, and contracts when it
gets colder in the evening. So to solve this problem of the wires'
greater resistance at night, we had brought heavy ropes with us.
Crouching on the ground, we used them to pry apart the wires at
the bottom of the fence so we could crawl through. In this way
we safely passed the first fence and crossed the road. But if we
had walked straight ahead, we would have been seen by the guards.
Stretched out flat, we rolled along the ground until we reached the

second fence. Here we proceeded in the same way, and again at the next fence. Then we came to the minefield. Lately, in some places, besides the mines, they have rigged up Vietnamese-style booby traps. These are holes covered over, with sharply pointed spikes inside. If you fall on one, you are impaled and killed. So even if you make it past the mines, they can get you that way.

At first we thought they had the kind of mines that exploded when you step on them. But we found a different kind. At night, looking from above, you cannot tell they are there. As we crawled along the ground we came across a very thin wire, so fine you could hardly see it. We noticed it because of the reflections from it visible from our close-up position. The wire is attached to a detonator and when you break the wire at any point, it explodes. Carefully feeling our way along, we came to the next series of fences, where there is less surveillance. Remember that we had been eating next to nothing for a long time and that for the past two days we had had no food or water. Our lips were so parched that they were cracking. Added to this problem were the thorns that got embedded in our bodies. These accumulate because the area around the base is deliberately not cleaned up so that it is harder for people to escape.

As soon as we passed the remaining fences we saw the American guards. On their side they patrol in jeeps, since there's a greater distance between the sentry posts than on the Cuban side. A few more meters and we reached the American fence, a Peerless chain-link. We climbed over the top and in our joy cried out, "Finally, we've reached freedom!" Then, exhausted, we lay down without worrying anymore, and waited for the American patrol to come.

We did not start walking around inside the American base because we were not sure what they would do with us. Eventually, when we saw their patrol approaching we walked into the middle of the road. A few minutes later we signaled to one of their trucks and it stopped, leaving some distance between them and us. A short black man in an olive-green uniform dismounted. When we saw him, we said to one another, "Oh my God, get ready to run," thinking that someone in those clothes must be from the Cuban army. We preferred being killed while running than being captured. But the soldiers started speaking English and asking if anyone else had come with us or had been wounded. We said there were just the four of us. One of the guards took us to the post until someone came to pick us up. They started to take care of us, removing the thorns from our bodies. The only thing we asked for was water, which they offered us from their canteens. Soon all the soldiers came out to welcome us. They gave us food and clothing and brought us to the United States. Two of the fellows who escaped with us and went to Miami returned to Cuba in the hope of rescuing their families. They were captured and imprisoned.

"If You Have Eyes, Don't See Me"

At the moment I was ordered to change jobs and work in agriculture, I forged in my mind the idea that it would be preferable to die trying to be free rather than to live like a robot controlled by individuals with neither hearts nor any spark of human feeling.

Bernardo
Interviewed August 1976
New York, New York

Bernardo is a short, wiry man of thirty-five with curly black hair and light-brown eyes that turn into small half-moons when he smiles. He is still slightly dazed by his survival. In the hotel room where he is temporarily staying he sits upright in an armchair rather than settling back comfortably, as if he cannot yet afford to relax. He begins haltingly but gains confidence as he relates the rapid sequence of events that led to his escape.

I USED to work as a truckdriver for an organization of public works. One day a commission arrived from the Communist Party in the region where I lived, Holguín Tunas Puerto Padre. They required the workers of our brigade to fill out forms answering questions like the names of our parents, the number of brothers and sisters, the place we lived, where we worked, to which political party we belonged before the Triumph of the Revolution, and whether I was happy with my salary of forty-two centavos an hour. The last question they asked me was to which organization of the Revolution I belonged, to which I replied, MICONS [Ministry of

Construction]. But they wanted to know which organization for the Defense of the Revolution I had joined—the Committees for the Defense of the Revolution, the Civil Defense or the National Militia. When I said, "None," they stared at me until one finally asked how I could be driving a truck without being "integrated" into the Revolution.

I was told to report to the office of the Communist Party in another town, where I was informed that I was going to be given an opportunity, for they had noted in my file that I kept my equipment in good condition. (They had also added in red ink that I was "not integrated into the Revolution.") I didn't trust their offer because I knew what happened to people who weren't members of any revolutionary committee. Frequently a person's truck, tractor or other machinery was broken by party members, who accused the owner of sabotage. The Revolutionary Court then sentenced him to punishment he didn't deserve.

I returned to my job, but after they gave me time to join a revolutionary organization and I did not do so, they summoned me and told me my truck was being given to the military and that I was supposed to begin work on a farm in another area. At that point I made up my mind to escape.

I left in a truck for the town of Guantánamo and arrived there one Friday in June. I stayed the night and got a ride the next morning as far as a beach called Yaterita, about forty kilometers from Guantánamo Base. We arrived so quickly that it was only seven o'clock. When the driver dropped me off there, one of the border guards was suspicious and did not take his eyes off me. A little while later a truck appeared, one of those designated for transporting sugar cane. The driver went to the cafeteria of INIT [the National Institute of the Tourist Industry]. He returned right away because he could not find breakfast. He stood on the beach eating something and when he passed by, I asked if he could take me to a village twenty kilometers away. He said he was prohibited from doing so but agreed once I showed him my driver's license and ID.

After driving about eight kilometers, we were intercepted in a fishing village called Tortuguilla by a pair of soldiers belonging to the town. They asked the driver if I was the guy he had picked up on the beach and the driver said yes. I had evidently been watched since the border guard first spotted me. We drove to police headquarters, where they asked me who I was and what I was doing on the beach. I gave my name and occupation as a truckdriver and said I was doing what people go to the beach to do—swim in the sea and get some sun. They interrupted me brusquely to ask if I knew that it was forbidden to be on the beach before one in the afternoon. I realized then why I had aroused the guard's suspicion. They began to search me and turned my pockets inside out. After reading all my documents, one of them said to me in an ironic tone, "Mulatto, there's good reason to investigate you. Your ID says Holguín Tunas Puerto Padre, so what are you doing here, mulatto?"

At three in the afternoon I was put in a jeep driven by a soldier going through the village on the way to Guantánamo. I was now under orders of State Security. Since the soldier taking me did not know where the G-2 office was, he brought me to a local police station. After the sergeant read my papers he asked what I was doing there when I was supposed to be at State Security. He spoke a lot of words that made me tremble, and then called G-2, telling them to send a car because there was a case for them. Ten minutes later three agents appeared but could not stay because they were not able to find a place to park. They left, drove down the street and found a place in the middle of the next block. They sent a policeman to take me to where they were waiting. The policeman who came for me never had a chance to take me to the car.

I walked with him down the stairs and outside. After he was sure I was following him, he continued walking. We had to stop at the corner until some cars passed. I stood next to him. When the opportunity came, he crossed the street and continued straight ahead. I turned to the left, took a few normal steps and then started running. I ran five blocks, without anyone pursuing me, until I was exhausted and my legs began shaking. Finally I came to the yard of a house where I immediately heard the sirens of the police cars coming to look for me.

The owner of the house, a lady about fifty-five years old, saw me enter completely breathless and heard the sirens. I was paralyzed and unable to speak. Then, when I saw her shock at finding me in this state, I told her not to be afraid because I was not a murderer and had not done anything. She let me enter the house and sit down on one of the two beds in one room. She told me to sit next to her and explain everything. When she saw I was indecisive about telling the story, she told me to trust her as I would my mother. I lost my fear and told her point by point what had happened to me from the time I had my first commission from the party to the moment I found myself talking to her, when by luck I had entered the yard of this house.

A little while later her husband arrived. After learning all that had happened to me, he thought for a minute and then told me I had picked the most dangerous zone to enter the Guantánamo naval base, because a few days before, a freight train going from Guantánamo to the port of Boquerón had been intercepted. The driver was forced to drive as close as possible to the border separating the base from Cuban territory. A few of the border guards were killed and an equal number of people escaped. Shortly after, he met a man whose son had been killed in that escape attempt. Their only crime was to want to be free and live somewhere else without terror. I did not know anything about the incident, because in Cuba nothing is published in the press about such matters.

The couple prepared a bed for me in the room of their younger son, who was completing three years of obligatory military service. They explained that it was very risky for me to leave at that moment because there was a state of alert for all the chiefs of the vigilance committees of that zone. The members of the committees were checking every block. The two of them promised that if things weren't being as closely watched the next day, they would help remove me to a farm in another town. They advised me not to leave from that farm, since it was located where the military zone starts that surrounds the naval base. It is the most difficult road to escape, thanks to all the guards and battalions Fidel has dispersed throughout the area, yet it is the nearest route to freedom. Those who are caught trying to get inside the base are shot on sight.

The man and woman warned me about all the precautions I had to take and all that might happen to me. At any moment I could come across a trench filled with soldiers. The main road from the farmhouse to the town of Caimanera was patrolled constantly by troopers on motorcycles who had German shepherds with them. To pass from this farm to the main road and to be a prisoner were almost the same thing! At the entrance to Caimanera you had to present the sentry with a pass that only the residents had. For example, a person who did not live in the town but had family there had to be the responsibility of the head of the household he was visiting, and if this person went to the base, everyone else in the family had to go along behind him. If they did not, everyone would be arrested. The guards know when someone who comes to visit relatives goes to the base, because at the entrance to the town you have to say for how many hours or days you are going to be there and this is noted in a book and on the pass they give you. They want to be sure they can find that person in that house. Visitors have to return the pass when they leave town.

I went to the farm in a truck of those who look for people working on the farm. I got on in front of the civil hospital as if I were one of the farm workers. The truck went between a few houses until it came to some coconut fields, at the end of which is a river. The truck followed the river along the left side, bringing me directly toward the base.

Before I left the house where I was hiding, the woman had brought me a prayer, telling me that before I left I should kneel and in that position read the prayer three times and afterward keep it in my pants pocket. I remember only a few words of the prayer: "If you have eyes, don't see me; if you have feet, don't pursue me." I did what she said and later, once the truck had dropped me off, I waited until it was dark in the coconut field before starting on the road that would take me to freedom or death.

I began walking along the riverbank and had not gone one kilometer when I heard a voice saying, "Stop!" I threw myself on the ground and heard the voice say, "He's over there!" One of the guards fired about eight shots. I rolled along the ground until I fell into the river; however, I had not been hit. When my feet touched bottom, I lost a shoe, which remained buried in the mud. I swam underwater, lifting my head only to breathe, until I managed to get to the other side. The soldiers fired two Bengal lights and screamed, "Come out, you are surrounded!" The other words they shouted are unprintable. I answered them under my breath while I set out again. Walking along, I reflected on how I had crossed the river. Part of the way I had been able to walk on the bottom with just my head above water. I immediately got back into the river, trying to stay in the deepest part in order to walk as upright as possible, without having to incline my body too much. In the deepest places, where my feet did not touch bottom, I swam the way a dog does and tried not to make even the slightest noise that could reveal my presence.

I figured I had been in the water an hour when I heard a voice on a jeep radio saying that at Post One someone was killed but that they would have to wait until daybreak to look for the body, which was probably at the bottom of the river. The man answering on the radio said, "No son of a bitch will pass my post, because I'll kill him." At that moment I went by fifty feet from them.

I decided that if I continued, they would catch me, so the best thing to do was wait in the woods during the day and continue the next night. I left the river and crawled like a snake until I buried myself very deep in the brush. I stretched out, face down, looking toward the river, and began to scrutinize my surroundings. A white object caught my attention. It was moving up and down at regular intervals. I thought it was a duck; in the darkness I could not distinguish clearly what it was. Leaning on my elbows and resting my chin in my hands, I stayed there watching what I thought was a duck until the light was bright enough for me to see. Then I froze in shock. It was a border guard in a trench who was wearing a white handkerchief on his head as protection against the mosquitoes. Without taking my eyes off him, I inched back until I could no longer see him and he could not discover me. I tried not to get too far from the riverbank.

When I continued my journey I advanced with great difficulty because now I had to go through mud. Since I kept bumping into the shrubs along the shore, my whole body became covered with thorns that cut like razors. Being in the water was just as bad. There were barbed-wire fences stretched across the river. The wires were so close together that at times I had to inspect them very carefully to find a place where I could go through.

At the third fence I decided to take off my pants and underwear because in crossing I had to sink deep down and my clothes caught on a wire. While trying to unhook myself I had to come up for air. I tore at the wire and cut my thigh so badly that I needed five stitches later. I confess that this was one of the moments when I felt the most terrified.

I kept advancing, completely naked now, since at the first fence I had left my shirt on the wire under the water and my one remaining shoe in the mud. I should have removed my clothes at the beginning. From the moment I disposed of them I progressed with less difficulty and greater speed. In the distance I saw the brightness of the base above the trees, but I could not see the base itself because the river had so many bends.

I climbed out of the water when dawn began to break, and as day advanced slowly, the truck arrived bringing soldiers for the change of guards. It stopped near me, but on the other side of the river. After they changed the guards and I heard the truck leave, I started to pick some leaves from the trees to make a cushion to sleep on, but I could not close my eyes because there were so many mosquitoes. When the sun came up very strong they disappeared as if by magic. Then I started to sleep and had a good rest, because I needed it. When I woke up, I went over in my mind everything that had happened but I was not nervous about my situation. I told myself I was sure to accomplish my objective—to cross to the base. I did not miss food or water, even though I had not had any for twenty-four hours. I could not drink the water of the river, because it was salty.

Night started to fall and the mosquitoes did not leave me alone. I had to pass my hands constantly over my face and neck and arms. When I decided it was dark enough I went to the river again, twisting along the ground on my stomach, moving forward little by little. When I reached the salty water it was very painful because of the scratches and mosquito bites all over my body. One arm was completely red and I couldn't keep back tears. As time passed the pain disappeared.

I crossed the river because I knew the guards would be there soon and I wanted to be as far from them as possible. I made good progress. When I came to a fence I figured I was near some guards and took precautions to avoid making any noise. I moved more easily now.

I withdrew slowly until I thought it was safe to go faster. Up ahead, closer now, I saw the brilliance of the base's lights and while watching them I felt anguish for the first time. Then I calmed down and told myself this was not the moment for anxiety, that I should keep cool now more than ever. I continued advancing, able to do enough without anything getting in my way, until I started to feel like sneezing. I had been in the water so long that I caught a cold. The sneeze surprised me and I could not prevent it. At that point I was very close to the guards. I heard, "Stop! Who goes there?" The words were accompanied by shots but they were far from where I was. Luckily the guard was on the other side of the river.

At this point I began to see the empty space with just trees that surrounds the base and Cuban territory. I saw the fence that separates the base, and the bridge with an American flag in the middle. I thought that was the last guard I was going to have to pass. After I had gone about a kilometer into that empty zone I decided to come out of the river and I started walking on the bank. I knew that in case the Cubans saw me they would not shoot in the direction of the base.

Suddenly I was in the focus of a reflector from the bridge and I did not hear a word. I continued to walk. Then I saw a marine motioning to me to approach him. When I came and they saw the condition I was in, they shook their heads in sadness. Somebody gave me cigarettes, a carton with six packs. About ten minutes later a jeep arrived with some marines. One spoke Spanish and told me all my suffering was over, that I could say I was a free man again. At that moment I started to cry like a baby—I couldn't help it. When I had calmed down, I saw some food and a plastic container full of milk and asked if they could give me something to eat. They said it was not allowed because they did not know what my state of health was. If I ate immediately, it could be harmful. They said a doctor would check me right away and then could order food for me.

I have come to the end of my story. Right now I do not have any idea what the future holds for me, but I am happy that I will have some choice in deciding what direction my life will take. I have faith that one day my country will be free, and when it is, I will return.

The Invisible Boat

We were lucky that a man who later escaped with his wife and son had two outboard motors and lent us one. He told me that if I survived, I could return it to him afterward in Florida. Six months later I found him and gave him back the motor.

Leonardo
Interviewed February 1978
New Jersey

On April 12, 1964, twenty-one Cubans escaped from Playa el Salado, a beach to the north of Havana. Skillful teamwork enabled them to assemble a highly unusual boat and to avoid detection until the last moment. But in spite of their adroitness in carrying out a novel idea, and the good luck of having better provisions than most of the other escapees, the group encountered unexpected problems and nearly didn't make it. Leonardo is a short, thin man with light-brown hair, fair skin and blue eyes. He tosses aside the cloth with which he has been shining the top of the bar where he works, and comes around to greet us, smiling. Since it is late afternoon, we are able to sit at a table in the corner, undisturbed, as he recounts his adventure.

THE LEADER, Orlando, who organized our escape, was thirty-four. Among the rest of us there were four women; two children, aged one year and a year and a half; and others from thirty to forty years old. I had no relatives in the group, just friends. I was eighteen at the time, and like the others, I came from Havana. Once before I had tried to leave Cuba. I was supposed to escape from Cardenas in a boat belonging to a lawyer who smuggled people out for money. But the day before we were to go, he changed the plan and did not take anyone. I never found out why.

Different people in our group each lent something for the escape. Someone had a truck, to which we attached a trailer. We invented a special disguise. The roof of the trailer was actually our boat. It was made of wood and zinc and was about fifteen feet by seven feet. A friend who worked at an INRA [National Institute of Agricultural Reform] warehouse let us in at different times to build the boat in secret. Although we used a soldering iron to seal the boat, while we were at sea it began to leak a little bit.

Many of our friends had been escaping from Cuba and we used to hear about them on the Voice of America broadcasts. We heard about those who had come by boat. Every day we learned that three more had arrived, that ten others had made it. These successes inspired us. Nobody in our group was pessimistic. We were not worried about being caught at sea. The main thing on our minds was to get safely out of Havana. The other thing we thought about constantly was being free and working to better our lives. What I objected to in Cuba was the total repression, the feeling of being a slave. You could not think for yourself or express your thoughts openly. I hated the fact that the government pried into every corner of your life—that there was hardly any privacy. If you are not a member of the Communist Party or other organizations of the Revolution, they make life impossible for you.

I had begun working against the Revolution and, of course, if you are caught, you go to jail. At the time, I was a student. During the day I worked in my uncle's store and went to school at night. I joined a clandestine organization because a friend of mine was a member. It was a group of young Christians who held meetings to discuss the political situation in Cuba. Our organization began to grow, until eventually there were 150 in it, all of them young people. Since the only information and news allowed was what the government put out, we used to make copies of articles in American newspapers received from the United States. Then at home we put them together into pamphlets and included letters from different people telling how they had escaped from Cuba. Because people were spied on by the neighborhood Committees to Defend the Revolution, our work was very dangerous, but we managed to distribute our booklets in churches. Each of us took about ten leaflets at a time and passed them carefully from hand to hand.

The afternoon of our departure, the truck dropped us off in small groups in different places. Too many people going anywhere together would have created suspicion. By five o'clock all fourteen of us arrived at the beach. We acted as if we had come to fish and pretended not to know one another. Then we noticed seven boys, ranging in age from seventeen to twenty-one, watching us the whole time, observing every movement we made. At first we thought they were in the militia, but later we found out they weren't. When they saw our camper arrive, they probably thought we were planning to do something, so they hid.

When we started to take the boat down they came at us, threatening us with sticks and knives, and saying, "Take us with you or you won't get out. You have to take us or we'll make trouble for you." In the end we had no choice and took them, although we did not think the boat could carry so many people. The motor was only 35 hp and was not intended for that heavy a load. And we had enough food for only fourteen people for three days. We carried a tank of five gallons of water and little crackers. The only thing we had enough of was fuel, because little by little each of us had been saving gasoline and oil. Once all of us got on board it was incredibly crowded. We were packed together with scarcely an inch of extra space. We discovered that the boys, who were students and factory workers, had planned to steal a boat from the militia. But when they arrived, they found it was gone.

We left the beach at nine o'clock, rowing at first because we wanted to avoid the noise of the motor. Fortunately the night was very dark. There was no moon and the sea was calm. But soon we were in trouble. After going one kilometer we saw a Cuban patrol boat coming. Five weeks in advance we had checked exactly what hour the patrol boats changed and had calculated our departure time for eight o'clock. Running into those boys had delayed us an hour and we would definitely have been caught if a stroke of luck hadn't saved us.

About thirty kilometers out we came across a tugboat scooping sand from the sea. We hid behind the tug until the patrol boats changed. We had to wait a half-hour until they were gone in order to row one more kilometer. During that time the children were asleep because we had given them sedatives so they would not cry and give us away. Finally we started the motor, but the boat went in reverse. Then the propeller broke and we had to pull the motor inside to repair it. Luckily we had spare parts to replace the broken one. It took us forty-five minutes to fix it. We continued, but could still see Havana and were terrified. If a patrol boat had spotted us, they would have machine-gunned us.

A few hours before dawn we stopped only to put in more gas and to cool the motor for a short while. Throughout the trip we were so nervous that we were not hungry or even thirsty. Several of us were dizzy and vomiting. Orlando's wife got seasick and was worried about her baby. She kept asking for Orlandito, whom I was carrying. The whole time, we were anxiously searching the horizon.

At dawn we finally saw something through our binoculars that looked like a bird. With a little piece of mirror we started signaling it, in case it was a plane. Thank God it turned out to be a plane from the U.S. Coast Guard. It signaled us to go in the direction of a smoke bomb it dropped. We continued toward it and then they picked us up thirty-five miles south of Key West. They told us to take the rest of our water and belongings and leave the boat, which they sank. They had to go on with their work and then they took us to the base at Key West. With the little English we knew we explained our situation and were taken to the Immigration Department. Afterward Orlando's wife received some injections and soon felt better, but another woman who was pregnant at the time of our escape later lost her child.

"I Don't Want to Remember"

I want to live, if only to do what is good. It is really a miracle to find myself alive.

William
Interviewed November 1972
Miami, Florida

William is the sole survivor of a group of eight Cubans who fled on a raft in November 1972. During his third year at the University of Havana Medical School, William asked about the possibility of leaving Cuba. As a result of this request, he was forced to end his studies and do construction work instead. While he was still in the hospital after arriving in the United States, William gave the following account of his escape.

MY ONLY acquaintances among those of us who went on the raft were Dr. Ángel Tasis, a veterinarian; Dr. Cosme Huerte, a doctor; and his mother. I did not know the rest because of the secrecy with which the trip was prepared. We left from a place on the beach of Santa Fé, which is where I am from. Our raft was made of boards and tire tubes. Among the poignant things I remember is that Dr. Huerte's mother took a small dog with her and it started to bark as we set out. The memory of everyone appears to me clearly now. Mrs. Cosme was the most spirited.

The night we left was propitious, since it was dark. We took some cans of powdered milk—you cannot imagine the work it cost us to obtain them—and water and crackers. Nothing more, because we thought the crossing would be short. No one thought that what unfortunately took place would happen. I don't want to remember it . . . I'd like to explain that I needed something to believe in and I think that I succeeded because God gave me the strength. He allowed me to return and tell about our odyssey.

As the days went by, our frail raft became weaker. We were already sensing great troubles. How far we were from knowing what the end would be! A simple sign from a boat or an airplane would tell us that we had been discovered. The anxiety began to weigh on everyone.

We all talked together and when my turn came I suggested that we begin to limit the food and water. There was still hope, but the days continued to pass, increasing our desperation. And then what we feared so much happened . . . that the raft would break. We knew it would come to that, but we could not do anything to prevent it. In the meantime, by day, when there was no sun, there were the waves that made us hang on to one another to avoid falling overboard. You can imagine how it was at night. The cold made us huddle against one another and cover ourselves with the driest clothing we had. Then the moment arrived. When the raft fell apart all of us took whatever tire and wood we could because we needed to hold on to something in order to survive.

You will remember that I told you there was a very nice dog with us. The poor thing had behaved very well every day we traveled on the raft. All of us began to take care of the dog, which had become very dear to us. There were tears in our eyes when we saw it submerged in the water. I don't want to remember . . . In the end, we could not do anything to save it. Mrs. Cosme had carried the dog with her, burdened by the task of keeping it from falling overboard. You can imagine that when she had to hang on to a tire, there was no way left except, with grief in her heart, to let the dog swim alone. The poor thing swam with us the best it could, with its head above the water. When it could not do so anymore, we saw it moving away from us little by little until it disappeared. I turned my head away. No one said a word.

As time passed, the desperation among the group grew. For the moment the waves separated us from one another, making us try to keep as closely united as possible. But the hour arrived when death began to surround us. My friendship for Mrs. Cosme made me offer her all the aid possible. We became debilitated, our strength reduced to a minimum. The first to die was Dr. Tasis—almost in front of me. I saw in his face that he was doing his utmost. Suddenly raising his voice, he said, "William, son, I can't do any more. I hope God—" And he disappeared in that instant before our eyes through the center of the tire that he was using as a life preserver. You can envision the spirits of the rest of us. Who would be next? I don't want to remember.

Then night enveloped us. The breeze blew gently and we slept a little. The other people had been separated from us since the first moments, when the raft broke, kept at a distance by the waves. Our remaining little group tried as much as possible to stay together in a circle, using the rest of the raft and tires to support ourselves.

When morning came, a dense fog began to enclose us. The sun appeared faintly on the horizon. Suddenly I felt someone pulling me strongly by my clothes, saying to me, "William, I believe my time has come. I am sinking fast. I try to hang on but I don't have the strength. I am too old. I believe I have lived enough for my age. I am going to ask you only one thing. Save my mother for me. For God, save her . . . save her . . . save her . . ."

Little by little Dr. Huerte began to move farther away into the middle of that gentle mist. One can imagine that he withdrew from us to prevent our having to witness his death. His mother burst into tears and began making superhuman efforts to save him. She tried futilely to hold him up. But he was completely exhausted and there was little or nothing I could do . . . First he disappeared through the center of the tire and instants later ascended, floating for a second. Then he began to descend gradually, leaving above only one hand, which moved slowly. He remained like that for several minutes until he disappeared before our eyes.

The situation became even more desperate. Now I had the responsibility of caring for the doctor's mother and my own safety.

This stage was more critical. Hanging on to the tires and the boards that surrounded us, the poor . . . I made another small, movable raft with the tires and planks. Laboriously I got on it and with great effort pulled her up against me. We remained in this position for several hours until she recovered a little. We did all of this in silence. I believe we were able to cope because we saved our energy by not talking. The thing now was to survive.

The sun, burning ferociously, made us delirious. At times I woke up and it was dark. At other times I woke up and there was light. Now my concern was to be able to arrive with her. But nobody appeared. We were hidden by waves; besides, we had nothing, nothing with color that could stand out and distinguish us at a distance. We had to trust ourselves to luck, and pray. There, at that moment, I understood that something exists—this God who at times seems not to hear our supplications, our entreaties. I confess that when I had a moment of lucidity I began to pray to God. What greater force he gave me! Thus the first day passed. On the second I heard a muffled sound. I could not imagine that Mrs. Cosme's end was nearing. At times I was trying to hold her and move her, but her strength was failing. I cannot forget the look on her face and her gratitude. Her eyes spoke more than words. She had struggled hard to keep herself and the others alive, and now she, too, was dying.

Suspecting the end but still making an effort, she said to me, "Fight for your life and try to save yourself, son. If you succeed, tell all of this journey so that the world is informed. We died trying to be free. God wants you to succeed, son. Thank you. I am going to sleep a little. Don't wake me." And thus she entered her eternal sleep.

I moved slowly, in a daze, and drifted off to sleep. I suddenly awoke remembering her death with a shock. Then I discovered that I had been bitten by a fish.

I believe it was God's will that I survived. I don't say this only now that I have been saved. I had faith all along. As the days and nights were passing and I stayed alive, drinking ocean water and putting my head in the waves for relief from the burning heat, I was sure I was not going to perish. Although it was like a frightening novel, I knew someone had to endure to bear witness. This idea stayed with me during the remaining days I had to survive until a fisherman found me. How did I do it? I cannot explain it to you. Toward the end I was unconscious and the only thing I remember is having to cover my buttocks and thighs with the tire because I had been badly bitten by fish several times, probably because they smelled the blood of my first wound. But fortunately I am alive and here to relate this voyage of drifting for two weeks between Cuba and the United States.

On the Run

If they catch you trying to escape from jail, they shoot you, not to wound but to kill. That's why I always watched carefully for the right opportunity. Many of those who tried to escape were shot in the back and ended up in wheelchairs. Many others lost their lives.

Manolo
Interviewed November 1977
New York, New York

For some fugitives, freedom is a distant light or a blessing finally attained. For Manolo, liberty is the birthright you snatch back every time it's denied to you. This stance made his life in Cuba a continuous saga of confrontation, imprisonment, escape and pursuit until he had earned a sentence of forty-nine years by the time he left.

A twenty-five-year-old black boxer, Manolo is pure sinew and cunning, the skin on his face stretching tautly over high cheekbones. Everything about the man seems molded to fit a powerful will. He punctuates his fluent monologue with animated gestures and laughter. His energy is radiant but controlled, his tone of voice coolly ironic most of the time. The wonder of Manolo's story is that he survived so long before escaping. Constant bouts with the authorities over what he considered infringements on his personal rights landed him in jail or sent him into hiding numerous times.

People who accomplish unusual physical feats are often disappointingly inarticulate about them; athletes are not always the best commentators on their sports. Manolo is an exception. With the alertness and concentration of a man always ready to act decisively,

Manolo scarcely pauses to deliberate or search for words, and there is an air of youthful bravado in what he says.

YOU SEE, *chico*, if you're born like me under the Revolution and don't have the spirit of fighting, then you get acclimated to the system. Many young people in Cuba say they are not going to leave because their families are still there. So they accept the situation in order to live without difficulty with the government. But others resist in any way they can. Remember, I am a boxer, so that whatever the police did to me, I tried to do back to them!

I worked as a truckdriver and stevedore for 200 pesos a month. I transported liquor kept for tourists and food from the main warehouse in Havana to the hotels. Since in Cuba you can't show what you really feel, I often got in trouble for disagreeing with the system. For example, the police sometimes stopped me for speeding, but I would not pay the tickets because I didn't deserve them. Sometimes the judge accepted it if I didn't pay the fine, but usually the police's word counted more than mine, and when I still refused to pay I was arrested. One time I went to jail because I had a fistfight with a cop. In 1976 the government ordered people to cut their hair and I refused. I fought and escaped and stayed in hiding while they were looking for me to put me in jail. But the main reason I was in and out of prison was for refusing to do military service. One of the greatest terrors facing Cubans is the thought of being sent to Angola, Mozambique or other countries in Africa. Blacks are particularly affected because more of them have to go there so that they can blend in with the Africans. Another reason many people did not want to serve in the army is that they felt they had no future. In the Cuban army if you operated radar or were a mechanical engineer or did a simple job, you got the same 7 pesos a month for three years. That's not even enough to buy cigarettes! Your food was rationed just as it is for everyone else, and there were no special privileges. Or I should say that you have privileges if you belong to the Communist Party or the Young Communists, or if you're a *chivato*. Then you're given a number of things you want. In other words, if you denounce your comrades, you get to live a little better than they do. Now the military service is improving slightly. If after you finish the required three years you say you want to continue for three more, you can make a better salary depending on what you're doing.

I resented many things about life in Cuba. There is still a caste system in which members of the government live like rich people, with good cars—the latest models—and the rest of the people see that. Most people can't get enough food and clothing with the ration books, so they buy on the black market. Then, too, there are problems with the Russians in Cuba. Many of us hated them. We constantly felt hostile to them because they give the orders. They are a privileged class in our country—the directors of different enterprises like mining and sugar manufacture. The Cubans are the employees and the Russians are the technicians.

A situation that provoked many people was that the Tourist Industry decides where you will be sent if you are working for them. In many cases they send people to another province and you have no choice. Or if there isn't enough work for you as a driver, they put you in construction, building roads. Many refused to do that kind of work because they were only drivers. To prevent people from refusing to work, there's a law against being unemployed. To enforce it the government checks your ID card. Usually when they find a person isn't working, they send him to one of the state's *granjas* to do forced labor.

Something that gives people outside of Cuba a false impression is the celebrations of the Revolution, which are held on May 1, March 13 or July 26. It may look as if everyone is happy to be there, but that isn't true. If Fidel or any member of the party was going to speak at the Plaza of the Revolution, everyone had to leave for work early in the morning so that by noon they could all go to the square. If you didn't go, you didn't get paid for that day's work, and you would immediately get marks against you for being an enemy of the Revolution. They used to take everyone by bus or truck to the square. The whole city was immobilized except for the rally. Traffic was stopped and everything else shut down. The only buses working were those that took the workers to the plaza. When I was a driver I had to pick up people in my truck from the different work centers. But when I had dropped them off, I disappeared. I left them at the square and went home in my truck. I didn't care. I stayed in my house, kept track of the time, then went back for the people when I thought the ceremony was over. When the people there applaud, some really mean it, but others do so because they have no choice. For instance, if I'm at a rally and I don't cheer or clap, other people look at me and know I don't favor the government. People like me applauded but without agreeing, and to avoid this problem, we looked for excuses to leave.

I was in a number of prisons in Cuba and saw many terrible things. I was lucky to be able to avoid what so many others experienced. One of the most rigorous prisons is in Pinar del Río. Usually, if you're sentenced for refusing to serve in the military and you escape, that's where you go, but I was sent to one in Camagüey. The prisoners called it *La Humasa* [The Smoker] because the cooks always burned the food, even the milk! The real name was the Military Unit to Help the Revolution, and then they changed it to *Columna Juvenil del Centenario* [Youth Centennial Column]. Before being sent there, I was in the army only one day. When I arrived they said, "Here's your helmet, your shirt, your pants, your boots and your bed." And they gave me a number. It was 120, the last in the unit and the last in the formation. I deliberately tried to get that number to be in the back so I could sleep longer. Then I asked myself, Why should I care about being the last number if I'm not going to be here a long time, anyway! After they gave us everything, we started marching. At night I went to the kitchen and asked the cook where the nearest town was to buy cigarettes. He gave me directions and the minute he finished, I took off. I met a farmer along the way and asked him for an old shirt, pants and sneakers, and a few pesos to get to Havana. Dressed in these civilian clothes I was able to go to my aunt's house, but three months later, after they had tracked down my relatives, they found me. They caught me sleeping and sent me back to La Cabaña, in the military prison.

In La Cabaña there are two yards, one is for the military and the other is for political prisoners, where they have the *paredón* [firing-squad wall.]. Sometimes the political prisoners are even put in "drawers." These are big boxes like coffins built inside the wall with the prisoner's head outside, used as a knob. The G-2 has *jaulas* [small cages] made of iron where prisoners are kept sitting on the floor, bent over, with their hands and legs tied together so they cannot move. When they make you stay like that for five hours you are likely to confess to anything they want you to say. In the dungeons built by the Spanish hundreds of years ago, the old *bartolinas* [punishment cells] are still used. You have to stand inside these cells, unable to bend or sit. There are holes through which water from the sea enters. It is very damp and you are constantly getting wet. Many prisoners die of pneumonia from these conditions, and others are beaten to death.

There are also the *tapiadas*, punishment cells that are completely walled in with only a hole for food to go through. The door, made of iron, is soldered shut. The prisoners inside are there for an indefinite time. If someone dies, the others call the guards, who unseal the door, remove the corpse and seal the cell again. There is a faucet for water and at certain times during the day they let you have the water and then they shut it off. *Tapiadas* may be for five, ten or twenty people, and sometimes only for one person.

One time in Baracoa, a town in Oriente, the jail was set on fire. When we were protesting the beating of two kids by going on strike, the guards came and beat us up. We threw whatever we had in our hands at them—stones, tin cans. Then the warden opened containers of gasoline and poured it all over. He set a match to it and seven or eight prisoners were burned to death.

As soon as I got to La Cabaña I began analyzing the situation and watching the change of guards. I figured the best thing to do was to get a job outside in the yard. Fortunately, I ended up working in the kitchen so that I could walk outside all the time during the day, in the afternoon and sometimes at night. Then, one visiting day, I started sweeping the public area. I was very accommodating to the guards and this encouraged their confidence in me. I quickly took advantage of the situation. It was raining and someone else escaped, which caused a commotion. They shot and wounded the man, and an ambulance came. When it arrived and they were putting the prisoner in, I crawled underneath and held on to the frame. I clung to it until the ambulance stopped at the naval base and they took the injured man into the hospital. Once they were inside, I dropped to the ground, jumped into the grass and went to the section called La Vibora in Havana, where I stayed seven months. Eventually I had to go back to prison, and once I was out

I was unable to return to my previous job. They would not give it to me because they said I did not behave myself. Then they promised me the job on the condition that I pay for my studies myself and that I join the mass organizations. I said, "No, I'd like to be an engineer. I don't care about politics at all. I have no interest in joining any organizations." So, like the end of all my stories, I had to go back to jail.

While I was working on the *granja* cutting sugar cane I met Eduardo, the man I left with. We did not talk then about escaping, but his feelings were similar to mine. One day Eduardo said to me, "I can't take it anymore. I want to leave the country." We were thinking about going right away, but that day my mother came with some clothes and I had to give her most of my money, so I did not have any for escaping. The little I had I gave to Eduardo and told him to go to Havana. After twenty days I had some money to meet him there.

As soon as I got away from the camp I sneaked back to my previous job where I had worked as a truckdriver. I stayed just long enough to take two inner tubes from the rear tires of a truck. Once I had them I asked a friend to get me two more. Then, with a piece of canvas from the top of the truck I made a covering like a pillow-case to hold the tubes. From there I went to my mother's house to get a pump to inflate them. Eduardo met me and we built a raft from these materials, sewing the canvas around the tires. We assembled it at ten in the morning in some bushes near Guanabo Beach. Afterward we undid what we had built until the right moment for our escape. But every day we had to go back to make sure the raft was still hidden. Anybody could have used it. In fact, many people escaped on rafts they found. I know someone who built a raft and left it, only to discover later that another person had taken it.

We had to delay our escape because the weather was very bad. While we were waiting we made sure that the guards walking along the beach and others patrolling the area in boats did not see us coming down there so often to check on our raft. Meanwhile, for the next two months we prepared ourselves by swimming three miles every day, from one beach to the next. As part of our training we deliberately did not drink much water or eat much food to accustom our bodies to doing without either. At the beginning I weighed 196 pounds and knew I had to lose weight. By the time we left I was down to about 165 pounds. During this period the patrols did not pay attention to us because this was the beach season and many people were around swimming and fishing.

We knew the best day to leave was Thursday, when a lot of people—amateurs and professionals—are all fishing and we would not be conspicuous. After Thursday the patrol boats checked fishermen for their ID cards. We also figured this was a good time to get away because fishermen from Miami would be out in the Gulf and we would have a chance to be picked up by one of them. We could not go that particular Thursday, however, because the weather was so bad. There was a lot of rain and you couldn't see the stars to guide you north. The winds were wrong, too—*remolinos* [whirlwinds], which would have spun the raft around. Therefore we had to wait fifteen more days for clear weather. Finally I couldn't wait any longer and on Monday, June 19, 1977, I told Eduardo that although it was a bad day, I thought the weather would change. It turned out I was right. At about six that night it cleared. The wind was southerly and the sea was quiet and flat as a plate.

We took our raft with oars and a small sail from the hiding place. While we were carrying it through the bushes the mast caught on a branch and snapped, so we had to do without the sail. We waded into the water and started rowing. We took some nylon string and pretended we were fishing, but we were rowing like hell the whole time! We did so until six the next morning, and after all our effort we were only ten miles from the Cuban coast. We could still see the shore and the fishermen out in groups. Eduardo was worried and complained that we were too close. I told him, "Forget it and keep rowing."

Our hands were bleeding by now, but we had to keep going. We could not stop then and forced ourselves to continue. From the first day we had terrible weather most of the time. Just briefly on the second day the sun came out and it was beautiful. But at six that night the weather changed drastically. It got so cold that we started shaking. I kept rowing to stay warm but it was freezing and raining constantly. We were drenched from above and below, by the rain pounding down and the waves crashing over us. That helped us in one way, though, because with our bodies wet all the time we got used to the cold water. It's when your clothes start to dry and you get wet again that you feel worse. At that point you get furious and curse the sea. The only clothes we wore were light shirts with short sleeves and *pitusas* [jeans]. When we bought them they were white, but we had dyed them black so that no one would be able to see us; at night, white pants show up from far away. All we took for food was fifteen lemons. That was the only thing we ate during our five days at sea. Well, we knew lemons kill hunger, prevent you from getting dehydrated, and have vitamin C, which is good protection against colds!

The third day we reached a place where two different currents crossed. This let the raft go steadily and in the direction we wanted. It was a relief to be able to stop for a while and relax because at that point I had a bad asthma attack. We never slept once during our trip. Since the sea was so rough, we were tossed around all the time. It felt so good finally to be able to curl up and get some rest. Just as I was enjoying this new position and beginning to get warm, a big wave hit us. Eduardo thought I had thrown water on him and got mad. A little later another wave came and soaked us again. Eduardo started swearing and I told him not to bother, that the waves would keep hitting us. "Remember," I said, "we're in the middle of the ocean."

The weather was so bad that we were lost for the next two days. It kept getting worse and we were pushed into the middle of the Atlantic. Once a German ship passed and we signaled it. It went around us but did not stop. During this time we were followed by sharks. At night they were green and luminescent like other smaller fish. One of the tires started losing air but we did not worry about it and kept going. Then we saw a Soviet ship but made no signal and it continued past us. A Japanese fishing boat passed and went on. I realized it was rented to Cuba because of the Cuban flag on the back. Many times the Japanese ships in international waters don't have the Cuban flag but have three small triangular flags in the colors of the Cuban flag. I knew something about international signals from reading manuals while I was in the flotilla of the Cuban naval base on the Gulf of Mariel. While we were on the raft several planes passed but did not see us. Even the Coast Guard came close but missed us because we had no instruments and were very small. We had made sure not to take anything metal—except a knife, which I lost—so that we would not make any noise.

On the fourth day the weather improved. This was good in one way and bad in another. Good because the sun was shining and bad because it was so fierce. Luckily we had hats we had made, with long visors. That night the weather got bad again. I was caught off-guard and the raft turned over. I thought that was the end. Eduardo disappeared and when I called out for him he did not answer. Then I heard his voice saying, "I'm here." I felt much better and we turned the raft over.

We got back on and I looked around. I saw a big shark but did not tell Eduardo because he was afraid of them. As we rowed along, my oar kept hitting against something and I realized it was knocking against the shark. It was huge, but I did not want to say anything to Eduardo. At that point he was so tired that he was resting his head on my shoulder with his eyes closed. When he finally opened them, the first thing he saw was the shark. He yelled for me to look at it but I pretended not to see anything and asked, "What?" "Look," he said. "Isn't that a big shark?" I said, "No, that's just a piece of wood." He insisted it was a shark and later I admitted it was. "It's so big," he said. "We'd better row fast."

That day we were about forty miles from the Florida coast. The weather shifted again. We saw another boat and signaled it. When we got very close they started their engines and left. On the other side of us a boat sounded its horn. We changed direction and headed toward it. The boat disappeared. With this kind of maneuvering we lost the day. Next we saw an American aircraft carrier and tried to signal it by taking off our shirts and waving them. I told Eduardo they had probably seen us but could not take us aboard because it was a military ship. We thought they might call the Coast Guard to pick us up. But even if they had, the Coast Guard could not have reached us because the wind was moving us along too fast.

On the fifth day we were about an hour from Key West and started to see some yachts. I said to Eduardo, "Look at those boats. By the way they're moving I think they're fishing boats." I knew we were in the north close to the American coast because the water was very cold. The sun was directly overhead and I explained our position to Eduardo. I turned northeast toward Florida. At night we had been using the stars to guide us, following the polestar north. We had to rely on navigational knowledge like this because we did not have a compass.

Our raft was tossing up and down but we knew it would keep floating. When the waves threw us off course we used the oars to keep in the right direction. We started to row close to the boats, but two of them withdrew from us. About four hundred meters away I saw another boat and told Eduardo we were going to try to get close to it. But as we were watching it I noticed something strange. I did not trust the boat. Judging from the large size and construction I knew it could be American. But to play it safe, when the boat turned toward us, I told Eduardo we should wait and see what happened. When we saw they had electronic equipment Eduardo said, "Oh, now we're as good as in jail." Then, as we got closer, we saw women aboard. An American called out to ask us what we wanted and where we were from. I said I was Cuban and he asked if I wanted to go back to Cuba. I immediately called back, "No, no, no. I want to go to the United States." He said not to worry, that they would take us to Florida, only one hour away.

Once on board I tried to walk but found I couldn't. I had been twisted up for so long with my legs under me that they were too weak to walk. My friend was a little more comfortable than I because he's shorter and hadn't needed to bend his legs so much, but at first he couldn't walk either. Then the Americans started to take care of us because we were very badly sunburned." [At this point Manolo shows us raw pink patches on his leg even though it has been several months since his escape.] "I'm fairly tall, and after having to curl my legs under me to stay on the raft, the canvas rubbed off my skin. That and the sun and salt water irritated my skin terribly. Our arms were badly burned too.

Storm

We escaped from Cuba on an eight-foot boat containing two oars and two jugs of water. We were hungry and exhausted but we kept on without sleep.

Roberto
Interviewed February 1977
West New York, New Jersey

Roberto, twenty-eight, is typical of many Cuban escapees who slip into the obscurity of the bodegas, coffee shops and rented rooms of the Cuban communities of West New York and other cities in the United States. After an initial meeting to arrange an interview, he disappeared. He finally agreed to talk to us several weeks later when we came upon him by chance. He is a thin, shy man with a pale face and dark eyes that glanced nervously at us as we sat at a small table at the back of a bar, which was quiet because it was early evening. Many recent escapees share his attitude. They are reluctant to discuss their experience—and some refuse to do so at all—for fear of reprisals against family still in Cuba, or from the suspicion that they may be reported to Cuban secret-service agents. Many, like Roberto, do not wish to dwell on their flight. Survival was the main thing. After the jolt of success, the confusion of being in a new country, or the glare of publicity that greeted their arrival, they want to go on with life unobtrusively.

For many Cubans, safe passage entailed long-range calculations and months of covert maneuvering. Others, like Roberto, bided their time and then left abruptly when the right conditions arose. Despite the weeks of getting ready, his departure was totally impromptu. Roberto and his friend seized their boat at the op-

portune moment and jumped into it, wearing only bathing suits and
pullovers.

ESCAPED on October 23, 1976, at nine-thirty in the evening in
the midst of a terrible thunderstorm. I'm originally from Santa
Clara but moved to another city* in 1970, where I met Orlando,
who escaped with me. He is thirty-five and had worked in the
merchant marine. Since I was a lifeguard for the tourists from North
America and Europe, I knew the waters of the area very well and
had been planning to escape for three months. We were able to
practice rowing every day in one of the fiberglass boats from Spain
used by the tourists. Since the government made sure all these boats
were tied up at night with a steel cable and were guarded by watch-
men, we had to wait for a chance to take one.

Our opportunity finally came that Sunday in October during a
bad storm. At night while it was pouring we broke into the shed
where the boats were kept, cut the cable and stole a small boat.
Because the weather was so bad, no guards were around. We
carried the boat down the beach and set off, rowing away from
shore. The sea was very rough and there was no moon. This com-
bination worked to our advantage, although it made the trip
difficult. As we started out, we spotted the Cuban coast guard
eight kilometers away. Luckily they could not see us because of
the rain and high waves. Then, as we went farther out, the sea got
worse.

We had left immediately, without any food. All we had were two
oars, two jars of water, and some towels. As the waves kept rolling
over us, we had to use the towels to absorb the water and a jar to
bail it out so that the boat wouldn't sink.

The next day at four in the morning we caught the Gulf current,
which takes you away from Cuba. At that point we could not see
the island anymore. The weather was so bad that we had to drift
with the tide for seven hours. The waves were too high for us to
use the oars, but the current helped us a lot, carrying us along as if
we were on a river. By nightfall the ocean grew much calmer and

---

* Roberto does not wish to mention the place of escape in case others want
to try to leave from there.

we rowed the entire night without stopping. Fortunately my friend knew about navigation, because all we had as a guide was a compass from an old helicopter.

The following morning we began rowing once more, but not for long—there was another storm. The other reason we could not continue to row even when the sea was calmer was that sharks began to surround the boat. We thought that if we hit them with the oars, they would turn over the boat. Nevertheless, we were not afraid during our trip, which lasted thirty-nine hours. Many of the people who do not make it fail because they give in to fear. They panic and tip over their boats. You need steel nerves because when you escape in a small boat like ours there are moments when you don't dare move or else you would capsize. The boat needs stability, so one person must sit in front and the other in back and both must always be sure to balance their weight. You cannot afford to think about the bad things. You have to concentrate with all your strength on getting where you want to go.

Aside from the sharks, all we saw during our crossing were some birds and American planes. Seven of them came close but did not see us. Then, on the second day, we reached American waters and were about fifteen miles from Key West when we saw a ship coming in our direction. It was about 150 feet long and flying a German flag. Later we found out it was traveling from Havana to Canada. The minute we sighted the ship I ripped off my pullover, tied it to an oar and started waving and yelling. A passenger noticed us and the ship picked us up and brought us to the U.S. Coast Guard. Eventually we were taken to the Cuban Refugee Center, where we were given food, clothes, money for two months, and a place to stay until we contacted relatives in Miami. The Coast Guard returned our boat to Cuba. Seven of my friends escaped in the same kind of boat we used, also taken from a tourist center.

THE REASON I left was that I had no freedom. In my country they say there is freedom, but I never found any. If you want to visit another country, they will not let you go. For me, that's not being free. The other reasons I left are more directly political. They arrested me once by mistake. I had to go to jail because I was with a friend involved in politics. He was against the government, but I had nothing to do with his activities. They took him to prison, and me too, for no reason at all. I had to go before a jury, but in Cuba you can't have a lawyer to defend you. If they are suspicious of you, or if a member of the Communist Party says you are doing something wrong, or that you belong to some subversive group, that's enough for them to condemn and punish you.

I have a lot of friends who escaped and many who want to leave. One of the things that bothers them is that they cannot obtain the things they need. Even people with money have little to spend it on. I would say that most of the young people in Cuba want to escape. It's just that they don't all have the opportunity we had.

Inferno

It was a flip of the coin. Freedom or death. All my life I had thought of leaving Cuba. During the four years I worked in the port of Havana I watched and waited for a chance to escape.

Ernesto
Interviewed October 1977
New York, New York

Born and raised in Havana, Ernesto, who is twenty-three years old, has the look of a man who bargained with death and is still surprised he won. His thin body, delicate features and large, troubled brown eyes cannot contain his agitation. His escape from Cuba was clearly an ordeal that still hurts. It has not assumed an orderly shape in his mind. He cannot yet contemplate it with composure or discuss it with the volubility typical of many other Cuban refugees. Ernesto is at once nervous remembering his flight, vehemently angry at Castro's regime, and relieved that he survived. He is tentatively feeling his freedom, a swimmer testing the water.

Ernesto speaks softly and slowly, trembling sometimes. There are intervals of silence while he thinks about what he will say. He has a habit of glancing around and looking over his shoulder for fear that he will be overheard by the wrong person. Recalling his escape causes Ernesto anxiety because he seems to feel that somehow he might still be punished for what he did.

WAITED a long time before I could take advantage of my job on the waterfront to escape. But one evening, when a Latin American ship* docked, I had my chance. At nine o'clock on March 24, 1976, I hid myself in the smokestack I had been repairing. It was on a ship bound for the United States. I had decided that if I was caught, the government was going to have to kill me in that smokestack, but I was not going to let them take me to Security. In Cuba, the tortures of Security are well known.

The day before I left I got friendly with two men working on the ship and they told me it was going to Houston, Texas, after stops in Tampico, Mexico; Santa Clara, Colombia; and Buenos Aires. I explained to them that I was desperate to leave Cuba. They looked at each other and then said to me, "We don't know you very well, but we trust you. Up in the chimney is a space if you want to hide there, but you do it at your own risk. We don't know anything about it." I told them not to worry, that the only thing I wanted was to leave. Our agreement was that if the police found me, the men did not know I was there, and if I escaped, there was to be no mention of who had helped me. I assured them that I am a man who prefers to die rather than go back on his word.

Our conversation took place in their cabin with the doors closed. That night I slept there, woke up at four in the morning and climbed into the chimney, waiting nervously for the moment when the ship would pull out of the harbor. Normally you punch a card when you arrive at work, but I did not that day so that no one would know I was there.

From the moment I squeezed into the space between two platforms inside the chimney stack, I was terrified of being found. At one o'clock police boarded the ship. They searched everywhere until seven, looking for anything that needed repair or contraband. I could hear them knocking on the walls, checking for whatever might be hidden. At one point they stood only two feet away from my hiding place, so close I could see their pants and shoes. The only reason they did not find me was that they were being careful not to get dirty from the soot.

In the meantime I was turning completely black. The whole

* Ernesto does not wish to reveal the origin of the ship.

time I was waiting, the chimney was smoking from the laundry and the kitchen. It was hot inside, but not as bad as it was once the boat started moving. Something I had not known was that one of the pipes near me was connected to the horn. When the boat started to leave I got an awful scare. A sudden deafening blast of the siren sounded, followed by six shots. I was panic-stricken, sure that I had been discovered, but the signals were only to announce the ship's departure. We finally left, shortly after seven o'clock.

I felt miserable watching Cuba slip away from me into the distance. I could see the lights of El Morro Castle at the entrance to the Bay of Havana. The beams from the lighthouse swept over the ship. Each time they passed I had to duck down. This was the saddest time for me because that is the moment when it strikes you with terrible force that you have made a tremendous change in your life. You are leaving part of your body, your very being behind. You know that later, if you survive, you will wake up in a totally strange, unknown world. It is as if you have to be born over again into a new life.

I spent hours completely curled up in the smokestack. I could not stretch my legs and could hardly breathe because of the heat and smoke. But to get your freedom, you do anything. Finally I saw the lights of Cuba's coast disappear and thought the ship was safely in international waters. At dawn I left my hiding place to look for water because I was dying of thirst. The boatswain found me, covered with dirt and sweat, and brought me to the captain. I showed him my papers and identification. At that point the boat was in the Gulf of Mexico. It had been twenty-three hours since I crawled into the chimney.

The crew treated me very well. After showering off the sticky coating of soot, I was given food, water and clothing, and an officer's cabin. Then I wrote a letter of explanation to the captain, telling him that I wanted to live in a free, democratic country. The captain sent the letter to Washington and the United States government accepted my plea for asylum.

I do not know if you can understand my feelings about how things were in Cuba, because in the United States it is so different. The main thing I felt was that I did not own my own life, that I had to conform in every way to what the government demanded. When

Fidel took power, I was seven years old. I never really adapted to his system, but I had no choice other than accept it, particularly when I was older and needed to work. I did not, however, serve in the army. I managed to avoid it by pretending to be mentally disturbed. I felt that there was no reason to fight to defend a government I could not support. The frustrating part of life was that although I worked very hard, there were still many times when I did not have enough to eat. You get tired of promises that things will get better when you find that they never do.

Often the smallest personal choice can cause you so much trouble! For instance, once I bought some clothes from a sailor. When you are young and work hard, you feel entitled to something nice once in a while, just to be able to feel good. Well, when the police saw me wearing the clothes, they questioned me. They asked if there were any papers inside and when I said no, they looked again, saw a French label, and made me go put on something else and give up those clothes. Since they still were not satisfied, they came to my home and searched it, removing other clothes that were not made in Cuba. It enraged me that these men had the power to come into my own home and go through my personal belongings. While they are doing so, they are rude—pushing you aside and insulting you the whole time.

One of the big problems in Cuba is housing. Renting an apartment is difficult. I lived with my relatives in an old apartment they had before the Revolution. If you apply for a new one, you generally work in a minibrigade in construction for two years. After you have built the first building, the government may decide that someone else needs the apartment more than you do, and they give it to that person. Then the same thing can happen next year. By the third year you might get it, but you pay rent. It never belongs to you. At the beginning of the Revolution it was different. Once you had paid rent for land or a home for a certain number of years, it was yours. Now you get an apartment in which you can't even hang what you want on the walls! If you put up a picture of the Virgin, or have some figures of saints, for example, they throw you out and bring in someone else, so it is better to put up a picture of Fidel or someone like that. Often they prohibit you from having private parties, and visitors must leave at night. Then on Sundays you are pressured to attend political activities. Their intention is to prevent you from having any form of amusement or recreation on your own.

One of the worst features of the system—something I cannot forgive—is the fact that the government tries in many ways to turn people against one another, to encourage neighbors and friends to inform on one another. As a result, a person lives in perpetual fear, not knowing if something that was said will be observed and reported to the authorities. The ugliest part of this situation is that your own family is torn apart. In my case, my father and I were at odds because he supported the government and since I could not, the two of us have scarcely spoken to each other in years. To divide people in this way, to cut a person off from his own flesh and blood is a vicious, inhuman way to rule a country.

Winged Victory

Every day the people of Cuba lack more necessities, and they are poorer.
Instead of prospering after twenty years of the Revolution, Cuba is going
backwards. But if the present government fell, I would return to my country.

Rodolfo
Interviewed October 1979
Miami, Florida

*His hollow cheeks, large, dark, deep-set eyes and impish face sug-
gest a poet, not the passenger who recently alighted after a flight
from Havana in the wheel well of a Cubana jet.*

*When another refugee from his home town heard of the escape,
he arranged to meet Rodolfo, and the two are now co-owners of a
small luncheonette in Miami. Rodolfo brings us two thimble-sized
cups of rich Cuban coffee that abound in "Little Havana," lights a
cigarette, pauses to collect his thoughts, and then begins an account
of his adventure. As various customers arrive he darts from the table
to serve them. His body is small and agile, his gestures swift. As he
proceeds with his story, his face crinkles into a smile from time to
time at the recollection of some amusing detail. His calmness and
modesty are striking.*

I WAS born in Matanzas twenty-eight years ago and went to
school through the sixth grade. My mother, four sisters and
two brothers are still in Cuba. My wife, from whom I am
separated, and my son, who is nine months old, are also there.
Before my escape, on September 6, 1979, I was a machine operator
in a sugar mill in Matanzas. I had heard a little bit about another
escape like mine, and could have gone by some other means—by

boat, for instance—but since I don't know how to swim, I couldn't take that risk!

I left because the situation in Cuba is so bad. The worst thing for me was the repression. You live in a constant state of anxiety that you will be punished at any moment for the most trivial reason. If you say you do not like the government, they put you in prison. If you criticize something the government does wrong, they put you in prison. If you have a problem in your family and can't go to work but don't have time to tell them in advance, they put you in prison.

Cubans realize that everything the government tells them is lies, because the people are being starved to death. We have been lied to for twenty years—promised that next year we will have this, in so many years we will have other things, one day we will have everything. But what results is that every day they are tightening up more and taking away more. Do you know what it is like to live mainly on five pounds of rice a month? There *are* clothes in the stores but you cannot buy any because the prices are too high. For a pair of pants worth 4 pesos, they charge 25. Two or three years ago the people worked with more enthusiasm. But now they do not because every day they are hungrier; they have less to wear; they can speak out less. When Fidel talks, everybody has to go and listen. You are paid your day's wages to attend. But the people are discontented. They ask one another, "Why is there nothing in our country? Why do we spend so much capital helping other countries when our own people need so much? Why must the government meddle where it has no business being?"

The majority of the people do not truly support the government. Some do, with the objective of living well. For example, I have a good friend who is a member of the party. He said to me, "Look, *chico*, I can buy rice on the black market and get away with it because I belong to the party. I know the state prohibits it, but I have to do it. Do you think I am going to let my children go hungry? So I send my wife to buy it. I am a member of the party because it is the best way for me to live."

A very different reaction which is also typical is the one I encountered before I went to work in the sugar mill. The workers there told me about the problem they had been having. Every

morning at eight one of the machines would be broken and therefore they could not start work until one. The authorities came in
one day, changed the directors of the mill and took a lot of people
to prison. Then the trouble stopped. I concluded that it must have
been sabotage. In the past several years this kind of thing has happened frequently, more so than before, because the people are
angry. As a result, the government has been cracking down—
arresting more people and sending them to jail for longer terms.
You hear on the radio and read in *Granma* [the Communist Party
newspaper] all the time Castro saying that stronger measures must
be taken against delinquents, against those who destroy state
property. He encourages the Committees for the Defense of the
Revolution to be even more vigilant.

THE DAY I left I walked thirty kilometers from the mill in the direction of Havana. I was wearing my work clothes so that no one
would pay attention to me. Then, on the side of the road, I saw a
campesino working in the field and on the other side I noticed his
bicycle standing in the dirt. When the man wasn't looking I took
the bicycle and rode the rest of the way. Two days later I arrived
in Havana in the afternoon. During that time, when I wanted to
sleep, I had pulled off to the side of the road and hid with the
bicycle in the bushes. I ditched it when I got to the city and walked
the rest of the way to the airport. For a while I stood on a hill
there to watch the movements of the planes so that I would know
where to go, because I had never been there before.

I came down the hill, passed the entrance to the airport and took
the road to the right, where there are mango and avocado trees and
coffee bushes. The road borders the runway and is separated from it
by a wire fence and tall grass. I waited among the trees until it was
dark, then I crossed the barbed-wire fence. This wasn't too hard,
because the fence was old and many of the wires were broken. I
lay down in the grass where no one could see me. I had chosen a
point near the spot where the planes turn around so that I could
observe them carefully. About fifty meters away there was a sentry
post with a guard and two dogs. Luckily they were to the north of
me. The wind was favoring me, because at night it blew from the
north and therefore it could not carry my scent to the dogs.

In all this time the only thing I had eaten on the way was four little pastries and two *croquetas*. I had gotten them when I passed through a small town. It wasn't a problem, since I was dressed like a worker in soiled clothes and was riding a dirty bicycle. I had left my mother my ration coupons. When the sun came up I crossed to the other side of the fence and began looking for mangoes to eat. That whole day I stayed hidden, watching the runway and sleeping when I was tired. The next day I was so hungry I went to town to get something. Close to the airport is the bus terminal, where I saw an old lady. I told her I was from the country, new in Havana, and didn't have any money for food. I asked her for a peso, and she gave me five. That night I ate in the terminal and waited there till the following morning. Then I returned to the airport and went to the same spot, because the grass was high there. I wrapped some of the grass together to make a small shelter like a tunnel to hide in. Altogether, I stayed at the airport for six days, living mostly on mangoes and avocados. On the fifth night I was so tired I was falling asleep when I heard the sound of an airplane. I thought it was the one I should take and I ran toward it. When I saw it had propellers I realized it was not a jet and would not be going out of the country. I had to run back to my hiding place at the risk of being seen by the guards. I was breathless and trembling but managed to return unnoticed. That night no other planes left.

The next night the same thing happened: I heard an airplane, but could not see what kind it was. I ran out, crossed the fence and waited. When I got close I ran along under the plane until it came to a stop. But then I discovered that it was a Russian line, so I had to rush back to my hiding place a second time. I began thinking that I wasn't going to be able to leave that night either. I felt very discouraged and fell asleep. A few hours later I woke up and heard another plane. This time I said to myself, I better check first what kind it is before I run out. When the plane got close I saw it was a Cubana jet and I thought, Finally, this is the one! So once more I ran under the plane. I carried with me a paper bag with a mango and an avocado. They were big and round and beautiful! I wanted to show people outside Cuba that we grow these, not for Cubans to eat, but for export.

It was now about two-thirty. Under the plane it was so dark I could not see anything at all. And everything was strange to me because I had not been near a plane before, except for the two quick runs I had just made which had not given me time to see much. I did not get to bring my mango and avocado here because I needed them for something else now. I took the package and threw it up into the opening on one side of the wheel compartment. I waited to see where it went—if it would stay or drop down. The package fell out, so I threw it on the other side and there it stayed. I knew then that that was the place where I should go. All the while the plane was standing with the engines running, waiting for the signal to take off. The noise was so loud, I could not think. I just acted on instinct.

I climbed onto the wheel and hoisted myself up into the empty space above. I went up but could not tell where I was because it was too dark to see. On the side of the compartment I felt a bar and decided to get close to it. The plane, which had stopped for only about a minute and a half, now taxied down the runway and lifted off. I told myself, Finally, I've made it! Just then part of the floor suddenly flung open. Because I was so close to the metal bar I was able to hold on tight and avoid falling out. Then the wheel began moving inside slowly. Since I couldn't see very well, I reached out and touched it with my hand. By feeling it, I was able to judge the direction it was moving in and I shifted my position so that it would not crush me. The air rushing inside drove me against the wall. Once the wheel was completely inside, I was crammed between the wall and the wheel, which was pressing heavily against my ribs.

The flight took about forty-five minutes. I didn't sleep and it wasn't cold because the heat from the wheel mixed with the air outside kept me warm. The worst part was the noise. It was so shrill that my ears bothered me for two weeks afterward. I also had problems for a while with my stomach because of the pressure of the wheel against it. During the flight my mind was completely blank. I did not think about anything and I was not afraid. My feelings were totally numb. When the plane started to descend I was surprised how short the flight had been. As we glided down, I held on to the bar. When the bottom opened, I looked out but saw nothing because it was too dark. Then the floor closed again, with the wheel outside. The plane landed and when it stopped completely, and the motor was off, I stuck my head out to see where we were.

A man walking around with a flashlight checking the plane saw me. One of the crew came with him. Both were Cuban. When they saw me, one of them said, "What's that under the fuselage?" The other said, "I don't know, let's go check." Then they discovered me. I wasn't afraid of the airport employee because he told me, "Jump, quick!" But the crew member said, "If you jump, they'll kill you." I did not know what to do. When I asked where we were the crew member said we were in Matanzas. I decided the minute the guy looked away, I'd jump down and start to run. What else could I do? I believed that we were in Matanzas. But then I noticed, in the distance, a young fellow who looked like an American watching what was going on and he was holding a can of Coca-Cola. At that moment I concluded we were not in Cuba, because there you don't see soft drinks in cans. I asked again where we were and the man said, "I told you before, we're in Matanzas." I started to smile and he said, "O.K., now jump."

In order to descend, I had to climb down the wheel. When I jumped there was already a circle of four guys waiting for me. Two of them took me by the arms, and the other two led me onto the plane, by force. At that moment I did not care what happened to me because once I was inside the plane, I figured they were going to take me back. Inside, the captain asked me, "Are you crazy? Do you know what you've done?" I answered back, "Yes, I know." Then he asked, "Do you know where we are?" I said I didn't and he replied, "Well, we're in Miami."

With the captain there was a short, fat mulatto from State Security. He said to me, "Well, we're going to do something. We're going to talk man to man." I answered, "*Bueno, chico*, you won't find more of a man than me to talk to!" The guy said, "Yes, I know, but tell me the truth." I told myself, I have to play with these people. I can't be rebellious now.

There were six of them from the Cuban crew. I knew I couldn't do anything, so I started looking around, acting fascinated by the plane and asking, "What's this thing for? Really, this is beautiful." I was trying to make them believe I was stupid. Then the agent said,

"Tell me again. Where do you want to go?" "Look, *chico*," I said, "I want to go to Puerto Rico." The guy asked me again, "You don't want to stay in Miami, no? O.K. We're going to do something. In case Immigration talks to you and asks you, you say that you took the wrong plane, because you wanted to go to Santiago de Cuba, and that you just left Mazorra Mental Hospital four days ago." I said, "O.K. Perfect."

Meanwhile, I was stalling for time. I had to play with them because they were playing with me. Then I heard the captain whispering to the agent, "This doesn't mean anything. Before we go back to Cuba, we're going to get rid of him." The agent said, "I understand we have to take him to Immigration, but that won't hurt Cuba any. Or if he wants to stay, let him." The captain said, "No, no, no! Besides being the captain of this plane, I am a lawyer. I am going to do things the proper way." Then the security officer said, "O.K. Do what you want." He turned to me and said. "Have you eaten yet?" I said no, that I didn't want to. Of course, I was tremendously hungry, but I did not want to accept anything from them. The guy told me, "Well, we're going to feed you, anyway," and he brought me a big steak. That was to deceive me; then they would take me back to Cuba.

The captain saw me looking the plane over and asked me if I liked it. I said, "Yes. How long does it take to learn to work on a plane?" He told me it took about a year and a half. At that moment a stewardess came into the plane and told the captain that some officers were looking for him.

A tall blond American policeman entered with a Cuban, González, and two women. The officer said we all had to go to Immigration. The captain told him everyone could go except me. But the American insisted that they had to take me because that was the law. The captain objected, saying that I was on Cuban territory, that he was not only the captain but a lawyer who knew what to do in these matters, and that under no circumstances would he hand over the stowaway. The policeman disputed with him saying that they had arrested me on American territory. The captain answered, "No, no, no. He came up here voluntarily and doesn't want to stay in the United States. If you don't believe he came with us willingly, you can ask him." González looked at me and asked what I wanted to do. Since I knew I was finally safe, I smiled, touched his hand and said, "If it's not with you, I won't leave here." At that point the security officer exclaimed, "Why didn't you say so before? If you'd told us that, we would have been finished with this conversation." I could see that now he and the captain were nervous.

When the captain told the American they weren't going to give me back, the officer said, "Well, if you don't leave him with us and go to Immigration, we're going to retain the plane." The captain still said that he would not release me under any circumstances. The American looked at his watch and said, "Listen, I've waited here almost an hour for you to decide and now we have to do something." The captain said, "All right, let me call Havana and see what they say. In the end, the word from Havana was to hand me over to the Americans. The captain told the officer he could take me. I started smiling and walking out. Everyone else went ahead of me, but when we got to the door of the plane, the last one in line turned to me and said, "You go first."

Alone

My parents knew I wanted to leave the country, but I did not tell them ahead of time when I would be going or how. The day I escaped I just said to them, "Father, Mother, *adiós*. Maybe forever."

Domingo
Interviewed October 1979
Miami, Florida

His voice is musical and liquid, with spaces between the words. It is light as a moth as it weaves through the grayness of the air and the syllables of rain flickering outside the window. Beneath a wispy mustache his lips curve down and his mouth seems to be tasting again the bitter texture of his past life.

Domingo is a twenty-two-year-old mulatto from Uvero, Santiago de Cuba, the town where one of the important early battles of the Revolution was fought. A word Domingo uses many times is "nostalgia." He is still haunted by loneliness, by the crushed feeling of a man searching for what Hemingway termed "a clean, well-lighted place," betokening wholeness and somewhere that is home. Domingo's was a solitary flight, and now, having just arrived in Miami, he is for the moment estranged from the world around him, without the reassuring presence of relatives or friends.

FELT great repugnance for the government of Fidel and decided to risk my life so that I could live and work in peace. In Cuba you cannot have a mind of your own. For example, whenever Fidel speaks at a rally, you have to go. And when he says, "This is like this," then everybody has to say yes. If you don't, the person next to you asks, "Don't you agree?" So you say to yourself, "I don't like what he's saying, but I better put up my hand and go along with it." Under the system they have, a man is also a slave to work, but he does not receive in return what he is supposed to. Although people work very hard in Cuba, the salaries are so low that most of the time you spend all you earn just for food, a pair of shoes and other things you need. For young people like me, there was no relief from the same pattern of work every day because the government tries to control your free time as well. There are few amusements you can enjoy on your own. You need money to get into clubs, where each beer costs 1½ pesos. My only diversion was going to the beach sometimes.

At the time of my escape I was working as a swimming instructor at a pool in Santiago de Cuba, although I had been trained as a mechanic. Before that I had received a scholarship when I was twelve to study in Havana. The government gives young people scholarships, but what good are they when you feel that your life has no value, because every minute you are being told what to think and how to act? Later I did obligatory military service for three years. This is another way they take advantage of the people. In the army I earned 7 pesos a month. In the morning you are given a machete and you go out all day to cut cane. At night, when you come back, you do military drills. During my service I was also sent to Pinar del Río to harvest tobacco.

When I came out of the army I went to the Ministry of Labor to apply for a job in petrochemicals. They told me I could not find work in that field because I was not an *integrado*. That was always a problem for me—I could not accept the system and people knew how I felt. My parents were not sympathetic to the government, but they did not influence my attitude or tell me how to think. My father has worked hard all his life, doing the same thing before and after the Revolution. He is a maintenance mechanic for heavy equipment and earns 130 pesos a month. My brother, who is thirty, is a Communist. He works as a political instructor and has never married. His whole life is politics—he is totally involved in it. My four sisters are integrated into the Revolution. Nevertheless, we feel great love for one another. They used to cry when they saw that I could not adapt to the system. They love me a lot.

I had tried once before to leave the country with a friend who was fifteen at the time. He was the kind of guy who did not keep his feelings to himself. You have to be careful, though, because you can go to jail for something you said and afterward you have no chance to explain anything. Every day the two of us would go to the beach to practice swimming. Our idea was to swim to Guantánamo Base. When we were ready to leave, my friend stole a jeep from his uncle. At the control point of Mangito in Santiago, the *fiana* [cops] stopped us. I told my friend, "Don't stop. Keep going!" But he got nervous and stopped. Then about fifteen guards came behind us with pistols drawn. We were carrying some inner tubes, no gun, and nothing else. They put us in the *jaula* [police van] and brought us to headquarters, an underground tunnel where they interrogate you. They try to frighten you, and some people talk. I said nothing except that I was trying to escape. My friend explained the rest. Before we left he had told his aunt we were going to leave the country. She worked for the State Security and that is how they were able to catch us.

They kept us in jail incommunicado and then gave us each two years. In 1975–1976 I was in Boniato Prison, in Oriente, San Ramón, and Kilo 7 and San Francisco, which are in Camagüey. They treated me very badly in jail. The system is designed to degrade you, to rob you of your manhood. In the eyes of the guards you are not even a human being and therefore I felt great hatred for them. I could not suppress my anger. They were worse to me than to other prisoners because I insulted them and tried to strike back. I worked as a welder and believe me, they make you work very hard. Much of the agricultural and construction work all over Cuba is done by prisoners.

Because I had trouble controlling my temper I had many problems. Sometimes if a guard asked me a question, I answered in a hostile way. On one of the *granjas* there was one particular guard who was always spying on and mocking the prisoners. For example, when we were going for food, he would stand in line offending the prisoners by calling us women's names. One day I was there without a shirt. Since I had only one, I needed to wash it so that it would be ready for work the next day. I did not want to be in line without a shirt, so I stood off to the side. Seeing me out of line and not wearing a shirt, the guard asked me why and *si yo tenía la luna* [if

I had my period]. When he said that, I got so mad I jumped on top of him. I had to hit him! I struck him a few times, but he did not even know how to fight back. He was garbage! Instead, he went off and brought other guards, who took me outside in handcuffs and beat me with sticks and iron rods. They hit you all over, man, until you're left there almost dead. Then they pick you up and put you in the *calabozo* [cell] or take you to the hospital. In my case, they put me in solitary confinement for six days. It was a dark cell under the stairs—a cage made of iron bars. Whether you sit or stand, whatever position you're in, it hurts because the iron on the floor is rough and they left me in only underwear. Afterward they put me in another punishment cell. Inside when there's a breeze, you freeze because you have no clothes on. And when it's very hot, you get asphyxiated from the heat. The toilet is a hole in the floor. Under the door they pass you a little *rancho* [slop]. It is completely dark. You can't see anything. I had to stay there twenty-one days. There were a lot of mosquitoes and other insects. In the Cuban jails, prisoners suffer from many illnesses, especially asthma and stomach trouble. In my opinion, they put something in the food to make the prisoners sick. In protest, young people like me who were not in the rehabilitation plan put tattooes on our bodies. This one I have is the head of an Indian woman from the Caribbean.

Once I got out of jail I had trouble finding work. Whenever they discovered that I was against the system, they fired me. Then, because I could not get a job, they put me back in prison for another year for being unemployed! I could not continue living in this way, so I concentrated on escaping. After my first experience I decided to make my own plans and tell no one about them. I asked someone I knew, a *muchacha perdida* [lost woman, i.e., prostitute] if she could find out which boats were leaving the country. I told her I wanted to send a letter to a friend in a foreign country and that if I mailed it, Cuban authorities might read it. She found out for me that a Greek ship, *Maya*, was going to Barbados. After she gave me this information I went to customs to find out more and prepare myself.

When I arrived at the customs office at the port of Santiago, I did not go through the main door, but walked around in a place nearby where there weren't too many people. After a while I spotted the ship, walked toward it and entered as if I were a customs employee. I slipped through a door that was on the side where the railroad is. Once on board I found some cement and covered my work clothes with powder from it so I'd look like a worker on the boat. Before I left, I tied a rope I found to the ship and threw the other end in the water. I had also chosen the place where I would hide.

I went back to my home and waited there until night, giving them time to check the ship. At about ten o'clock I returned to the dock and had to swim to the boat because there were guards watching on land. When I reached the ship I used the rope I had thrown over to climb up. Then I groped my way along the deck in the dark to the hiding place I had already picked out. It was where they had cement stored in sacks. I rearranged them to make a little tunnel for a shelter. I had to hide because before the ship left Morro Bay, the coast guard came up with flashlights to check the cargo again and be sure no one was hiding there.

While I remained inside the tunnel, which was very hot, I was terribly thirsty and hungry, but did not dare go out during the day-time. Since I did not have a watch I could only tell what time of day it was by observing the shadow coming under the door of the storage place where I was hidden. After the shadow passed I started to calculate the hours until very late at night, when I finally came out to look for food. On the third day I saw a sailor, so I went back inside again. I was afraid that if they saw me, the ship would return to Cuba. From that moment I was too frightened to come out, al-though it was hot as an oven where I was. Later that night I could hear the sailor walking above me. By then I was so hungry and thirsty that I decided to come out, anyway, even as I heard the steps above me. When I began climbing the ladder, I slipped and fell on my knee. I hurt myself so badly that I saw stars. Right there I began crying because of my pain and thirst. I wanted to call some-body for help, but my voice wouldn't come out. Then I fainted.

When I awoke I decided to go up the ladder, anyway, but I was too weak to climb it. Luckily, during all this time no one had seen me and I returned to my hiding place. When the ship finally reached Barbados on the fifth day it could not stop there because of Hurri-cane David; the winds were so strong that no ships could enter the port. We went on to Trinidad and Tobago, and returned to Barbados three days later. During the eight days of my trip I had managed to go out only a few times to get some water. I had not been able to find any food.

At night while the ship was anchored three kilometers from Barbados I went above. No one was around. I jumped from the deck about midway down the ship and swam for half an hour, when I reached the shore. I was carrying my clothes in a plastic bag tied around my chest. Once on land, I dressed and started walking in search of the American embassy. I spent that night and the next day looking, but I could not find it. I didn't know what to do. Everyone spoke English. And after all I had been through I was *sonso* [dazed] and blacked out two more times. As I wandered around, lost and alone, I was consumed by nostalgia.

What I soon found out is that once you have escaped, still more problems lie ahead. The days while you are waiting seem endless because new troubles happen that you did not expect and you have to think and act fast. There is no time to plan. You just know that after coming so far and in spite of how sick and confused you feel, you must make it! You cannot afford to fail. To come so close and then lose it all would drive you insane. You are still like a cornered animal until that moment when you are actually walking in freedom.

Finally I decided to surrender myself to the authorities of Barbados, thinking they would give me political asylum. Instead, they put me in jail for ten days. A guy there who spoke a little Spanish explained to me where the American embassy was. At the trial I was accused of entering the country illegally. The judge told me I could stay there only one month and that then they were going to send me back to Cuba.

They took me to Immigration, where they gave me nothing to eat and just a bench to sleep on. In the afternoon the interpreter who had been translating everything for me left and said he would come back in the morning. I was there with a guard at the door who spoke only English. As I walked by him he started saying something and I told him I did not understand. When he took me by the hand, I told him to be careful. I could understand a little of what he said. He was asking me where I was going. I said in Spanish that I was just going outside for a little while and would be back. I continued walking and he went inside, probably to call someone. When I reached the corner of the street I started running and finally arrived at the American embassy. The American consul sent for a priest, who took me to a Catholic church. While I was there I did not do anything. I was free inside the building, but they did not allow me to go out. They told me not to let people outside see me. I think they were afraid there might be Cuban spies around, especially since the country has relations with Cuba and may follow in its path. At the end of a month the American embassy sent me to Miami. Now that I am here in the United States, I hope to be able to study naval engineering.

Together

I taught in school without desire because I was never a Communist. What I taught about the Revolution was obligatory. The director and the evaluators passed by and checked the classes to see if we were teaching what we should. If they caught you saying anything to a child against the Revolution, you went to jail right away.

Teresa
Interviewed October 1979
Miami, Florida

Teresa has smooth, brown skin the color of old bronze, and dark hair drawn back on top of her head. Her face is a palimpsest, prudence and reticence showing prominently at first. As the interview proceeds, warmth and laughter gradually emerge, and her initial reserve fades. She is still feeling ill from her escape, but as she talks her strength revives.

I AM twenty-two years old and I come from Marianao, a suburb of Havana. I was a substitute teacher in a boarding school for girls and boys, where I was in charge of the fifth grade. My salary was 4 pesos a day, which came to 118 pesos a month. I taught the children about the Revolution—the rebels who fought in the mountains and why they did so. We discussed the martyrs of the Revolution and the bad things the Americans did. I had to use a textbook and stick to it. We were told that those were the things we had to teach first, before anything else. I also had to meet with the parents who did not send their children to school; who spoke against the Revolution; who did not encourage their children to want to serve in the army because some of them had religious beliefs against that. My job was to call the parents to school to create a revolutionary consciousness in them. Some would say their child was sick but they had no papers to show that. Or they defended their children by saying their sons or daughters did not like the school and complained about the food given to them. It is true that the food is very poor, and there is not much variety in their diet. They give fish—*merluza* [hake]—rice and very thin powdered milk. They force the children to drink that milk, telling them it makes them strong and is necessary for good nutrition.

I was a Young Pioneer and a member of the Women's Federation. In Cuba you have to be integrated into everything, because if not, the people on the block see you as a bad person. You have to belong to the CDR and to have a job like mine you must be integrated into the ranks of the Young Communists. The Women's Federation helps women find jobs, particularly if it's a woman alone with children. They also assist with economic necessities. In these ways women have benefited from the organization. When my father left for the United States, my mother became the head of our small family and was unemployed. The first job she was given was cleaning the streets. She earned about 70 pesos a month and it was not enough. Then she started working in a laboratory as a *revisadora*, handling paperwork. Now she is employed in a jewelry-making factory and receives 100 pesos a month.

In Cuba the salaries are too low and there is too much work. In our family we received meat one week and chicken the next. They allowed only half a small chicken for my son and me. I gave all the meat we received to him and rarely tasted any myself. The rest of the family helped in the same way. I worked every day, and on the weekend I went to the shop to buy our quota. They sell you your food for the month and that's all. Now they charge you for water in Marianao. Recently they told the people the water is contaminated and that they have to boil it. I don't know from what, maybe Hurricane David. I lived in a building with a motor pumping water up. They gave it to us twice a day. Therefore you had to keep water in containers to use when you needed it later. Otherwise you had to wait till they pumped up more. You pay for the amount you consume.

The lines for everything were *mortales* [killing]. I spent my life running all the time. When I was on the morning shift I had to get up at five because I was working very far away from the day-care center for my son. We had to wait hours and hours for a bus. Often the choice I had was to come late to the day-care center or late to work. Even if I took my son to the day-care center early, I would still be late for work sometimes. Then you get a red mark against you. Eight o'clock is the hour for entering all work centers. If you do not arrive on time and have red marks for tardiness, or if you cannot come one day because of a problem at home, they dock your salary.

Your work shifts rotate—either from eight to four-thirty or from eleven to seven. I used to run even more for the one starting at eleven. I had to wake up early because my son had to be at the center. If I didn't come on time, they wouldn't let him in. Then I went home to clean the house so that it would be ready when I returned at night. Then I ran to work. At seven I had to rush to pick up my child because the center closes at that time. Sometimes I had to ask my husband to leave his job early or get someone to keep my son in their home. Later I would have to hurry to pick him up. Afterward I had to wait long hours to get a bus to return home. Then I had to wash and iron the clothes. This was my daily routine. In the day-care centers the children learn songs, drawing and how to get along with other children. That part was good, but the meals were bad. The only food I ever saw there was very soft rice, like mashed potatoes, mixed with a little ground-up meat, a bit of banana, a little milk, and some water.

When my husband told me we were leaving, I decided to go without looking back, in spite of the fact that my mother and two sisters are still in Cuba. The specific reason we left was that although we were married, we had to live separately because there was nowhere for us to be together. My husband slept in his house and I slept in mine. My house was too small for the two of us. His was bigger, but he has many brothers and there was not enough room for me. Since our salaries were low, we did not have money to stay anywhere else. All we could do was talk to each other. We had no privacy. Most young people are in this same situation. Many marriages end in divorce as a result of this kind of boring life. Sometimes we had to go to the *posadas,* to rent a room. My husband knew some people who worked there and we went to a place close by. But we stopped going because it was very unhygienic. The sheets were never changed. They just let them dry out and then they put them back on the bed. They were dirty and the towels were filthy too. My husband was afraid we would get a disease. So we had to stay a long time without contact.

I used to look at the couples who could live together and I envied them. Those people had their own home. The majority of the people who do are *pinchos*. They have good jobs and are well placed in the revolutionary government. They have privileges like houses and other things. That hurt me a lot and I used to comment about it, because if we are all supposed to be equal, and we are all revolutionaries, why shouldn't we all live the same? In Cuba the government says there are no more privileges, but they still exist. There is a bourgeoisie. There are still the haves and the have-nots.

My husband and his friends planned everything for the escape. For many months they were arranging the trip, without my knowing anything about it. He told me quickly the day we were leaving, just like that, and I said, "O.K. Let's go." I understood that in the United States I could have what I dreamed of, to be together with him. Do you understand? Our odyssey was terrible in that I was afraid, not for me but for my child. My son knew how to swim a little, and I knew how to swim because for five years I had been in sports and was a diver. My husband was a lifeguard. Well, at about three in the afternoon we were on the coast at Cojímar waiting till nine o'clock for the boat, which was out on the water. Then we swam to it. I was the most afraid at the moment we jumped into the water. I knew it was deep and I was afraid for my son. Later, once we were on the boat, we had to move along carefully because there were many Russian ships around. We were worried that they would see us and send us back. That was the other most frightening part of the trip for me. Fortunately my son slept most of the time, but I was ill and vomiting because I was unaccustomed to being on a boat. I was praying the whole way because I was afraid someone would see us or that the boat would sink.

Teresa's husband, Danilo, who planned the escape, is a tanned, muscular man of medium height with a blaze of sun-bleached blond hair. He takes evident pride in his four-year-old son, delighting in the boy's intelligence. In a waiting room of the Cuban Refugee Center, the child is glimmering in his own world of antics and discoveries. He is inquisitively checking his new surroundings and entertaining a group of Cubans who watch him work his way neatly through a chocolate bar, nut by nut. His chewing, miming and laughter go on at another end of the room while his father describes to us the preparation and different stages of their trip.

AM twenty-four years old and was born in Havana, where I have lived all my life. I worked as a lifeguard, earning 118 pesos a month. I did not tell my wife about my plans until the day we went because I did not want her to worry. There were ten of us altogether: the father and mother of the guy who worked with me, and his wife, plus two sisters, and one other person. The friend who worked with me and lived in Cojímar called me once because he trusted me. He said, "I have a plan to leave. If you agree, let me know." I said O.K. and we started planning, but it was really he who made all the arrangements. His father was a fisherman in Cojímar and was the captain of a boat. He did not own the boat but used it to earn his living.

My friend talked to his father about the plan and the man had to ask permission to go fishing the night of our escape. Then he waited for us on the boat about four hundred meters away from the shore. In the meantime my friend and I had arranged a password. By noon of the day we escaped, my wife and I were in Cojímar. I left her in a park and went to my friend's house, talked to him and told him we were all ready. We went to where my wife was and walked around the town to get something to eat. Then my friend took us to the place and explained that it was the area we were leaving from. I did not know the rest of the people we were going with. He said, "You'll find a boy fishing. They call him *el Chino*. When you get close to him, try to be sure his name is *el Chino*—that's our code— and ask him anything you want to know." I agreed and stayed there

on the coast. My wife went swimming with our son like the other
people who were around there. For part of the time I went to a cave
to hide. There were some rocks where couples were staying to be
by themselves. Later, I lay down on the ground for a while, waiting
for the night.

We had not gone to work that day and gave no notice. This
caused some problems for my wife because they sent someone to
her house to see if she was sick. They did not discover anything,
however. We stayed where we were until eight in the evening. About
that time we saw a guy coming with a pushcart. My wife came out
of the water, dried off and we put on our clothes. There were still
a lot of people around and we would have been in trouble if any of
them had noticed we were not from the area. I saw that the man
with the cart had a tank of gasoline, a tire and grass covering part
of it. It looked like rubbish he was going to throw away. Then he
stopped the cart at the edge of the water and put the inflated tire and
the tank in. I don't know what he was doing, but it looked as if he
was planning to escape, too.

Finally all the members of our group started to assemble. We
went to the water with our clothes on. I had given my son a sleeping
pill so that he would stay quiet, but at that point he was still
awake. I explained to him that we were going fishing and he paid
attention to me. The boat was anchored and the old man was fishing. He did not look at us. He had the special light on that fishermen
have to use. It is a bottle with petroleum inside and it hangs on
top of the boat. If you turn the light off, the coast guards come
to check. We swam around to the other side of the boat that was
not visible from shore. But we could not get up on that side because
there were many fishing boats around. We had to wait for them to
go farther out. Once we were on the boat we had to steer in and
out to avoid the Soviet boats. As we moved along, we kept cutting
the wick of the light down with a knife so that the flame would get
smaller and smaller. We did this so that they would think we were
farther away than we were. If we had turned the light off immediately, they would have noticed something was wrong and would
have come over. We continued going out and finally turned the light
off completely.

We had gotten a weather report beforehand and found out that the weather would be good. We had also managed to collect thirty-six extra gallons of gasoline from friends who had cars and coupons to buy it. As we went along that night we had to be very careful all the time because many Soviet ships were arriving in the port of Havana, and if they had seen us, they would have reported us. We kept going north. I sat in front with a compass to guide the boat, and took turns with the guy at the helm. The women were trying to sleep on the bottom of the boat because they were very nervous, and I put canvas on top of them so that they would not be bothered by the night dew and get sick. Our trip lasted eighteen hours. We knew that the boat went five miles an hour and that is the way we calculated how long it took us.

The main inconvenience we had was passing two merchant ships, but we were able to avoid them by moving in another direction and turning off the motor. We discovered that no one on the ship was looking out. Probably they were sleeping. We were still afraid, although we did not know what country they were from. After about sixteen hours we realized we were in American waters. We saw a sailboat and headed straight for it. As we watched it we noticed fog very far behind it. We could not tell if there was land there or not. As we got close to the sailboat we asked the American where we could find land. He signaled us to go straight ahead. Farther on we found a tourist boat which guided us until we arrived at Big Pine Key.

I LEFT BECAUSE the salary I made in Cuba was not enough to support my wife and son. Because there is so much hunger I had to go fishing and sell what I caught to buy rice, even though this kind of thing is prohibited. I had to buy beans and other food on the black market. And you know what happens to you when they catch you doing that—you are put in jail. I used to carry a shopping bag with me to be able to buy what I needed whenever I happened to find it. I was lucky they never stopped me, but you are afraid all the time. I planned that if they ever caught me I would say that a friend had given me these things. The government, however, has its own system, too. They check to see if the rice or whatever you have is the same as your friend's. You just have to take the chance, anyway.

There is much repression of all kinds in Cuba. Every day when you are at the bus stop they ask for your ID. If you walk with a package they ask to see what is inside. If they notice a few of you on a corner, they tell you, "Go on. Scram." I decided to be very "integrated" into the Revolution because I had plans to leave. I spoke well all the time of the Revolution. I said everything was very good. Meanwhile my mother was filling out forms to leave the country, waiting for the right time to present them. She asked me if she should fill out my forms and I told her, "No, I'm not going anywhere. I'm staying here." I told her that to avoid arousing suspicion, my plan being to bring her over once I had escaped. If she had turned in my form, that would have removed my mask as an *integrado*. At the time of my escape they had already taken my blood and done a physical exam for me to join the Young Communists. Before that I was in the military service for eight months and then they put me in the reserves.

I will give you one last example of the kind of things the government does that made me want to leave. When the meeting of Non-Aligned Countries was going on in Havana, many of my good friends were picked up and put in jail, only because they had been in prison before and had problems with the Revolution. The government did not want their guests to have any contact with people who do not accept the system. They got those people out of the way in order to feel more secure in front of visitors from other countries.

"Don't Jump Yet"

Before we left, five friends who worked on the docks with us tried the same thing we did. They hid on board a Soviet ship. But as it got close to the U.S. coast, the men were so hot and thirsty they went to look for water. When they came out, they were captured, beaten and taken back to Cuba and are now serving five years in jail.

Martín
Interviewed October 1979
Miami, Florida

A twenty-one-year-old who looks younger, Martín has long, sandy hair and is wearing tinted, wire-rim glasses that seem incongruous because most of the time his expression is serious. They are a touch of whimsy, an amusement for him now that the exacting, colorless life he describes is over. With his slight physique and thin legs it is hard to imagine him working as a stevedore. He begins his story by explaining this anomaly.

AFTER finishing high school, I studied mechanics—repairing diesel engines. But when I completed my training they had no jobs for me as a mechanic, so I had to work as a stevedore. They give you a one-year contract and after that time you have to find another job as a stevedore somewhere else. When I had worked eight months in one place, I left because I wanted to be a mechanic. But since I still couldn't find a job, I went back to being a stevedore, this time in Regla, in Havana, the town where I was born and raised. It made me angry that although they train many engineers and technicians, they don't have enough positions for them. What good is it to become a mechanic and then go to the Ministry of Work and be assigned to agriculture or construction, for which you're not prepared. Actually I was lucky to find a job on the wharf because I refused to do the work they told me to do. Imagine after studying mechanics for three years, the job they offered me was digging graves!

I was born under the Communist regime and because I grew up with that system I did not think about leaving the country until a few years ago. Like many Cubans I kept thinking that the system would progress. We did not believe things were going to be as bad as they are now. But in Cuba there is much misery, a scarcity of all kinds of things. A typical day for me meant working eight hours straight at the port. There were no breaks because the work at the pier doesn't stop, and it was very strenuous—carrying heavy sacks of coffee, lard and iron. Then I would go home and often there was nothing to eat. I would see the children in the house going hungry. There were nine of us in my family living together. We could buy only two liters of milk every other day and three quarters of a pound of meat per person every fifteen days. You can't always get meat—they give you chicken instead. After twenty years of promises, things are getting worse every day. They are rationing more, even the milk for children, and bread, too. I used to visit many of the homes of my friends who have children and sometimes they hadn't eaten anything but flour mixed with water for four days. That hurt me all the time I saw it.

They have put a lot of effort into medical care, but there are still problems. For example, my mother is a diabetic and they gave her a special diet to follow. But because she could not find what she was supposed to eat—it just wasn't available—she had to have the same food as everyone else. Medicines are very expensive and most of the time you can't get the ones you need. At one time they will have a lot of one kind of medicine and if it happens to be what you need, then you are all right. If not, you have to wait.

You live like this day after day, and there are no diversions. I did not make a big salary—152 pesos a month, but it was more than most people earn. The average pay is 85 to 120 pesos a month. Since the quotas of things allowed just aren't enough, you are forced to buy on the black market, even though it is illegal and therefore dangerous. If you are young and want a pair of jeans, you pay more than 100 pesos for them on the black market. The government does not sell enough things. So if a person is working in a bakery, say, and does not buy under the counter, he steals lard because he has none at home. As a result the bakery is short of lard; they can't put enough in the bread they make and no one can eat it. For reasons like this, many products sold are very bad. If things were readily available, people would not steal a little bit of coffee here or something else there because they do not have the money to buy it.

People cannot always buy on the black market. In my case we had more because the pier was nearby. We used to do business with the Russian workers on the ships. We bought and exchanged things with them—like Soviet perfume for 5 pesos a bottle or head scarfs for women. The Russians are just like the capitalists. They sell contraband goods, making sure the captain and crew of the ship don't see them. When the Russians go to the United States they buy jeans. New ones in Cuba are sold for as much as 150 pesos. When I bought from the Russians, I paid 50 pesos for a pair.

The government uses different tactics to manipulate the people. They will remove certain goods altogether for a while and then start selling them again. For instance, once they eliminated cigarettes completely, so one pack went for 20 pesos on the black market. We called 1970 "The Dance of the Millions" because there was a lot of money but nothing to buy. A contraband chicken cost 100 pesos! Then the government started making things available again, and a pack of cigarettes for which we had paid 20 centavos sells for 1.60 pesos. A pair of pants costs 30 pesos and they are of such poor quality that the material disintegrates. When I was working at the port I saw tobacco, rum, fruits and preserves leaving Cuba. There is a huge difference, though, between what Cubans eat and what they export. I only wish the people could have what they send to other countries, but they don't know what it is to eat shrimp or lobster, which are shipped out by the ton. Almost all of the factories make things for export. In Cuba you can't get things like products made of mangoes or preserves of coconut or guava. These go abroad. Infants receive only small portions of baby food and no juices. Spain buys a lot of Cuban tobacco and England sends us chicken, but most of the trade is with the Soviets. When they had the meeting in Havana this year of the Non-Aligned Countries, that was the time the people of Cuba felt the poorest. So much went for the visitors that they reduced our food rations even more, and what small quotas we were entitled to were often not available.

My friend Luis and I boarded a Soviet ship at two in the afternoon on August 31, 1979. The day before, one of the Russian workers on it had told us it was going to New York, and Luis and I decided to hide on it. I had tried once before to escape. I had a connection with a foreigner who was going to take me out of the country, but since it was a Western ship, I could not get on it. The only way you can board it is if you are working on it. Even then, you have to present an ID card authorizing you to be there. Then, when you've finished work you have to return to the office to get your ID back. Obviously if you don't do so, they know you are still on the ship. Thereafter, when our five friends were arrested for stowing away on a Soviet ship, we were afraid that we could not get out that way either. We were scared they would start checking Russian ships, too, something they had not done before. The reason they did not, however, was that it would have seemed disrespectful to the Soviet crew.

Now Luis and I went to the ship together before our work shift started. Since we knew all of the workers there, we just went over as if we were working too. We tried to avoid attracting notice because if their boss had seen us, he would have sent us out, knowing it wasn't time for us to start working.

We walked to the back of the ship because there were large metal containers there for the cargo. When we were about to hide in one of them, two Soviets appeared. We decided to make friendly conversation with them. Just to be sure, we asked them where the ship was going and they said, "To New York." I don't speak Russian, but I know a few words and we talked with gestures. They told us that the work on the ship was finished and that it was almost ready to go.

We went inside the ship and entered a cabin, where I saw a trap door in the floor. Underneath was a storage area in which they kept cables and tools. We climbed in and while we were hiding we heard people walking and working overhead, but no one came down. The room was so crowded with equipment that the space we had was very narrow. We could not lie down on the floor. Later the twisted position we had to stay in while we were sleeping made our legs numb. While they were working above us we had to be quiet. We had brought absolutely nothing with us—no food and no water. I started thinking that if we stayed too long, in case something was wrong with the ship and it was delayed, it would be dangerous for us to be without water. Since everyone at that time was working, I told my friend it would be safe to go for water.

The workers bring water in a bucket and so Luis went to get one. He found one and brought it back. It was lucky he did, because the ship did not start moving until midnight. I had a watch with me and at two o'clock I decided to go up to look outside. We figured that since it was so late, no one would be up and around, that they would all be sleeping, and that with the deck so full of containers we would not be visible. I came out alone because Luis did not want to go. As I looked out, I saw the lights of Havana in the distance. I went inside again and told Luis that we were finally on our way to the United States.

At about one o'clock at night on Sunday we were close to the U.S. coast. It had taken forty-eight hours and in that time all we had had was water. Now we had no more. We left our hiding place and hid inside a crane, from where we could watch the other people work. We could also see the other ships and the lights of the city. The loudspeaker started to give orders in Russian. Then the boat turned and we saw the coast of what turned out to be Houston. The ship stopped and we thought that the next day the ship would begin to enter the port.

Once the workers had all gone down into the boat, we climbed out of the crane and hid in one of the empty containers, staying there until the next day. All that day we remained in the same place and were without water again. We got very thirsty waiting while the Russians continued working. When night came we decided to go outside for water. We went to the back of the kitchen looking for some. We saw a fountain near the door of a cabin, but when we tried it, no water came out. Luis looked around and found a hose that was connected to a water tank. We tasted a few drops and found that it was fresh water. I took the hose and started drinking fast. When I finished and turned it off to pass it to Luis, we heard a door open. I threw down the hose and froze in fear. Luis got ready to run, but I held him back. I pulled him to me and embraced him hard while the Russian passed by without stopping. I had held Luis against me, patting his head to calm him down and had only seen the Russian from the waist down. Either he did not see us or he thought we were a Russian couple—because of my long hair and the fact that Russian women were working on board. At that moment we were in front of the stairs. The man passed very close to us and then walked up. Now it was Luis' turn to drink but I didn't let him. I said, "Come on, hurry up," and we ran back to our hiding place. We waited all the rest of that night and the next day. At night we took the bucket and went once more for water. This time we waited till three in the morning. Since the cabins had small windows we had to stoop down as we ran in case anyone was awake and could see us. We found four bottles of juice that were empty and filled them with water. We each took two and I told Luis that if any Russian came, we'd throw the bottles at him. One of us would jump on him and the other would run out to leap overboard and inform the American authorities about us.

Once we were back inside the container I told Luis that I could not wait anymore. I saw a lot of ships around that weren't too far away. I could not tell if they were American, but I knew they weren't Russian. I said to Luis that we ought to start preparing some kind of raft to throw out on the water so that we could approach one of the ships to take us to shore. We had arrived during Hurricane David, which is why it was not so hot where we were. Naturally, this was a help to us, but there was the problem of very high waves. We took two life preservers from the side of the ship, one for each of us. Even with that, Luis didn't want to jump, but I was desperate. We went back to our hiding place and took some wood and wire to reinforce the life preservers and to try to make a little raft. It was now nearly dawn.

I told Luis, "Here's what we're going to do. At about four o'clock we're going to jump." He was afraid because the sea was so rough and we had to go to another ship that was far away. Luis was worried that the current would drag us off. I told him that if we jumped at about four and couldn't make it, the sun would rise and some boat or someone would see us and pick us up. The coast was way off in the distance, the lights just tiny specks. During the day the land had looked blurred, like a cloud.

We tied the two life preservers together. They were red, with the name of the ship on them. After we made the raft, we prepared a rope and threw it down. We took two shovels as oars so that we wouldn't have to put our hands in the water, because we were afraid of the fish. As soon as we had dropped the raft overboard, I asked Luis, "Do you want to jump first, or should I?" He said, "No. You go ahead." I climbed down the rope, which we had knotted so that our hands and feet could grip it. The other end of the rope was tied to the raft. When I finally mounted the raft, it wouldn't support me and sank. Even if it had stayed afloat, we could not have used it because it kept flipping over. I decided the lifesavers were probably just to use in an emergency if there was nothing else because they were made only of light cork. In the water I felt very heavy because my clothes were all wet. The barnacles on the side of the ship cut my hands while I was holding on, trying to stay on the raft. I suddenly realized that I was down there without knowing how to get back up. I didn't think I could use the rope because the boat was so high and I didn't have enough strength to climb, especially with my clothes weighing me down.

I was lucky that I noticed a ladder hanging down—two ropes crossed by slats of wood as steps. It was way at the other end of the ship. I called up to Luis, "Go get that ladder and throw it down." During the time he went to get it, a Russian appeared on the deck, at the place where the crew gathers to steer the ship. When Luis threw me the ladder he called quietly to warn me to be careful and pointed to where the Russian was standing. By that time I did not even feel like being careful anymore because I was so tired. When I finally got back up, Luis came close to the container and said, "Stay there. Stay there. Don't move." I kept going, anyway, without caring if the guy caught me. He did not see me, though, and we returned to our hiding place. When Luis had gone for the ladder, he let our rope go over the side so that no one would discover evidence of our attempt to escape.

The next day the ship started moving again. By now it was our fifth day and all I had eaten was some coffee at home and some ice cream before getting on the ship. We started feeling happy as we saw the ship heading toward the pier. Then it moved away in a different direction. When I saw the coast disappearing I told Luis,

"I'm not waiting anymore. I'm going to jump! These people must know we're on the ship and they're returning us to Cuba." He said, "No, no, no. Don't despair. Don't jump yet." He tried to calm me down, but each time I put my head outside the container, I saw more open sea. I told him, "Listen, now we're going to go to Cuba for sure!" Soon we started to see posts in the sea with numbers on them. It looked like a channel. Then I noticed small fishing boats around, crossing very close to the ship. I said to Luis, "Come on. Come on. Let's jump." But he did not want to. I resigned myself and said, "O.K. If they're going to take us to Cuba, let them."

We saw land again and the boat started to enter a channel. When I saw those narrow channels, I wanted to jump. Faraway I could see factories and tanks of petroleum. Luis kept telling me, "Take it easy. Don't get desperate." The sun came out from behind the clouds and it began getting warm. It was about two in the afternoon and the crew started anchoring the ship. After they finished, we kept waiting and drank all the water we had left. We were standing and began weaving from dizziness. We opened the door and looked down. On land we saw some barracks. We waited twenty-five minutes and then it started to rain. We waited for it to rain hard because then the Russians would not be outside and we could leave. It wasn't raining heavily but I told Luis we'd leave, anyway, because we were in American territory and the Russians couldn't do anything to us.

We left the container and saw how high the waves rose and we were afraid to jump. We got another rope and tied a lot of knots in it. We were going to go down on the side facing land, but a few Russians appeared on the stairs and some Americans started coming aboard. We threw the rope into the water on the side facing the open sea. We were close to the front of the ship. Meanwhile, there was a Russian preparing a rope. As soon as I tied our rope I hurried to climb down it, while Luis was watching the Russian. After I got down, Luis threw the two bottles he had into the water and started to come down. Luckily the Russian didn't see us. Once Luis hit the water we started swimming toward land.

In front of us was another Russian ship and on the land side a lot of people had seen us jump and were watching us. They were workers from the factory. As soon as I touched shore I started running. Then I turned around to look for Luis but I did not see him. I ran back for him and told him to hurry up. He said to wait, that he couldn't run. He couldn't catch his breath and his legs were shaking. I held him up and walked to where the people were. When I approached them I thought they were all American and asked if any of them spoke Spanish. There was a Mexican and we told him we had jumped from the ship and wanted to know where the police were. The guy said, "*La policía*? We don't have any police here." I asked him to tell us how to get out of there. An old man came over and told me the way to go: "You'll see a little house over there with some guards for protecting the factory." While we were walking in that direction two policemen came over to us, probably because they saw us so dirty and wet and thought we were two crazies! We noticed they were both Americans. Then when we started talking they did not understand us and we did not understand them.

I tried to explain and pointed toward the ship, but they didn't know what I was saying. Then the old man came over in a little truck. He translated what I said to the guards and I heard them calling Immigration. We had gone through the worst part and now were beginning to feel tired. I felt so dizzy I had to sit down. The people asked us if we were hungry and we told them we had not eaten in several days. They gave us a bag of Fritos, a can of beans, some meat spread and a Coke. Then Immigration talked to us over the phone, asking all kinds of questions. The guard finally took us to his home. We removed our wet clothes and he gave us each a clean shirt. Afterward we were interrogated further and spent a night in jail. We stayed in Houston a few days and then they put us on a plane to Miami. A group of Cubans had given us clothes and collected money to pay for our plane fare.

Troubadour's Song

We are not valiant. We are just determined—people of action who came here in order to live a decent life. Some people are more afraid than we were. Others are worried about their families. But almost all of the youth of Cuba want to leave, and if they could, they would.

Lorenzo
Interviewed October 1979
Miami, Florida

Their clothes are ragged and sweat-stained, and stiff with salt. Their faces are burned pink and are marked by several days' growth of stubbly beard. Their hands are raw with blisters. One young man is shivering violently despite a heavy denim jacket and a cup of hot coffee over which he is hunched. This group of Cubans who have just arrived comprises Lorenzo, thirty-one, a singer; Oscar, twenty-five, a railroad electrician; Marcos, twenty-one, a mason and plumber; Alfredo, twenty, a labor supervisor at the port of Havana; and León, thirty-nine, an automobile electrician.

Lorenzo, the first to speak, is a rugged man with a shambling, bearlike gait. He has long light-brown hair streaked blond by the sun, and candid eyes that look like chips of bright-blue sky. He is a man with a precise view of his world and a goal he kept firmly in mind. Reconsideration or wavering are luxuries he could not afford to indulge in. Lorenzo speaks plainly, without much elaboration, chiefly because he regards his trip as a modest accomplishment. For him it was a necessary action carried out expeditiously with the collaboration of friends. Once they finally assembled the rough paraphernalia of escape, fortune smiled on them, and they were able to proceed directly without delay or setbacks.

WHEN I was singing one night in a town on the coast of Havana I met some of the members of our group through the sister of one of them. Later I went to that friend's house and we started to share our ideas about escaping. His father had a fishing license, but not a boat, so I tried to find out about buying one. The one I heard about was being sold for 1,500 pesos. You can imagine—1,500 pesos in Cuba is like saying a million pesos here! I myself couldn't buy the boat, but my father could, since he is a fisherman. However, I could not put the money together for it. Although the money was an impossible obstacle, I still decided to leave the country in whatever way I could.

For a while we thought of getting a truck to take the boat down to the water. But a truck, too, was out of the question. Like the boat, it just didn't appear. Then one day when I went to the house of some others in our group, they told me they had spent several days building a boat. I did not expect that! So I put on this shirt because it has always brought me good luck. "Let's go," they said, and so it was. We left.

What they had made was a kind of wooden box—like a coffin, only larger. It was square and came to a point in the front. On the bottom was a big slab of metal, and inside, it was lined with cork. Hard cork. Not the kind used for bottles. It floats well and keeps out the cold. The outside was wood. The whole thing was painted, and later, when we got the parts to the beach, we nailed them together well and secured the boat with wire. There were also four oars.

At about nine o'clock at night, we met in a deserted lot. Then we went to a very isolated part of the woods, where it was dark, to finish working on the boat. At one point we were alarmed by a family on their way somewhere. The children called out, "Look Daddy, a boat!" We just ignored them and went our way, praying that they would not be curious and follow us and that no one else would appear. The dangerous part was crossing the highway to bring the boat down to the water. Since it was very heavy, we could go only for about a meter and then we had to rest.

Finally we reached the water and set out. At that time there were no guards in the area, which was a fishing village. I was from there and had noticed that the guards usually passed by at nine or nine-thirty. Things just worked out for us, thank God. None of us had experience rowing but we managed, anyway, particularly because we caught the current and it helped us along. We did not even take food, only water, which ran out on the first day. By the end of the second night we were very near the United States. We were too exhausted to row anymore, so we fell asleep. We had a compass —an old Boy Scout one—to guide us and we had kind of an idea where Florida was. As we approached the coast, we saw an American boat and shouted to it. They came and helped us ashore.

For thirteen years I had been a singer in a group. Because I was not "integrated" and sang in English, I was blacklisted by the government and could not appear on radio or television. Another reason for this measure was that I was a practicing Catholic. In Cuba it is difficult for Catholics to attend mass. You can go to church, but they note it down and count it against you. The repression there is so bad that the police have the right to take everything from you, even your life. Since I could not get contracts to sing, I had to find another way to live from my profession. So, on Saturdays and Sundays I went from place to place singing at private parties. It was difficult traveling around like that. I sang rock 'n' roll, which is the most popular kind of music among the young people. It is part of today's reality. The government, however, tries to push Cuban music, but with no success. There is nothing novel or interesting happening with it anymore. I was paid well—70 pesos a night —but there was nothing to buy. Anything beyond the merest essentials—a pair of pants of poor quality costs 150 pesos, and a bottle of rum 24 pesos.

What I want is to live as a free man. Life in my country weighed heavily on me because under this regime there is no respect for anyone or anything. There is so little dignity possible for a human being in the conditions that exist in Cuba. It is an enormous problem, for example, just for two people to be alone, in peace, together. Instead, you are dehumanized. What they have are *posadas,* but of such poor quality—in crumbling old buildings! Things there are dirty. Often there is no running water. The owners charge high prices to reserve a room— three hours costs 2 to 5 pesos, and everything is filthy and broken! Graffiti all over the walls. Although it is not allowed officially, everyone there and in other jobs takes tips— on the sly, but they take them. The other alternative to going to these places is for couples to live with their families. This arrangement is hard on everyone and often leads to divorce. Adultery is now common. The tension of life is so great that the majority of the population drink a lot to forget their misery. There is a big racket in alcohol and drugs as well—not heroin, but marijuana. Frequently, people mix a lot of pills with drinks to get a high. They are only human, after all.

After twenty years of the Revolution, the economy is a disaster thanks to the mistakes made by the leaders. But the state does not care. It owns the capital and the people—who have to pay for the consequences of the government's errors. Anyone with any vision, anyone with any intelligence, sooner or later, in the short run or the long run, has problems with the system. I grew tired of suffering from this form of life that does not offer the least incentive for effort or accomplishment.

THE OTHERS in the group add their comments to Lorenzo's account.

MARCOS: I was the one who made the boat. It took me three days but I could have made it in one if I had had the materials. My reasons? I had tried to escape before, when I was seventeen, but the five of us got caught. I was in prison for six months and then managed to break out. Later, I was recaptured and sentenced to eighteen months. In different work farms, where I worked eight to ten hours a day. There were about five hundred other prisoners in the last one, from which I eventually escaped. Practically speaking, everyone in Cuba is a political prisoner. All you have to do is look at a policeman the wrong way. The government has no trust in the people. Fidel goes around in an armored car and a bulletproof vest. One day I saw two little kids stealing a piece of fruit. The soldiers came, separated them and hauled them away as if they were murderers. I know another case of a man who got six months in prison for not swearing allegiance to the flag. There were so many abuses like this all the time. What you have in Cuba is a system that really makes man hate man.

OSCAR: I studied for two years to be a vet. But when you are finished, you have to wait months before they call you for a job. I have friends who finished five years of their training and they are still waiting for work in their field. Of twenty people I know who studied to be technicians, only three have jobs. The others are drivers, clerks or do various kinds of work that have no correspondence to what they were trained to do. This is one of the reasons that the government sends technicians abroad. Fidel says, "We can now export intelligence because there is an abundance." In the meantime, the work in Cuba is not being done. I worked in transportation, which is in terrible condition. You travel from Havana to Santiago, as I did, and it took two days because the equipment kept breaking down. Well, one time a fellow worker was trying to repair a train by putting in an engine from another train that had broken. You have to improvise like that because there are no spare parts for repairs. Afterward the engine caught fire and my friend was arrested for sabotage. This is a system of slavery! How long can it last?

The reasons I left are simple: for liberty and democracy. Neither exists in my country. All opinion against the government is silenced. They have what they call a Socialist Constitution, but it means nothing in terms of protecting people's rights. Everybody had to vote for it or he or she would have been persecuted. Even though I had to leave behind what I love most—my country, my family—I did so because the system is so oppressive that I could not bear it any longer. My family knew that what I was doing might cost me my life, but they agreed that it was worth a try. A person like me who does not belong to any organization, who does not go to assembly meetings, has created a dangerous situation for himself. I have seen people get two-year sentences for nothing—*por pelegrosidad*, just because the government thought they were dangerous. Nevertheless, the Cuban people are beginning to lose their fear of criticizing government officials and denouncing the bad state of affairs in transportation, housing and food, and all the orders given to them in their daily lives.

ALFREDO: I left because I did not want to be brainwashed by Communism. It is so well organized. It is a sickness, a plague. After you work all week, they urge you to study at night and do volunteer work on weekends. This is their way of keeping the people occupied even during what would be their free time. It is politics and propaganda all the time, for pre-school children as well. That is all that is permitted. There is no freedom of the press, because all the newspapers are written by the government. They can put you in jail for no reason. In my case, I was at a party one night and some officials came and asked for my ID card. Since I did not have it with me, they took me to prison, to one of the work camps.

Because of such things, which happen all the time, the young people in Cuba are rebellious. They call the police "anti-youth." During the International Youth Festival last year, the slogan created by the government for visitors was "Citizens of the world, this is your home." At night, spontaneously, without being organized, young people scribbled over it: "I would trade it for yours."

LEÓN: Nobody respects what Fidel says anymore, because Cuba has been physically and morally destroyed. There is a new class in the government. While the children and workers do not have breakfast in their schools and work centers, the *mayimbes* drive the latest cars and sit at special tables reserved for them at the Tropicana, where they drink bottles of rum without paying for them. All of Cuba is their private estate. As a father I was worried about the low level of morality developing among some of the youth. I worked at the port and used to cry when I saw girls of twelve and thirteen selling themselves to foreign sailors in exchange for a blouse, a pair of pants, or a can of imported food.

Bloody Hands

My family were combatants in the Rebel Army fighting against Batista. A brother and an uncle of mine were captains, and another uncle was a *commandante*. Nevertheless, Fidel's government took away our land, removed us from our farm and imprisoned us.

Alejandro
Interviewed October 1979
Miami, Florida

Four o'clock in the afternoon, the sky turning pink. This stretch of Miami Beach is deserted, with just a long sweep of ocean and palm trees, whose branches are already starting to look like large dark spiders against the horizon. A small room inside one of the hotels reverberates with Alejandro's vivid personality. His bristling Afro-style hair and bright-red shirt suit his emphatic way of speaking and his life-loving sense of humor. The words go by at a rapid clip with frequent exclamations and knife-thrusts of irony. He is celebrating a hard-won victory, without self-consciousness. Along with his toughness there is an underlying innocence—an unwillingness to compromise, but no desire to impress.

I WAS born in Trinidad, in Las Villas province, in 1956 and worked as an auto mechanic. There were eleven brothers, of whom I am the youngest. My family was humiliated by Fidel's government, although they had fought in the Revolution and supported it in the beginning. My family eventually turned against the system because they saw that what was happening in Cuba was not what they had struggled for.

There were many reasons for their anger and disappointment.

In the early 1960s the government went back on its promise to distribute land among the *campesinos*. Instead, even those like my parents who had small farms had to give them up and those farmers who had never owned land just became paid workers of the state. The government claimed that the collectives it was organizing would be more efficient. But sending in managers who knew nothing at all about farming, and who did not even know the area, created terrible confusion and waste. The supervisors came in with their plans, which often had no relationship to the actual physical conditions of the land. Their ideas of what could be planted, and how it should be done, did not work because they had little or no experience with farming. It is an awful feeling to see the land being ruined and harvests failing, particularly when the people of the region were not consulted about how to do the work. They were just given orders. The people could do little and if they argued or tried to explain the proper ways of planting, they were accused of being counter-revolutionaries.

The same kind of thing was going on all over the country. It was not the original revolutionaries who were in power, but Communist Party members who were suddenly taking over in the government, in the unions and in the schools. The freedoms that Cubans had fought for were being taken away—with the newspapers and television and radio stations run by the government, and people arrested and sent to prison only because they were suspected of being against the government. Many of them were revolutionaries. They were *not* opposed to the Revolution but to the methods being used to force everyone to agree with whatever Fidel and his followers said. They removed my family to Havana and put my father in jail for nine years, one of my brothers for seven years, and another for six and a half years. They sent me to a reformatory because I was too young to go to prison. Afterward, I went to schools in Las Villas, Camagüey and La Habana.

In Cuba the police don't leave you alone. They tell you that you can't be without a shirt; that you can't have long hair. The young people don't receive anything decent for their work. There are endless lines for everything, and even on the beach there is nothing to eat. You have no aspiration for anything. You can't even work to be able to afford a bicycle because there aren't any available. Here, if I want to buy a car, I may have to work for ten years, but I know that at least I will be able to buy one. In Cuba there isn't a future of any kind. Always they talk about tomorrow, but if you don't have a present, you can't have a future. Here you are able to afford what you need because the prices are lower than your salary. In Cuba you make, for example, 200 pesos, but it is not enough for the month and there's nothing to buy, anyway. When you go out to eat, you have to stand in line four or five hours, but by the time you get in they have run out of food. There are few clothes to buy, so you look for contraband. That exists in every country, and even more so in Communist countries because they don't provide enough. The reason there is so little in Cuba is that they export almost everything.

Every day the rationing gets stricter. Food and other things go to Angola, Ethiopia, and elsewhere. Any time a country comes out from there and needs an egg, Fidel sends it! And all the time he talks in the plaza, he tells us what he is going to *take away,* not what he is going to give us. The terror is so great that Fidel has made a human machine of the people. Not because the people want that; it is Fidel's terrorism. You have to raise your hand and say yes to whatever Fidel wants. Otherwise they put you in jail sooner or later. Even with the sugar! He said he was taking away one pound of it from each person's ration to send to another country. Then the authorities came with a piece of paper that you had to sign saying you wanted to give it. If you said no, they took it from your quota anyway.

The people I knew did not support Fidel. They think he is a criminal, *un sangriento* [a man drenched in blood]. He was the one who separated Cuban families. Why doesn't he allow the emigration of all the people who want to join their relatives in other countries? Let him keep only the ones who want to stay. Or let him have a system that works. Let him be adaptable. Cubans who come here have been welcomed and given work. The money Fidel charges Cuban exiles who go back to visit—850 pesos—is *un descaro* [act of effrontery]. Before, tape recorders were selling for 43 pesos and he raised the price to close to 400. He does not let people bring anything into the country. He forces them to buy what the government sells in Cuba. That is how he is taking money from other Cubans. It is a market. He runs it like a business.

The young people just are not with Fidel. *Seguro! Seguro! Seguro!* [I know this for sure.] The people who support him at the rallies are primarily older people in the government who do not want to lose what they have, like a house or a car. And as a result of their behavior, whatever those people ask for, they can get right away without waiting, unlike the ordinary people. Those who are with the government constrain, subjugate and exploit the rest of the people. They are the guards who watch everyone else. I don't know what they are watching! Because the people who steal over there do it so that they won't die of hunger.

In Cuba you are forced to steal in order to exist. And even if you go legally to buy extra things, because the ration was not enough, they put you in jail. You have to rob in one way or another just to survive. For example, I stole a machine part from my job to sell outside to another citizen who had an old car. The state would not sell him the part because the car was for private use. Therefore, stealing that part benefited both of us.

My salary was 150 pesos a month. I had trouble paying for food, let alone going out with my girl friend. At my job they did not provide any meal, not even milk. During breaks, they give you a tamarind, or *natilla* [sweet pudding], or egg and rice. You work like hell for eight hours and you do not even have the proper tools to do your job. Then, when you are finished for the day, naturally you want to do something to forget your problems. I am young and need some recreation. When you work and have some diversions, then you feel good and life goes along well. But we had none. It was all work and then at the end of the week was "Red Saturday and Sunday"—volunteer work. At your work place if you protest that there is no food, they shove you up against the wall and humiliate you. They make you the scapegoat and blame you for everything that goes wrong or for whatever gets lost. You can't live in these conditions!

I decided to come here because there is freedom of thought, and expression. Since I did not belong to any of the mass organizations in Cuba, I had trouble. They fired me from jobs and when I tried somewhere else, they would check my political record and not hire me. Then when I went to another place, they would give me the excuse that I could not work there because I had long hair. I would go somewhere else and they would say they had no jobs, but it was because I did not have any friends there. I wanted to become an engineer, but it is very hard for the average person. It is almost always possible, however, if you are the son of a *pincho*. Then you can go to the university and have a career in engineering. Or, for example, if a person wants to become a lawyer, he has the chance of being one of three chosen from a thousand. If he does not make it, they send him to learn agriculture. In the present system the blacks are often the most rebellious because the government says the blacks deserve everything—and then they give them the worst jobs. From above they say there is equality. Fine. Go see the Politburo in Cuba. There are almost no blacks on it.

The government says that education is free, but in the secondary schools in the country you have to work in the fields. I know about them because I was in one. There are about five hundred pupils in each. In the morning, half of them study and then go to work in the afternoon. The other students do the same thing in reverse. The truth is that with the work they demand, you pay ten times over for your studies. They have work quotas, for the girls as well as for the boys, and you have to meet them. If your boss helps you, he is penalized, often with a fine. Once my brother aided a young girl who did not feel well. Because she was weak and he helped her, they fined him 110 pesos. They told him the assistance he had given did not make for a good worker—that the girl had to do the work to develop herself. I don't understand. The girl was not physically strong enough to meet her quota.

I was in the military service for three years, earing 7 pesos a month. They call it military, but I never touched a rifle! It was forced labor. You were practically a slave. When we were cutting cane, the machine to collect it often could not get the cut stalks because of the mud, so I had to pick them up by hand. After we finished in the fields late in the afternoon, the only training we got was marching. There was never any rifle practice. Because of this system many soldiers are sent off without experience to Angola and other places. They give you a uniform, but I would not wear it. I dressed in work clothes. They put that on the report, too! Practically speaking, it is obligatory to wear a uniform, but because we were working I gave the excuse that it was too hot and that it gave me a rash. I did not tell them the real reason—that I just did not want to wear the uniform. Others did the same.

There is propaganda that says the Poder Popular takes care of the people's problems. For instance, if my roof is leaking, the Poder Popular is supposed to give me cement or tiles, but they don't give you anything. They put you on a list and several years later you may get two tiles, which aren't enough to solve the problem. In the future maybe they give you the cement. Of course by then your house is already ruined. If you need six sacks of cement to fix your house, then they give you two and you have to steal the rest—not because you want to, but because you have to. You can often find some in a place where it is just lying around getting spoiled. At the same time, you see that the *pinchos* have in their homes more commodities than anyone else. Yet if you steal and a *pincho* sees you, you are finished. He is the only one who can steal and get away with it. If you go to an assembly at your work center, as I did with a friend who is also a mechanic, and you tell them you need oil to repair a part, they give you water. If you say, "No, we need oil," they tell you, "It's already being taken care of. We're resolving that problem; we're on the way now." But they don't settle anything and they don't give you what you need. So everything keeps declining. At the same time, if you go into the house of a *pincho*, you see everything. *Todo. Todo. Todo.* But if you need a fan and go to a store, you have to wait for three months. When you get it, the price is high and it has defects. If they bought it on the world market for 10 pesos, they sell it to you for 300 pesos.

To give you another example of how the system operates. One of my brothers lives in a house in a small town in Camagüey province. While he was out some people got into a fight in the backyard, which has no fence. The son of a member of the party was cut with a knife. No one inside the house had been involved in the fight. But when my brother passed by at that moment, the police, who had been called, arrested him and took him to the station. They told him that the fighting started in his backyard and someone had to be responsible. They gave him a document to sign and because my brother is partly illiterate, he could not read what it said. If it had been me, I would not have signed it. But he wrote his name, with great difficulty, and for that he got two years in prison.

When he went to the trial, the judge said, "You signed the paper saying you cut the boy." We went to the offices of the party and to the other organizations, but no one would support my brother, since they knew we were in disagreement with the government.

I just came a few days ago, at a time when life in Cuba is getting worse and worse. There is more work and more misery. All of the young people are in some form of rebellion. Look, the people who are "integrated" do so because they want to subsist. They may not have the will that I had to jump into the ocean and come here. Five of us left, without food, without water, without a compass. Five days of rowing and we got lost on the sea. The integrated ones often don't really believe in the system. I know that many thought the way I did, because we used to talk among ourselves about these things. You see, you go to a coffee shop over there and you ask for a glass of water. They say, "No, there's no water. It's too warm to drink." Go to eat and you get bread and no butter, or they have butter and no bread! You go to work and the truck takes forever to come. But to pick you up for voluntary work, the truck gets there before you do! At three o'clock in the morning they knock on your door. To come back, however, you can't find a bus. The same with the food trucks. They are always breaking down. If by coincidence the truck comes, you are lucky if you get rice and an egg to eat. Afterward you go to do voluntary work, for which they assign you norms. Everything is drudgery and slogans, and for tomorrow, not for now. Why? Everyone has a right to live. But they don't even make an exception to give us enough chicken or a liter of milk. They tell you that the children are the future. But what future is there going to be if the children are starving?

For the sake of my people I would like to say all these things to a captain of the army, to the Politburo, or to Fidel himself. I, who was raised there, want to tell him to his face all that I have just said. See if he could deny any of it. I was born in Cuba. I am a son of the Revolution. If I can understand all this—that, excuse my language, it is all shit—what can people say who are forty or fifty years old, with more experience of life? I grew up with the system and nobody can make me change my mind or my feelings. Just today I heard Fidel on television addressing the United Nations as the leader of the Non-Aligned Countries. Who could not agree with him that the world must act now to solve the problem of hunger, which still exists in so many places? But I would like to ask Fidel how at the same time he can allow his own people to go hungry while he spends so much for arms and Cuban troops to fight for the Soviet system. I would like to know how Fidel, as the head of a poor country, is acting differently from the imperialist powers.

I had been planning to escape from the time I was in the military service, but I could not find anyone to go with me. People thought the way I did, but they did not have the courage to try. Most of them wanted to go in a motorboat, but to steal one is a big problem. Also, the radar can pick you up right away. The patrols locate where you are, don't tell you to stop and then they shoot at you. Obviously I did not want to die, so I looked for a way to fight and escape. The three times I tried to get a group together, I failed. We did not even get as far as the water, just to the discussion stage. Somebody always came up with "buts." They did not have the valor to try. They would talk about it but they did not want to make the sacrifice.

Finally five of us got together and made arrangements during the week before we left, September 21, 1979. One guy worked with me, one worked on the railroad, one who was eighteen was in the military service, and the last one was from La Juventud Cubana [The Cuban Youth]. He was known as an excellent young Communist, a fine worker and a good revolutionary. I was the leader. Our idea was to steal a truck one evening at eight from the park of San Juan de Dios in Old Havana. For some reason the owner took the truck away and we did not find it until several hours later. We really liked that truck because it was closed in back and we could hide the boat we stole on it. We found a tent inside, which we used to cover the part of the boat that was sticking out in the back.

At midnight we took the truck and went to a lake, La Presa La Guayaba. I had gone there myself two days before to check things like what time the place closed, and whether they sold anything to eat or drink. I asked a few indiscreet questions to find out where they stored the oars for the boats they rented. I discovered that the place closed at six and that they locked the oars up in a shed. After checking three other lakes, I chose that particular one because it had the advantage of being very close to the main road and to the beach. They rent boats there for 2½ pesos an hour. They used to keep those boats on the beaches, but Cubans stole them to escape and therefore the government had them moved to the artificial lakes they've made. We took seven oars in case some of them broke and we got the boat from the water.

While some of our group were breaking in to get the oars, the rest of us dragged the boat up with great effort and put it on the truck with much difficulty because the truck was very small. Half of the boat, which was ten feet long and made of plastic, was sticking out. There may have been guards around but we did not encounter any. Possibly they saw us and did not want to intervene because we looked very determined. Finally we started driving the truck toward the north coast. We left the province of Havana and proceeded to Matanzas because the vigilance there was less strict. In Havana, for example, they have El Morro Castle with the lighthouse and many coast-guard patrols stationed there. I had never been to the place we left from, but it seemed to be the right spot for escaping. I had chosen it from a map. The rest of the group agreed with my decisions. We took nothing: no water, no food, no milk, and no compass, which is a very difficult thing to get in Cuba. I figured that if they caught us with any provisions, they would know what we were planning to do. I thought it was better just to steal the boat. On the way if they had found us and asked us what we were doing, we could have said that we had been sent to deliver the boat to Matanzas.

At two o'clock we lowered the boat into the water. It was hard because we had to climb down a cliff. We left the truck on the side of the road, got into the boat and headed for the States. At first the weather was good, but the trip was very bad. Our clothes were dark so that they would not attract attention, but we wore shor-sleeved shirts—mine was of gauzelike cotton—and these weren't much protection. I knew how to swim a little, but some of the others did not know how at all. When we started we did not even know how to row. One oar went one way and the other another way. Then the boat kept turning around and tilting. We couldn't go straight! Finally we caught on to the rhythm of rowing. We rowed without stopping, two of us taking the oars while the other three rested. At night we guided ourselves by the moon and the stars, and in the day time by the sun. We rowed all day Tuesday and then all the next day and night. By then we had advanced a long distance.

The following night it began to rain and we had a storm. When we couldn't see the moon, we had no sense of our direction. We had no orientation that night. It was raining so hard—the drops fell with such force that they burned my face. There was such a strong wind that we lost control of the boat. We couldn't row, so we tried to sleep. We could not really manage to because the boat was so small and the water around us was high. Also, if you were not awake, you could tip the boat over. This was the most frightening part of the trip. When we couldn't row we felt helpless, whereas while we were rowing I knew we could make it. We had heard about people coming on rafts, which is harder. And we had also heard about people they caught and others who disappeared. When a lot of water poured into our boat, we tried to bail it out with a boot. We had not even brought a can because we did not want the radar to pick it up.

Wednesday morning the weather improved, but the sea was still very rough. The storm had driven us back toward Cuba. But we began rowing again, saying, "To Cuba? Not even dead!" We lost a day rowing east to west and in our confusion missed going north. Then one fellow held his hand up to the sun when it rose, and noting that point as east, he figured out the other directions. We turned the boat the right way and rowed all day Thursday. The sun was very strong. All we had was salty water to drink. Some, like me, only wet our lips with the water. Sometimes because we were so hot and sweaty we put our heads over the side of the boat. One time when we did so, big sharks came around us and followed our boat for a few kilometers. In desperation we threw our shoes at them. After that we stopped leaning over the side to splash our faces. While we were rowing we saw boats far away but had nothing to make reflections with. When we tried signaling one, it did not see us. Then another one coming in our direction detoured. Meanwhile two of our friends were very seasick, nauseated and retching but not vomiting, since we had not eaten anything. For a long time they were too ill to row. By the time we reached the United States our hands were all bloody, and so were our behinds. The skin on our legs was peeling off.

We continued rowing Thursday night under a full moon. On Friday morning at seven we were in sight of Lighthouse #6 in Miami. The arrival was very nice! When we came to the lighthouse, we tied up the boat. Then we lay down to sleep. We did not even know where we were. One of the guys said we were in Pinar del Río! I said, "What! If we're in Pinar del Río, we're going to start rowing again because I'm not staying here." A few minutes later, however, an American tourist and his wife came over in a boat. We called to them and they waved back. We shouted, "No waving. Come here!" Then he came over to us. Two in our group spoke a little English. They told the people we were from Cuba and wanted water. Then we explained that we had escaped. The American picked up the radio and called the police. He gave us some food, and divers in another boat gave us some sandwiches, apples and Coca-Cola. They took us onto their boat and let us sleep there until the police came in the afternoon to take us to the Coast Guard station. There they questioned us, took us in a jeep to the Miami airport, filled out some forms (like provisional passports), and gave us food and clothing, since we had arrived in rags and without shoes. It is so hard to get used to the idea that we are finally free. What remains for us now is to begin working as soon as we can.

"Let's Pretend..."

In my country they say that Cuba is a zoo because it is ruled by a horse (i.e., Fidel, "*el caballo*"), and that they starve people to death and then the funeral is free.

Vicente
Interviewed October 1979
Miami, Florida

Clusters of dark curls, bold brown eyes, arms slicing the air. Vicente, a thirty-five-year-old mechanic from Havana, has just arrived in the United States. The grueling physical struggle, the anxiety, and the suspense of his escape are fresh in his mind. His is an exuberant performance of that drama. Joy at succeeding overpowers other emotions. Strokes of humor and touches of poetry illuminate his story.

IRST I must tell you that when the Revolution began, I was entirely with it, wholly in favor of it. That was in 1959. But I quickly noticed that it was just no good—the lies of the government, the deceit, the disillusionment, *el engaño* [the deception]. These were all self-evident. It's like being here for just a few days, even, and not seeing that things are different. In Cuba we used to run out of everything: paint, cement, food. Such a lack of tranquillity and such great discomfort. Then began the CDRs, the hunger, the little wars all over. Later we began to help other countries while we, ourselves, were hungry.

The reins were tightened. The distance and fear between the people and the police grew. We began to be afraid. Then we worked not from a sense of duty, but from fear. Everything that is done in Cuba now is done in fear. At the beginning everything seemed fine. For a year, a year and a half. As a student I used to do voluntary labor for two months out of the year. Often I enjoyed it. It was nice to get away from the city and be in the country. And of course, when there is a bunch of young people together on a bus, you have a good time. It's the same for people anywhere. Fidel exploits this for propaganda. That's why you see pictures of Cubans laughing and looking happy on their way to work.

I did not join any of the different organizations. One of my observations about the people who were members of the Young Communists was that many were people with some kind of problem, and quite a few of them were handicapped. I think that being a member of a group gave those who were troubled about themselves, for whatever reason, a sense of importance. What I disliked was the way those people talked. They would repeat exactly what they had been told, without even understanding it—just mechanically. It was all rhetoric and no comprehension.

Well, then began the trading with Russia. There was hunger but food rotting in the stores, while some places, like Cardenas, exported almost all of their goods. All to the outside. What you have to realize is the problem that started at that time and that has lasted until right now. There is terrible, maddening inefficiency in transporting food. People would see crates of tomatoes just sitting somewhere, not being delivered and spoiling if they stayed there. But there was a law that you could not touch them, even if they were going to waste! Naturally, whenever people could, they would sneak off with some.

Anyway, by 1961 it was no longer a revolution of the people. There was the *calderos* [frying pan] incident. Men and women took their frying pans to the streets to protest hunger. It was a strike for food. That was the first protest. Instead of giving us food, they beat us. Afterward my sister hid me and tended to my bruises and wounds. The people were rebelling against the system. The second problem arose in Camagüey with the Matos Case. Matos wanted autonomy for Camagüey and not to have Communists infiltrate the Revolution. There was a protest about what happened to Matos, but it all died there. The intriguing involved was all that remained. Soon nothing was known about him. Of course there were stories circulating—that he kept to himself, that he was a prisoner, etc. This has been going on for twenty years.

When I was starting school, it was different from what it is now. You did not have to be a Young Pioneer, and because priorities were elsewhere, there was less indoctrination than today. I remember, though, getting confused; when we studied our country's heroes in history class, we would be taught to admire a particular leader who had fought for Cuba's independence. But then the next week it would be decided that no, he was a bad guy for he had cooperated with the Yankees, so we were taught to hate him. Sometimes I was not sure what we were supposed to think because they kept changing their minds. What I really wanted was to think on my own and not just put down cliches, but you cannot do that. You have to write what they want to hear.

Later, when I was about to join the army, they told us we were going to school to study. But instead of studying, we were taken in trucks, given an initial checkup and assigned to guard duty. Mine was to guard Military Unit 1700, near which there was a Soviet unit. This was in 1963. They had about two thousand Soviet soldiers there. We barely communicated with one another. We had almost no contact with them. The government does, but not the people. Cubans hate the Russians. They act as if they own our country. They walk down the street without seeing us, looking right through us. Their mentality is like that of the Fascists who occupied European countries.

Well, I got bored and tired, since I was not studying as they had promised. I stayed in the army about a month and then left. I went home and in a week's time I was caught. I was taken back to my unit and given a trial. I was sentenced to thirty days in prison for the five days I had spent AWOL. I must explain that before I was drafted, I had been caught trying to escape. At that time I was sixteen years old. I was arrested with a friend when we were on our way to Guantánamo Base, with the idea of eventually arriving in Miami. They found us before we reached the base. Since I had never done anything illegal before, my sentence was six months and twenty-one days in La Cabaña Prison. The lawyers on both sides are Communists and are assigned by the government. I was kept in a special room at the end of a trench, where they put people before the firing squad. Although they insisted there were no murders in Cuba, every night there were mass murders, sometimes thirty in a night. We heard it all. People crying before their execution. Voices calling out, *"Viva Cristo Rey"* [Long live Christ, the King]. This went on every day for those six months. From nine in the evening, when the gun went off until two or three in the morning. No days were quiet. I was horrified, shocked. I just wanted to get out of La Cabaña. Even the head of our *galera* was shot. His name was Luis and he had been a captain in the Rebel Army. I lived in constant fear that it would be my turn next. Without reason, really, since I had not done anything, but I was afraid. Meanwhile the newspapers kept saying there were no shootings, that the citizens were respected, even those who had been caught.

Life in Cuba continued to worsen. There is a bourgeoisie now, the *mayimbes* and the *pinchos*, who work their way up in the system. They live well, have new cars and other luxury items. They are the ones who have Cuba in the grasp of their hands. They can do whatever they want. My house was in terrible shape. It was not fit for a human being. But the *mayimbes* live in the new houses, and in the beautiful ones where the well-to-do lived before the Revolution. Their children also live well. When I worked on a yacht I was sent to take their kids on trips and I had to go wherever they pleased. I used to feel like a slave, like a dog. They love to say that we are all equal, but we, as ordinary citizens, workers, ate a miserable meal outside on the porch, while they feasted inside. Regular Cubans used to say, *"Tu eres pincho y yo te engancho,"* ["*gancho*" is a safety pin; thus, the pun "You claw, but I get back at you"]. It is a known fact that the *pinchos* feel pride in being called by this name. They are the phony revolutionaries, as we call them—"*el revolucionario artificial.*" We have another term, "*el colcho,*" for the one who always drifts around, "*flotante*" [floating]. He arrives in a factory without knowing anything and in fifteen days he is the boss of the place. Fifteen more days, and he is an administrator. He is always criticizing the work of others. That's how he gets where he is. We used to call him "*el perro*" [dog], too. When the *Communidad* [members of the Cuban community in Miami] came to Cuba, the joke was, "*Se echo a perder Cuba*" [Cuba has gone to the dogs]. Cuba was rejuvenated by the arrival of the exiles. The youth had been ready to throw in the towel. Then there was a rebirth. One could have something. Youth heard the message and *la furia* [the fury] followed.

You have to realize that for the last twenty years the propaganda against the United States has been incessant. It is all negative— only about millions of unemployed, or people not having any rights. Then comes the "Community," erasing these stories. You can imagine the impact. A spark was lit with the new ideas and they became the basis for new friendships based on common interest. Pablo, one of the three others I escaped with, and I began to hang around together. We had thought before of escaping, but this brought us together as a group. We ate the same food, from the same plate, we slept in the same bed. You cannot discuss these things with just anybody. You have to be careful. But at least 50 percent of the young people were convinced by the presence of the exiles that the government had been lying to us. We had been told, for instance, that the United States didn't want immigrants, that they would send back boats of escaping people. We had been led to believe that there was an agreement between the two countries not to accept any Cubans in the United States. The people are kept in ignorance. The broadcasts have a loud whistle that covers all news that is not bad. Of course, the newspapers tell even less. It is a huge cover-up. Cuba, the Island of Terror, as we call it.

The first thing a person must have is freedom. We would like help from the United States, but freedom comes first. You can't imagine what it is like to grow old not having any material things, but even worse is not having freedom. They promise that in the future all one will have to do is ask for what one needs, but God, who wants to wait till we have grandchildren? I was born to take care of myself, and I count. Yes, fine for my grandchildren, but I need things now. You cry when you see things here in the stores that you know your children cannot possibly have. When will the day come for my two little girls? But things are changing. Once they called us "*gusanos*" [worms]. We were militant. Today they are accepting the militants a little more. As part of their rebellion they dress in American clothes bought on the black market. I think that the time you can say to Cubans, "This is for the coming years," is over. Now is now. People don't trust anymore. They have a saying that what the government says in the morning is not believed in the afternoon. In the past year there has been an important new development. Underground groups are organizing in different work centers—in Havana, Santiago de Cuba and Cienfuegos. Manifestoes have been appearing to demand rights for workers. They are asking for decent transportation to their work centers; safe, hygienic conditions at their work centers; pay for extra hours of labor and for additional time spent getting to work when transportation is delayed. Workers are also insisting that they be allowed to change work centers, that leaders of the workers be genuine representatives of the people, not of the Politburo, and that workers have the rights to free assembly and to strikes. Workers are being called upon to reject Cuban intervention in other countries, the guards of the CDRs, "Red Sundays" (required "volunteer" labor on Sundays), and the dictatorship of Fidel and the party over the people. The slogan has become *"Independencia o Muerte"* (Independence or Death).

In my opinion, the solution for Cuba is not getting imports from the United States. It would just become international tourism and also the goods would just go right out. The problems in my country have to be resolved by the people themselves, by the individual. The U.S. embargo caused great emotional turmoil at first, but then it lost importance. Let me explain. The Cuban is the prototype of the guy to whom you say, "Let's cut cane," and he goes. But when he gets home and there is no food on the table, fire comes from his mouth! It is true that Cuba is not a developed country, but it is time it was. The sweat and labor that the Cubans have given certainly ought to be enough to provide us with a better way of life. We fought for our freedom and now Cuba belongs to another power and we have nothing.

My two friends and I had met and discussed escaping. One day when we went down to a beach on the north coast we saw a young man we did not know standing there. We took a chance and talked to him. As it turned out, he, too, intended to escape and told us he had a boat. He could have been lying and planning to report us, but we risked believing him. Likewise, he was afraid of us but gambled on our telling the truth. We agreed to meet there the next night.

We arrived at six the following evening. I went there with great fear. I cried. What I expected to find was the police in jeeps. We could not see clearly. The fear one has, the terror one lives in cannot be explained. The man was waiting for us, but we still did not trust him completely. We were terrified of being taken prisoner. There was no problem, however. We went up to the boat hurriedly and prepared it in great haste. We took off the branches that were covering it and we cleaned it well. We left at about ten of eight, October 8. The weather was bad and continued that way until about three in the morning.

We rowed about thirteen miles to one of the keys belonging to Cuba, El Pino. We stayed hidden there to work on the boat. We had two very poor oars that we had made by hand. Since I am a radio technician, I had made a compass from an old radio my sister had given me. We worked as furtively as possible behind the bushes. The mosquitoes were killing us! We put on a mast and a sail made from a sheet, just to give us a chance to stop rowing for a while. We had to be very careful because the boat was plastic. We had to improvise when we drove in the nails. A machete was all we could use. Everything was difficult. Primitive.

I told the others, "Let's pretend that we have been dead three or four days. If we arrive, fine. If not, what is lost? At least we will have been trying to get to *'la tierra de libertad.'*" It was *una noche brutal y revuelta* [a brutal and tumultuous night]. That evening we did not eat anything. We decided to row to another key, El Sombrero. In the meantime, quite a bit of traffic went by—fishing boats from a cooperative. So we decided to stay hidden on the key. By the next afternoon, hunger got the better of us and we caught some pigeons. We took the feathers off one and ate it raw. We had nothing, no salt, nothing. What counted was that we would endure one more day. We took two pigeons for the trip, for when we would be starving again. As it turned out, they died, rotted, and we could not eat them. The poor things died of hunger. We were afraid to eat something that had starved to death.

It began raining and a bad storm came up. We started to row again, anyway, and the storm helped by carrying us about seven or eight miles. When we began to see some lights we thought that we were still not free. We took a look and thought that we really had only ten minutes of life left. We came across boats like the ones we had seen sunken on Varadero and other beaches. Full of bullet holes. We were afraid we would also be shot at. Even death would not be a respite. To be killed like that in the middle of the sea, not being able to defend yourself! There were three of those boats and we were terrified.

Then some Soviet boats appeared. We would go one way, and one of theirs would go the other way—on like that until one of the boats stopped. There was a lot of activity. I said, "Let's row harder." Then we thought that maybe they were after us because they were suspicious of the sail, so we threw it away. *"Que nos cojan remando!"* [Let them catch us rowing!] I told the others and took a couple of oars. Pablo took the others. All this was done *agachos* [stooped over]. We kept rowing and in about ten minutes the boats disappeared. At this time it was still night. The boats had been big ones. Not fishing boats, but the kind used by the merchant marine. The ones that guard the coastline. Since there was often trouble in this area, it was well patrolled so that no one could pass.

Vaya pues [let's go on with the story]. With *el nerviosismo* [a word Vicente coins for "nervousness"] that we had, we did not try to do anything, to tune in the radio, nothing. We just kept rowing. We had forgotten everything else. We just knew that we were moving. I was trembling that night. It was black. We had some gloves that Pablo's sister had given us and they helped protect our hands for a while, but eventually they wore through. We rowed all night. Then at six in the morning *la luz destellaba como un faro* [the idea suddenly dawned on us] and we said to ourselves, "It can't be that just rowing we have arrived in one night. It can't be." "Hold on," I said. Then the rays of morning light came out and I saw a firehouse. "Hey, guys," I said, "we are once again in Cuba!" Yes? No? We were mad, crazy. We could not take it anymore. It couldn't be. Tears began to roll down my face. We were still in Cuba. I told the others, "We must not lose our spirit." We crouched down and filled the boat with water so we would not be seen when another Soviet boat appeared. It was now daytime. Just like that, stooping, we rowed. Christ! We were still in Cuba! With no food. Nothing.

Well, we had to abandon the idea of submerging the boat because it was taking us too long to move ahead. So we said, "All right, if they catch us, they catch us. That's all. If they see us, they see us."

There is a limit to fear. I wish you could have been there at that moment. All one wants is to be picked up and be locked in jail. So at least one can eat, can sleep for a little while. Or just die. We all felt numb. But then something happened. *Algo nos vino* [something came to us]. I do not think for a moment we stopped believing in God. Something grew in us. *Me heriza* [my hair stood on end—the way an animal's hair bristles when it is frightened or ready to attack]. Yes, it was in that very moment. A hope. A force. It was as if we were just leaving Cuba. I said, "Let's pretend that we just stole this boat. Forget all the days of work and hunger. Let's pretend that we have eaten, relaxed, and here we are ready to steal this boat." And so it was. Little by little we each took hold of an oar and rowed.

Up ahead we saw something made of wood, very big. It was round—it was a boat used by the merchant marine. Then from a distance we saw something like a duck drawing near. It was coming very fast. It was a fishing boat. We did not know from which country. At this point we were about fifteen miles out and could no longer see the coast of Cuba. It was seven-thirty, maybe eight in the morning. We figured these were international waters and that they did not belong to Cuba. The government here respects those boundaries and after twelve miles they do not go after you. But in Cuba, they do not respect these waters, even thirty miles away. The law is theirs. They make their own.

We continued rowing till our hands were covered with calluses. Then a storm began. The sea and sky turned black, but we could still travel. It was raining and the sea was thrashing around us. But it was all in the cards, I tell you. Never had something like this happened to me, never in my whole life: suddenly the ocean became completely calm, I tell you, and there was not a drop of sea water in the boat. The only water that fell was from the sky, but not a drop from the ocean got into our boat. Calm. Calm. The sea in absolute repose!

Now we were about thirty miles from Cuba. It was one o'clock in the afternoon. We continued rowing for hours. Then a little light at a distance. We could hear nothing We just rowed *a lo loco* [like crazy]. Then we remembered the radio and the compass and did our best to get a reading. We had five batteries, but Cuban batteries are very poor. We had big ones and were thrilled when the radio and compass did function well. By now it was almost night. We tuned in and realized that we were too far east. About fifteen miles off. Well, the breeze had pushed us. We had intended to go north, then to pull to the east. Somehow, we would run into the United States, Miami. We went like that for about four more days and met no one. We had nothing to eat or drink. The two remaining gallons of water were polluted and stank. Our mouths were dry inside and out from drinking sea water.

On the fifth day we saw a yacht. I shouted to the others, "Don't signal to them. It could be a Russian boat." Fear. Fear. But at a distance of about two blocks we discovered it was American. I could see the bottom was painted green. In Cuba, it's red. The paint here shines. But in Cuba the paint is not that good. All the boats there are spotty, semi-rotten. We began to signal. Then we saw a woman standing, and a man. He said, "Bye, bye." I said, "Bye, bye, nothing. Come here!" He called on a loudspeaker. Then the woman opened a refrigerator and took out a gallon of water and a box of cookies, a big one. Anyway, they collided with us. She gave us those things and we asked for the way to Miami. She said, "Ah, that way," and pointed with her finger. "Bye, bye" is all they said and were lost in the distance.

We did not insist. We did not ask her to take us. We wanted to get there in our own way, under our own steam. We were even afraid the boat might be going to Cuba. You can picture how our imagination went. The nervous tension. But at least we had something to drink and we threw out the spoiled water. We had spent only about ten minutes talking to the people on the boat and it was now about twelve o'clock. We knew that we were approximately thirty miles from the United States, but we could see nothing. We followed the general direction that they had pointed to, going north. I knew that the radio would eventually take us directly toward a station. In Cuba they muffle that radio station so that we cannot hear it. The whistling sound had stopped and we knew that we must be getting close. Now we needed to go east. These were our calculations.

There were some red lights. A big red light, a little red light in the distance. We rowed and rowed and rowed, till four in the morning. I had hardly slept in five days. Maybe for six hours, but I think less. I do not know how I withstood so much. I was the one who had to keep the others going. I would urge them to go on, saying, "We're getting there." They just did not want to row. One was lying down and could not row. Another was seasick. All he wanted was to be picked up. And there I was, not knowing where the coast was. The fourth was the only one with me, but he told me he could not stand up.

The red lights gave us hope. There was a white light, too. Then we realized that it must be a channel, with land ahead. But we lost these lights. We lit a fire with a cloth to find out if we could be seen. Nothing happened. Well, we had to arrive with our same little boat. One of us did stand up and saw another light. Then we thought we saw a bridge. We had heard in Cuba that there was a bridge that tied two pieces of land together. We were wide awake now, being careful not to run into the bridge. These might be the lights from the bridge. We rowed toward the shore and could see the coast. I thought I saw a motel, but it was a light shining from a house. That's the direction we took. We were all thrilled. We hugged one another. We said, "Hey, Pablo, let's open our eyes. It might be Cuba again! Who knows?"

We put down our mast. We did not know what to do and began fighting among ourselves. We could not agree what to do. Our nerves. I knew it was not Miami, because my sister had sent me postcards. I could not see any lights. No tall buildings. Nothing familiar. But Miami or not, we were going to get closer. We were right near a house, in front of the terrace. Well, we did not know it was part of a house until later. We got out of the boat. As we walked on the stones, we knew we were not in Cuba because we saw a beautiful raft lying on the sand. Nothing is left out that way in Cuba.

Big embraces, and we continued walking and laughing. We saw the streets. Everything was beautiful! But even after we saw some of the signs, we still were not completely sure whether we were in Cuba or not. Maybe this belonged to the officials in Cuba. In Havana. We were afraid again. There are tourist places in Havana which, although we are Cuban, we did not go to. We were still afraid. We were still seasick. We were not steady on our feet and had to sit down. Then we walked to a main street, not knowing which direction to take. We stopped in front of a store, and then we knew for sure that we were not in Cuba. So many things! Oh, if I had only had money. What a party!

There was a light in a house; it belonged to an engineer, who invited us in. We are so grateful to him. We weren't even hungry. The happiness had taken away our appetite. We had strength again. We could even walk. We cried and cried. Our happiness was so great, so strong! All we could say was "Police," to have him call the police. In five minutes they arrived in two cars. They took good care of us. They gave us milk, coffee. We left the boat where it was, although we did want to keep it as a souvenir.

We have what we need now, but have still not begun working. Soon we will. Everyone has helped us. All the Cubans here are like one big family. I sometimes walk around and think I am in Cuba. We are all close. No one really changes. We plan to study and work as mechanics. I am going to work with someone and then maybe I will have my own shop as a radio and television mechanic.

Fever

One of the jokes you hear in my country is about a visit Fidel made to
Bolivia. He was introduced to the members of the Cabinet. The President
presented the Minister of the Interior, the Minister of Labor, the Minister of
Agriculture, the Minister of Commerce, and finally the Minister of the Navy.
At that point Fidel interrupted, "How can you have a navy when you have
no ocean?" "But, Fidel," answered the President, "*you* have a Minister of
Justice!"

Aurelio
Interviewed October 1979
Miami, Florida

*The three men who recently arrived in a raft from Cuba have re-
covered from third-degree burns after treatment in a Miami hospital.
Blisters still cover their hands and legs. But it is another kind of
burn that afflicts each of them in different ways. Aurelio, the first
to speak, is a tall man with a mournful face and shoulders drooping
in fatigue. The pent-up fury smoldering in him shows in the hurt,
hunted look of his large dark eyes, the accents of disgust that mark
his speech, and the repetition of certain words that mirror feelings
of oppression and degradation. For Aurelio the tension of life in
Cuba was so great that escape became an overwhelming obsession.*

WAS born in La Habana province and am twenty-five years old.
I was raised away from home and at the age of eleven returned.
Thereafter I went out on my own, working and earning a living
right up till now. I took whatever jobs I could to support myself.
The last one was in a foundry, where I maintained and repaired the
cauldrons for smelting metal. At first I received the minimum
salary—95 pesos a month. In order to get an increase you had to

turn out an excellent performance and do extra work. My wife and I and our two children could not live on the wages we made. So I worked hard at night and went to school until my pay went up to 240 pesos. My wife made 117. Although this was a good salary between us, compared to those of other families, it was still not enough. All we could obtain were the barest necessities. Everything else we had to buy on the black market. We used to buy more food than we needed and sell it to make a little more money. That's the way we survived. Of course, it was illegal and we were constantly being watched. Of course, there were a lot of other Cubans doing the same thing. In fact, most of them did. And of course, the dyed-in-the-wool Communists did not do such things; they could afford to follow the rules and manage to live well. They had cars and could go to stores and get more things than the rest of us. Do you understand me, this kind of inequality is a maddening situation.

One can see how one people is being crushed by another. A whole country being ground down and no one doing anything about it! How is one supposed to see and hear how others live and not go crazy, crazy, mad! They don't seem to realize that it is their country that this is happening to. Even Fidel himself is a madman. He is just a lucky madman. He preaches that we are working for one cause, yet no one understands that we are going *backward*. No one seems to see that. They are blind—*ciegos, ciegos, ciegos*! Fidel boasts of this tremendous development and it is nowhere to be seen. It is all a terrible joke—like pretending that you like *chícharos* [peas]. Then one day in the future you look back and talk about how wonderful those times were when you had *chícharos*, when in reality you did not have them. Now the only things that seem to increase are the laws. They get more and more severe.

The latest law is an abomination. It is called the law of *peligrosidad* whereby if you are suspected of antigovernment thoughts, not even active rebellion, you are considered dangerous and constantly watched, and you have to report to the officials once a month. You have to tell them who visited you, whom you spoke to, whom you wrote to. They also want to know why you live beyond your means. They know how much you earn and they see how you live. Naturally, if you made only the money you are supposed to, you could barely eat and clothe yourself. Thus, the obvious conclusion is that you are doing something illegal. Those in charge are the DOPs [Departments of Public Order]. If they report you, you can get a sentence of from five to ten years. The reasons, of course, are that you are an unsavory character, that you are meeting secretly, but of course, there is never actual proof for any of these charges. They simply assume you are doing something wrong and convict you. This process can and does start all over again once you have served your term. So we must always be on "good behavior." Their idea of "good behavior," however, is different from ours. In prison, for example, not participating in their re-education activities was bad behavior. This trap continued forever, since you were under a sentence when in prison and also when you were out of prison. And on and on and on.

We were insane, crazy, mad to get out. Escape was all we could think of because we could not stand the incessant restrictions on us. We did not belong to any organizations and did not attend revolutionary meetings. We were, as they used to refer to us, *delincuentes*. We were in that frame of mind. We behaved as such, so to them, we were nothing but delinquents. I detested this labeling of people. We refused to integrate and thus we were constantly watched for our activities. Their eyes were always watching us—eyes, eyes, eyes. How it hampered our existence. And all the while time was passing. For thirteen years we had been singled out as "*rebeldes.*" I refused to go into the service. I just could not understand why I should have to serve, to defend a way of life which I did not support.

I was only four years old when this system began. When I was very young I did belong to the youth organizations, but it was like a game to all of us. It was most certainly not the ideas I understood. Naturally, you ask a child if he wants to join the Pioneers and he is excited. But even at the age of five I already knew what was happening. They spoke about the system day in and day out, but never offered an alternative. They used to talk about the past. They said that there was a great deal of corruption in those times and that the people were exploited, but I could not see what was different now. Where was the change? There was nothing now. I had the feeling, even as a child, that exploited or not, it was better to have something, not just mere verbal warfare against other ways of life. The conditions I lived under certainly caused a trauma; even now I nearly vomit when I think of them.

One thing that helped us understand was the arrival of members of the *Communidad*. We could see that they lived differently. *Nosotros podiamos palpar* [We could touch], we could sense another life, although we did not understand what kind of life it was or how the people lived here. Certainly, though, one lived much better here [in Miami] than over there. And that was one of the reasons I decided to come, or rather, it made me want more than ever to come. We did not know anyone personally from the *Communidad*, but they were friends and they all chatted, and of course, word got around. Let's face it—constant propaganda does have an effect on you and it did cause a certain amount of doubt in us. But now here were these real, live Cubans telling their own story. Things were visible, not just promises. People had money. They could do what they wanted. There was more liberty. There was opportunity for expression. It was different. That's all. Different. It was a different way of life. A choice. And that was the moment when the final decision to escape—the most recent one, that is—was made.

Before I could leave, they arrested me for what they considered delinquent behavior. I was in prison for four years. *Quien no cruza tras los muros de la carcel muere un niño* [Whoever does not pass through the walls of prison dies a child]. What I mean is that you really don't know Cuba until you have experienced the repression, the inhuman treatment, the lack of respect for humanity that prevails in the prisons. It is incomprehensible to people who have not lived through it. Of course, people who have not been in prison think you are propagandizing—everyone remains incredulous. While you are the one suffering the blows, the humiliation, the filth, the government is saying that in the jails and work camps prisoners are being rehabilitated by instruction and by doing productive work for society. You bet they are doing useful work. They are forced to! In fact, most of the hospitals, schools and many other structures have been built by prisoners, particularly political prisoners. The agonizing part is that when you try to tell people what you experienced, they don't believe you. They don't say so, but the feeling is there, in their eyes.

A tremendous gap grows between people, even between you and your family. They believe that prison really cannot be so bad. It was so hard to explain to them what it was like. The guards just don't feel anything. They seem to block all feelings, even though we were their own kind—that is, we were all Cubans. Some guards are more brutal than others, but on the whole they are animals, without decency, without a mind. One time they kicked me until I was hurt so badly that I had to be taken away. I was glad because for a while I could escape their cruelty.

One of the worst parts was the little bit of food they gave you—only spoonfuls. As a result, we often did not go to the bathroom, sometimes only every fifteen days. There were many who died. A friend of mine died, yellow with hepatitis. The lice and cockroaches are indescribable. It was an incredible state of hygiene. Only when you were very ill would they take you to the hospital, but many died anyway. One fellow was thin as a rail, and we tried to joke about it with him to comfort him.

I was traumatized by those years in prison. When I finally got out my nerves were so shot that every noise made me jump. It was a natural reaction. At night I couldn't sleep. I would hear a noise outside my house and I would be in anguish, as if I were back in that horrible prison. I was terrified all the time. I was filled with hatred. Yes, hatred. Not hate for Cuba, but for the system. How could they take a sixteen-year-old kid from the country and make it so that when he came out of jail, he was a different person? He was indoctrinated, terrified, another human being, undone.

I remember that they were showing a movie called *La Carcel de Grital*, which is about American prisons. As bad as they made them look, my friends and I who had been imprisoned in Cuba would have preferred twenty years in them. The crowded conditions in our cells were not to be believed. The mistreatment was unreal. They kicked us and hit us with chains and whatever else that was handy. One young kid tried to protest and was beaten so badly that his body was a mass of bruises. He was murdered. It was not death, but murder. After beating him they emptied their guns, firing on him three times. It was horrifying what they did to him. And after, they did not even pretend when the family came. They push people here and there, always with their mighty guns. They shoved the rela-

tives aside as if they were criminals. The family got the same treatment as the prisoners. If you don't do what they insist on, right then
and there, on the spot, they beat you. A person doesn't count for
anything. You can't even have an opinion of your own.

Of course, when you get out, you continue to be in a prison. On
the streets the vigilance is excessive, and it is constant. You are
obliged to report monthly in detail about what you are doing. Once
outside of jail, I sometimes went to my father's house to get clothes;
I had none to wear. My father works for the government. His job
is to look after delinquents and those trying to escape. People are
arrested in groups. If they resist, the police just fire. I know some
people into whose faces they fired. Everything is all right if you
don't protest.

You can imagine, then, the difficulty the three of us had in
planning our first escape attempt. We had to pretend all the time
so that no one would catch on. Little by little we pieced together a
float made of bits of wood and plastic that we gathered very carefully from different places. Then we went down to the beach one
night and threw ourselves into the ocean. Our effort failed because
the raft filled with water and we could not bail it out. Since it was
getting light we had to go back. We were afraid of getting caught,
so before we left, we took the raft apart. What a miracle that they
didn't capture us! It was miraculous to be able to take the thing
apart and get back home without being noticed. Since at least 90
percent of people trying to escape are caught, we felt extremely
lucky to make it back safely. Although you have to be very careful
what you say, escape is a topic that is well known and discussed.
We listened to all kinds of advice about where we could leave from,
but we had no success. We kept looking, but nothing turned up for
a while. Finally, though, we worked something out.

*Valentin, who narrates the escape, is a stocky man of twenty-seven
with light-brown hair and somnolent features. His mouth is sensuous
and there is a dreamy look on his face. His strength is veiled by a mis-*

leading indolence, the kind of protective covering assumed by a person who suffers some deep wound. Energy and sentiments are kept in abeyance, but surface at moments when he needs or wants to reveal them. At times he becomes so upset that remembrances well up and spill out chaotically.

OUR MAIN objective was to escape. We thought of nothing else. My wife took care of the food and our other needs, all in the black market. I had taught her how. She would go to a friend's house and sell what she had bought. Her father, who lived with us, also helped. For our second escape attempt we took a truck from a company and stole a small pleasure boat from a beach near Santa Cruz. We chose this place because it was fairly isolated. There were not many houses and only a few people around. We left at about two in the morning. I knew how far I had to go before the merchant marine stopped following us. This is common knowledge. Everybody talks about it. We started off and went fifteen miles or so, and then the motor died. Since a piece of iron that held the motor on broke off, we had nothing to power us. We did not have oars to row and therefore we had to go back. There was nothing else we could do. We were lucky that no one saw us and we arrived back at seven o'clock. Luck, just luck.

Afterward we gossiped, chattered and quarreled about the escape. There are many different opinions about how to do it, where to go, what to do. At a time like that you don't really think about your feelings. People become just like a pack of animals looking for food, looking for a chance, but there is a communal spirit. You do not arouse suspicion of escape as long as you have a job wherever you go. We went to different places to see the possibilities, and of course, everyone suggested a different one. While we were checking around, we were always careful to say the right things when questioned. We had to give plausible reasons for being in various places and sometimes we stayed in hotels. We went around pretending that we were taking a course. By the time anyone became suspicious, we had already left. It depended a great deal on the way you talked. If you pretended to be a Communist, everything went all right. It is easy to pretend when it is only a game.

We always had our identification cards. Since I did not belong

to any organization and had no place to report, I could go about
with greater ease. Sometimes I came home to sleep, but very often
I did not. We did not eat very much. In fact, we would go for days
without eating. Maybe just a slice of pizza. There again, we just
did not think about such things because we were consumed with the
blind desire to leave. We were busy with the plans; eating was just
accidental. In the process we lost a lot of weight—in my case,
forty-five pounds.

Leaving was what counted. Some incidental things happened
that affected our plan. One of the members of our group received a
telegram asking for information about a boat, a tourist boat called
a *cometa* [hydrofoil], that was supposed to leave with a lot of people. My friend was charged with "trying to escape," and the authorities tried to intimidate him and make him confess. They
detained him for a day and told him that if such a boat were to leave,
he would be held responsible. Of course, he had to defend himself
by saying that he was a good Cuban and a revolutionary. Knowing
that he was being watched, we had to consider yet another idea—
taking a taxi into one of the embassies, either the Mexican or the
Venezuelan. But after we thought about it, we decided that it would
almost be suicide because usually when you try to get into an
embassy that way, without a reason, they shoot to kill. After these
experiences, we came up with the plan of ordering a ladder from a
truck company. When it came we spent two days preparing for our
departure. We hid our things in my friend's house, because the
other fellow's mother was too nervous. Also, both of us lived in
apartments and it's difficult to build a raft in a place like that.
We had to be careful. During lunch and dinner were the best times
to work because everyone is busy then. My friend's house was
dangerous, though, for he was still being watched. The CDR in that
area was not as rigorous, however, as others so we decided to take
the chance. *Estabamos fritos* [we would have been done for] if they
had caught us, but that was the only choice.

The trick of the ladder was that no one would suspect that it was
going to be used as part of an escape vehicle. We attached three
tubes from truck tires to the ladder, which was three and a half
meters long. We left at about eleven at night, and luckily it was

raining. Also, since dogs were barking nearby, the guards could hear less. It took us about an hour to get everything ready and then we left once again from a place near Santa Cruz. We inflated the tires with a pump and put some containers of water and milk on the raft. We had made oars out of pieces of wood.

The hills in the distance were vague. We knew the area well because we had studied it. The marine patrols keep watch, but not every second. It was rather calm on the water. There was no great tide. The major problem at first was that there were two fishermen on either side of us. So we just decided to go in the middle, between them, that's all. We had some difficulty keeping our contraption from tipping, and with the constant swaying back and forth, from side to side, one of us got very sick and started to vomit. We had a lifesaver that we tied to him. Two of us rowed until four in the morning without stopping. Not for one second. We didn't even talk; we just rowed.

In the morning we were able to put up a stick and a piece of cloth as a sail. We realized that we weren't going in the direction we wanted, but it didn't matter. We were moving. We rested a little and continued to row. The third fellow was still not feeling well. We had two magnetic compasses the size of a penny, but on the second day we lost them. One got water in it and the other dropped into the sea. Thereafter, we had to just follow the stars.

The trip took six days and would have taken three if we had not lost the compasses. Also, our "boat" turned over at least twenty times. On the third day we did not see much, only a plane, but we could not make out what kind it was. All we saw was a star and a circle and from that we could not tell which country it belonged to. The plane saw us, circled, came down a bit, flashed its lights and left. After about four hours we realized that we were not going to be picked up. We continued to row. A storm caught us and we lost our oars. The waves were about three meters high. At that point we had to untie the tires from the ladder and move separately, each of us swimming in the middle of a tire. Having lost the oars, we had to push along with our hands. There was no other way to try to save ourselves. Although there were two storms during the trip, we were able to maintain a course. We knew which way we were going and that we were headed in the right direction. That is all that mattered. But at night we felt lost and huddled together in the darkness and crashing waves. Shivering, we took turns covering ourselves with the life vest we had tied around my friend at the beginning. The hours passed slowly in fear and cold and with the continuous surging of the sea around us.

By the fourth day we thought we were really lost, but we always felt that at least we were getting away. In the meantime, our bodies were badly burnt and the constant rubbing against the tires gave us sores. All we had left now was the can of milk. It had got salt water in it and so we had nothing to eat. Finally we saw something strange in the distance and then realized it must be the edge of a city. We did not know where we were. It could have been Mexico, La Habana, the States. We had no idea. We knew, or at least we thought, that we were going north. At night there was nothing to do but rest. On the sixth night, which was very cold we heard loud-speakers, American, and we began shouting and signaling with the can of condensed milk. We were about four hundred meters away. We realized it was silly to continue trying to attract attention because we were just too far. The fear hit us that by some crazy accident we might be back in Havana. If we had been, we would have just turned around and kept going. We finally saw land, what looked like sand, and a boat passed by. It had a red flag and a yellow star. I moved ahead, leaving the other two behind, and was picked up. The boat signaled for a helicopter. During all of this we communicated by signs. Then I told them more or less where the others were. By now I was afraid that one of them or both might have fainted.

I was dropped off in Miami and then they went to look for the others. I don't remember clearly. I just remember the ambulance and people talking, and that the others were finally picked up by a helicopter. Of course, as it turns out, they were worried about me, too. They knew only that I had gone ahead for help. It was a huge, huge area and I was worried about having left them behind. During our escape our greatest fear was not of the elements but of being taken back to Havana, having to be in Cuba for the rest of our lives. I would do it all again, if necessary, at any cost. God forbid that I should have to, but I would rather try again because it is better to be dead than alive in a place where you do not want to be.

Here it has been like a fairy tale, wonderful. Everything is so different. When we arrived everyone was very friendly. At the hospital we could hardly sleep because everyone was coming to congratulate us and test us for this and that. In Cuba I was never in the hospital, but from what I could see, they seemed to have the same cure for everything: penicillin. The treatment is adequate, but not warm. I never expected so much attention here. If Cuba were free, I would go back to fight to make life as wonderful as it can be. I would not turn my back on my country. Although letters were intercepted, my wife and children did eventually find out by word of mouth that I was all right. I hope to be able to bring them over here.

From the time I was very young, my life in Cuba was unhappy. My father is a lieutenant colonel in the army and is one of the hundred members of the Central Committee. When he came down from the fighting in the mountains, he brought another woman, with whom he has had four children. Since that time my mother has been alone and has not known any peace in her life. When I was five years old, I was taken from her for the purpose of indoctrination. I received a scholarship and was sent to a boarding school. I felt that separation very keenly. I missed my mother. The answer throughout my life was always a new school. I was sent to fifteen different schools. They all had the same message. My father's solution to any problem was to separate me from "unclean" friends and an "unclean" environment. I was to be properly influenced. That's the big key word in Cuba—*el ambiente*, the background, the atmosphere. What surrounds you, shapes you.

For one week I was on the Isle of Youth. It was not the fact that I was there that I did not like. It was the way in which I was coerced to do everything. This process of always being forced into a mold went on until I was fifteen years old, when I had the courage to confront my problem. It was, of course, embodied in the figure of my father. He reacted as all of them do. He put me into the army, although I was not really supposed to go till my sixteenth birthday. I tried to follow the regimentation but I could not. I could not take it psychologically. It was like not being a person. At the end of eight months I got out.

My father was respected because he was one of them; I was not. I could get nothing—not that I wanted special treatment. All that I ever got in life came from the black market. I finally was able to come home to my mother when I was eighteen. This stay lasted only two months, but at least I was able to talk to kids who had not been in the special schools I had gone to. Then two policemen came for me and I was back in the same situation: indoctrination, force, conformity. That's all that being my father's son ever got me—a constant deluge of pleading with me to change, to follow my father's ways. Then back to my *peregrinaje* [wanderings], hiding, being found, returning home again. I would always pretend to agree with what they said, and then as soon as I could, I left. The last time I was caught, I was at a party. I was taken to El Morro Prison, where I was wounded with bayonets, for not moving, for not doing what I was supposed to. The only comforting thing there was that I met a father and son who had been trying to escape. Because this was their third try, they had received twelve-year sentences.

The only thing that I considered for a profession was the merchant marine. By then I had the idea of escaping but I ended up in the army again. I seemed to have no escape from it, and I had to serve my three years. Here again, being my father's son counted against me. All those who were allowed to get out of jail for desertion were free, but I had to serve my term in the army. I guess it was their ultimate victory over me. They put me in construction. They wanted to see if I could stand it. I came to stay with my mother, who had always come to visit me in jail and wished that I would play the game as she had had to, just to have some peace, so that she would worry less. Thereafter I had various jobs— mechanic, driver, assistant in a machinery shop. I was paid to take a course, which I passed, and then I earned 95 pesos as a mechanic.

There was a law that Castro passed. We did not listen to his speeches, but we did find out the parts of them that pertained to us. Well, in this one he announced that he was not going to continue paying for educating the youth—that is, if they were going to become "unproductive delinquents." Where I worked there were some people who were not in favor of his ideas and they would try to defend those who needed help. They were not Communists, but pretended they were. They were very helpful. Of course, if they defended someone too much, they could be fined. So they, too, had their limits. There are many students at the university studying law, but I don't know how many or what they do, because I did not belong to that world.

Although there *is* work in Cuba, it is often not what you want. They send you to the country to work on a farm, to pick beans, but when you are twenty-five years old that is often not what you want to do, and thus you can end up unemployed. It is a question of what one wants to do with one's life. That is not what I wanted to do; there is no future in that type of work. It is all for the state, with nothing for yourself. I am a mechanic, but I was forced to do something else. And even if there are places that need your skills as a mechanic, once you have a reputation as a dissident, all your training is a waste. The absolute worst part of all of this was the constant indoctrination. I cannot be forced to do things! That is all. I cannot be made to do things against my will. All their speeches do not make sense. To defend the country? But what am I defending? The only alternative was to try to sabotage their way of life. To make jokes, at least. If we had tried anything really heavy-handed, we would have been out of luck.

I could not function in that kind of system of coercion, hatred and lies. It is not that Cuba is doing poorly because of the U.S. embargo. No. They just give everything away! No matter what comes in, it all goes out, just given away. When Castro wanted to give aid even to Santo Domingo, that country refused it, saying that it should go to Cubans. Trade is light. Most things come from Russia. It is all *nada, pero nada*! All indoctrination, from the first grade on. Who Lenin was, how bad things were before and how now the system is for the benefit of all. Russian is constantly being taught. They put it on radio and TV. English is taught in high schools as an international language. The great emphasis is on Russian. The supervisors speak only Russian. In the factories it is almost a necessity to learn Russian. Everything was done through interpreters.

My last job at a steel mill ended in an accident, in which I ruined equipment at a cost of about 3,000 pesos. I had to pay for the damages and then I was able to quit. There was a new law passed that if you were unhappy in your job, you could resign. I was unemployed for three months and had to live off the black market. After all that had happened, there really wasn't any other possibility for me. I had a small business. I would buy a tape recorder for 600 pesos and sell it for 700 pesos, or a tiny motorcycle for 400 pesos, which I fixed, painted and sold for 800 pesos. I finally had about 4,000 pesos, which was used toward planning the escape, for materials, and just general living. At this time my two other friends were also unemployed. We lived three blocks away from one another, had been pals for ages and thought alike. We liked and trusted one another. There is a feeling you share when you undertake such a venture as ours. The bond that develops is more important than any other kind of friendship. You are individuals dedicated to a common interest.

At first I did not tell my mother about my plans. You must remember what my mother, who is a very warm, trusting person, had been through—abandoned by my father and upset by my friends, who were different. She was under tremendous pressure. Just not knowing where her only son was eating and sleeping was a great deal for her to bear. At one time she tried to hang herself. The cord broke and she survived. She was put into a mental institution and afterward she went from one psychiatric hospital to another. Four different ones. She is sixty-two years old now. I finally told her about my first escape attempt and the second. I assured her that the next one would be safe, and that I would send for her. I have an aunt who has been trying to get out since 1968; they just won't let her leave. After I had prepared my mother psychologically for my trip, she did agree that I should go. I made sure that my friends would take care of her when I left. Any needs she had, like going to the hospital. She clings to certain things, like a habit of eating rice and eggs, rice and eggs. That is all she eats. In Cuba there is a general feeling of nervousness. A lot of people try to kill themselves—by hanging or setting themselves on fire. Of course, the reasons are never known. A great deal of secrecy surrounds these suicides. Even my cousin, whose wife set herself on fire, does not talk much and the reasons will never be known. Well, in the end, I left my aunt most of the money I had so that she could watch over my mother, and could even go and live with her.

Braulio is a short man with a hard, pithy body, and crisp features. Rage still propels him. He paces the room, sits down, stands up, walks around, sits down again. As he moves a coppery hue glints in his brown hair. His tone is alternately despairing and impassioned.

I AM twenty-nine years old, from the south of Havana, and worked for the State bus company. I was not an *integrado*, and for that reason they single you out as a rebel. They watch you more closely and classify you as being anti-Revolution. In Cuba we lived only to stay alive. That's all. There is no value in that kind of life. We seemed to go through the motions of living, but life had no real substance. Oh, sometimes I would go to public dances or to the movies, but I was not crazy about them, since 99 percent are Russian films. They are always full of propaganda, which meant nothing to us. The proof is that the theaters are always empty. The long lines happen only when there is a foreign movie, Italian or American. Then there is great excitement in the lines—*majaderías* [horseplay], fun, openness. The reason was that we knew they would not be just propaganda. It would be a nonpolitical diversion. God, the constant polemics of the Communist movies!

I am divorced, with two children. My wife did not belong to the party or "integrate." I could not and would not allow her to. I have two brothers, one who was not serving in the army because of a nervous condition that disqualified him, and a younger one, sixteen, who is studying engineering. He tried to fit into the system in order to live. What else could he do?

In Cuba everything was oppressive, physically and psychologically, without letup. The sense of being forced to accept everything is intolerable. There are no alternatives. Repression is organized and complete. They have total control over you through the CDRs, State Security and youth leagues. You can't move. You can't speak. You can't think. You are subjugated and can believe nothing that is different from what they demand. For example, everything is said to be bad in this country. *Todo, todo, todo!*

We are in a physical trap, too. Look, there are no clothes to buy. Youth likes to look good. God, to have something to cover up one's gloom. It is a matter of being a person—being a person, not an animal. It is a universal feeling, and especially Cuban, to want to please a woman. Women are not different. They feel all of these things too. They just don't think of escaping on their own because it is a very hard thing to do. There is a 90 percent chance of losing. It is difficult for them, because physically they are weaker than men. There is so much to be done in organizing an escape. All the materials have to be stolen. You cannot get them any other way. It is all part of the vicious circle of life over there. You have needs, you have no choice, you steal, they see you as a criminal, they put you in jail. It's five years for stealing any kind of vehicle for escape.

I served a sentence because of the army, not because I refused to join. But once I was in, it was the same story of control and more control. The army wants to own you. Finally I left and went to live with my parents and sometimes with friends. Always like a butterfly, yet not free. I could not be seen on the street. They would have asked for my papers. Since the list of deserters is published and available everywhere, the police can find you and arrest you. I finally got tired of playing the game, so that when they came to look for me at home, I turned myself in. I did not hide anymore. That's all. It's a prison, inside or out.

It is impossible to describe the treatment they gave me. It is inexplicable. They treat you like a dog. Not even that, because a dog can have more pride, more food, more choices! I was in El Morro Prison. *Miles golpes* [a thousand blows]. In or out, you get hit. My parents, of course, used to advise me to follow the rules because in their view there was nothing else to do. One cannot protest. After serving seven months of my sentence, I got out by chance. They passed a law that anyone who was in jail for desertion was automatically freed. There was just no more room for so many prisoners. It had nothing to do with mercy, as they liked to say. It was a practical problem. The jails had to be emptied somehow. At least 80 percent of the youth have tried to get out of the army. And then they are all imprisoned. To leave jail, big deal. You are only going into a bigger jail. The whole country is a prison. You are let loose on the street, but you are not really free.

ONCE I was out, I did not have a job. It is not that you get a job, but that you are assigned one. The title given to me was "production assistant." Although it sounds fairly good, it paid only 95 pesos a month. There again, I had a title but I had to do whatever they told me. Since I could drive, I was given the job of driving a truck. I did this all the time. I drove the truck around, picking up people and letting them off. When the truck wore out, since there were no more, they gave me twenty other jobs—painter, gardener, oven keeper, repairman, anything. None of which I was trained to do. That's when I began to do things so that I would get thrown out. For example, quite often I did not report to work. Anything to get myself fired, because at that time, you could not quit a job.

Finally I found work with a friend of mine who had a truck. Our arrangement helped both of us because he needed a good driver, and I was a good mechanic, too. When the truck broke down, I put it back together. There is no proper way to repair things. You just do whatever you can. The state does not frown on this kind of private enterprise because at least it keeps trucks and cars running. The logic, of course, is that if you own the truck, you are going to take care of it. You are going to repair it. If a screw falls out, you put a wire on, anything. Most of the cars are old, going back to 1958 and before, and they are still running. This benefits the state all the way around; it gives them a chance to control yet another part of your life. You can use the truck for work, and they need us to do so, but you can't use the truck for anything else. You can't take it for a vacation. You can't use it to go to the beach even. That is how they control you. Furthermore, gas is rationed and you have to report where you have been. It is all neatly arranged, with inspectors everywhere. If they find you where you are not supposed to be—a café, the beach—they fine you. And the fines are high 250–500 pesos and more. Well, they have a joke about all of these things. There is a conversation at a Communist Party meeting in

Cuba. One delegate says to another, "Comrade, how do you define capitalism?" The other fellow replies, "Capitalism is the exploitation of man by man." Then the first one asks, "And how do you define Communism?" And the second comrade answers, "It's the same thing, only in reverse."

Tattoo

I remember when I was a small child in kindergarten the instructors told us we were going to be Young Pioneers. They offered us a *pañuoleta* [neck scarf like that worn by U.S. Boy Scouts]. But I refused to be a Young Pioneer and wouldn't wear the *pañuoleta*.

Gabriel
Interviewed January 1978
Miami, Florida

Gabriel, a twenty-one-year-old with hazel eyes, fair skin tinged pink by the sun, and sparrow-brown hair freshly slicked down, seems a mere boy, slight and gentle. He speaks directly and matter-of-factly, without bitterness or histrionics. His room in a Miami boarding house is immaculate, giving a sense of orderliness and simple comfort in sharp contrast to what he is describing.

WAS born and raised in Caibarién, a fishing port on the northern coast of Santa Clara, and was only two years old when the Revolution came. One of my early memories is of children being urged to become Young Pioneers, but I was never interested in joining that group. Today, students automatically receive the *pañuoleta*, but when I was growing up, you were supposed to earn it by being a model child, by never missing a day at school. Frankly, the reason I attended classes regularly was that my mother insisted I go. Unfortunately, the time spent in school on mathematics and other studies was minimal. The majority of my class time went for learning Marxist theory and the way Communist governments function. Those who did not show interest in these political questions were sent to do compulsory military service.

We always found it hard to assimilate indoctrination. I can't really say why, but I think it depends on how you are raised. I always chose my own way of thinking, by listening to and observing many things, and I was lucky to have parents who never tried to change my ideas. In later years I was not "integrated" into the Revolution in any way. Of course I had to carry all the identification papers that everyone in Cuba has, but I had none for membership in revolutionary organizations.

After leaving school I worked in agriculture and was later imprisoned. In 1975 I planned to escape from Cuba with some friends by stealing a 20-foot boat with oars and a sail. We didn't get away that time because they caught us while we were getting the boat ready. They wanted to jail me for five years but gave me two instead in a concentration camp in Cienfuegos, Centro Especial #5, where we did construction work. There were 500–600 prisoners there, the majority of them young. Since this was a minimum-security camp, you had the freedom to move around, whereas in the maximum-security camps you stay in one place and work, for example, on prefabricated parts. The food was very bad, and sleeping conditions were poor too. You had a small folding canvas cot and one sheet. Since they mix the common and political prisoners, there were always problems, besides the constant conflicts with the guards. In my experience the ordinary convicts were usually low types who often tried to steal your belongings—behavior I did not find among the political prisoners.

Something that most people probably do not realize is that the young people in Cuba are lost—products of the system. When I say "lost" I mean that many of the youth are in jail. If a young prisoner didn't steal in order to eat, he robbed someone to get some clothes. People will break into houses to steal two or three pairs of pants or shirts, because they have nothing to wear. It is not for jewelry, but for food, clothing or shoes. I think the majority of young people in Cuba want to leave. I would say that 80 percent of the young are against Castro. They have no sense of youthfulness or hope, but they don't express this to anyone. They keep their feelings inside because of the terror that exists. The only explanation given about why we have so little food or other things is that we are an underdeveloped country. We are told that when a country is at this point we have to wait for a later stage when we can have what we need. I found, however, that the public did not want to re-establish relations with the United States because they believe that would only aid Castro economically so that he would be even more firmly in power. And it is uncertain how trade would help the people because Fidel warned that all we could expect from economic relations with the United States was to receive medicines.

In Cuba it is very difficult to study what you want. Not everyone can. If you want to go to the university, you need someone in the government to help you. If not, you have to be a member of the Jovenes Communistas. If you don't belong, you can't attend the university. Then, too, we did not have much incentive to work. Here in America, at least, I can choose where I work if I am qualified. In Cuba you must work where they tell you. They say, "Go work in construction." And if you say, "No, I want to wash dishes," they give you the choice of construction or prison. People often feel so angry about these things that in the larger towns they break public telephones or smash street lamps.

There are many people in jail now because Fidel issued a law against vagrancy. For instance, if you go to the Ministry of Labor [the governmental agency where people apply for jobs], what they offer you now is work in agriculture. Well, why should I work as a farmer growing all kinds of foods other Cubans and I never get to eat? But if you refuse to work, you go to jail for at least a year. There are also innumerable young people in prison because they don't want to go into military service, as many blacks as whites. I would have chosen jail rather than being in the army, and thousands of other Cubans feel the same way. They try to escape, get caught and are put in prison. Almost everyone in Cuba knows that a lot of Cubans have been killed in Angola. In many instances the dead bodies are not returned, or else they arrive in coffins and the relatives are told, "This is your son," "This is your husband," "This is your cousin." The young people know this and decide not to go. The soldiers they do send are often new recruits doing their obligatory military service. You might be taken into the army today and three months later they will send you to Angola.

Even the soldiers in Cuba aren't trusted. In the army each company is under one man, who is the only person allowed to have a gun. The others get them only if they are preparing for combat. At night on the base only the guards have guns. In case of a surprise attack, the others know where the guns are kept, but since the place is locked, they have to wait for the guns to be distributed. And in the street you no longer see soldiers with guns, except, in cases like mine, when they had me in handcuffs and were taking me to jail. Then one man had an order to carry a gun.

Something other people don't realize is that the way the system really works is different from how it appears. For example, the microbrigades that put up housing consist of people "integrated" into the Revolution. The whole thing is very competitive. If you want to buy a radio or a television set, or something else, you have to earn points for doing things like showing up for work every day, belonging to revolutionary organizations, or doing what is called voluntary work. In any town, the officials pick from each work center the few people who received the most credit for working. Then, after these people have finished eight or nine hours of regular work, they are incorporated into microbrigades, which also include people sent by the Ministry of Labor. The ones from the work centers put in as much voluntary work as they can, after their re- quired work, in order to accumulate points. They do so in the hope that in a week or a month, or perhaps longer, the government will send one radio, or one television set, etc., to their work center. There is just *one* item and everyone is given the right to ask to buy it. Everyone makes this request, but only the person with the most points can purchase it. In Cuba a Russian television set costs at least 750 pesos. The "winner" receives a ticket with which to buy the set. Depending on how much he makes, the work-center officials deduct a certain amount each month from his salary in payment for the TV or whatever he is buying. These products are not even very good; they're the cheap kind.

Something that makes Cubans particularly angry is the feeling that the Russians are the owners of our country. For them Cuba is a tourist camp. They have more privileges than we do. I am a Cuban and couldn't go wherever I wanted in my own country, but they can, and they may do whatever they want. For example, Cubans were not permitted to walk around in shorts, but the Russians can. The Cuban government provides special buildings

for the Russians, and they have no problems with food because
they are given good provisions.

As for entertainment for the young, there are block parties
arranged by local members of the party and the Young Communists.
These are held in the street or in a park until midnight, and there
is dancing and free beer. The music is mainly Cuban. Maybe you've
heard what happened when Fidel invited the popular Spanish
singer Julio Iglesias to Cuba. He refused to come, and so Fidel
forbade Cubans to play Iglesias' records. Movies are usually
Russian, East German, French or Japanese. The majority are
Russian and usually about war—the Russians against the Germans,
or the French against the Germans. I saw only three Cuban films.
Sometimes they show an old North American, Italian or Spanish
film, without announcing it in advance. Then the movie house fills
up. This happens just by chance. You never know when it will be
and you have to see many of the others before one of these comes
along. The books available are primarily political. If they sell a
book by a French author, for instance, it has been changed to favor
the Communist system, so you are not reading the book as it was
originally written.

Many of the older citizens in Cuba are also unhappy. Some are
confined against their will in asylums or subjected to strenuous work
because they are told they aren't producing anything for the Revolution. One of the concerns of older people is that they don't meet
with young people because the elderly are often treated like things
from the past.

TO TELL you now about my escape. After I had served one year
and eleven months in jail, I was approached by two friends who
had a plan they had been working on for three months. They needed
a third person to make the trip and I was lucky that they asked me.
They did so because they understood how I felt and why I behaved
as I did.

On two occasions I got into trouble with the guards. One day
when I was in the yard, they took me back to my cell. The problem
was that when you go to the eating area you have to be in line, and
I wasn't. The soldier threatened me with his bayonet and I told him
that I would fight back if he hit me. He struck me twice with his

bayonet, then sent me to a cell where I had to stay incommunicado. When you are in that one the food is even worse, and they give you less. Besides that, you have to sleep on the floor. At night they filled five-gallon cans with water mixed with kerosene and threw it on the floor. They did this every day before I went to sleep. When they saw the floor was dry, they poured in more water. When you live like that, you get sick. There is constant dampness, insects, rats all over, and crabs. There is no light coming in, just a little bulb they turn on whenever they want to, and water to drink when they open the faucet. In the cell there were eight of us and I stayed there seven days.

Another time, in 1976, the prisoners staged a *plante* [a protest], which I joined by removing my clothes—that means you are in disagreement with the plan—and insisting on being transferred to another prison. In response, the guards beat me badly. Then a few months later they offered me a transfer, provided I cleaned the prison. I told them I would not, that the only place I cleaned was where I slept and the bathroom I used! The guards asked me if I was in the rehabilitation plan and said that if I was, I would have to clean. I told them I was in the plan but that it did not require me to clean, and that if they wanted the prison cleaned, they would have to get someone whose job it was. The guards told me, "Well, you know what you have to do. Take off your clothes." I did as ordered and they took me to a place called "the tunnel." There, seven guards attacked me with bayonets and a stick inside a hose. I fought back until I couldn't anymore. At that point a tall guard kicked me in the testicles. Although I fell down and was too weak to defend myself, that made no difference to them; they kept hitting me even while I lay on the ground, dizzy and nauseated. Seven days later I still could not move around properly and had to walk with my legs apart. The skin on my back was peeling off from where they had beaten me. When they hit you with their bayonets, they use the side, but when you turn around to strike back, they stick you with the point. One of the guys who escaped with me has two scars from bayonet wounds, one on his arm, and one on his leg.

Finally on October 2, 1977, a Sunday, I was sleeping on my cot when a friend of mine came over to talk to me. He said to follow

him, that he had a *gofio* [drink made of flour and water]. I told
him no, that I wanted to go back to sleep. He insisted, telling me
that it would be good for me. I got up reluctantly and went with
him outside the *galeras*, where he and another fellow told me they
had an escape plan for that night, that they were going to Miami.
Their idea was to steal the truck belonging to the administrator of
the jail. It was the only one in the whole prison and could be used
only by the chief. I made my decision immediately, said O.K. and
started getting ready.

Fortunately one of the guys I escaped with worked as a welder
so he had all the tools we needed. As an excuse to leave the barracks
we showed the guards our cards and said we were going to help our
friend work. Once outside we were able to move around because
security wasn't very strict. Since I had a watch, we could keep
track of the time and calculate exactly when to carry out each step
of our plan. At seven o'clock that night we began fixing the truck,
which had a broken generator. We were able to work like this
without attracting attention because we were behind the barracks
and no cars were passing. While the director was on duty and
waiting for someone else to do the repair, we took the opportunity
to do it for him!

The first thing we did was walk to another car from which we
quietly removed the generator. As my friends were installing it in
the truck, my job was sawing off the lock on the main door of the
gate. I had to work fast but carefully so that no sound of metal
echoed in the night. The only guards around could not see me because they were fifty feet away on either side and the place where
I was doing the cutting was hidden by darkness. As prisoners we
were wearing the standard light-gray clothes of a very bad quality
material. *Es un fenomeno!* You wash them twice and they disinte-
grate!

By ten of nine I had the lock cut. I stayed at the gate while the
other two got in the truck. When they drove up I opened the gate,
let them leave, then got inside. We passed under the sentry post
knowing they would not shoot because the only person who drove
the truck was the warden and the guards did not know he was not
inside. At nine sharp we were out.

After we had been driving for a while we heard a clanking sound and in one of the small towns along the way the truck broke down. We discovered the generator was loose and we had to tighten it, so we pulled over to the side of the road. We crouched down in the dark trying to get the generator back in place. Just then a jeep from the revolutionary police slowed down.

We managed to stay calm when one of the men called out, "What's wrong, *compañero*?" My friend just waved back, saying, "No problem, *compañero*, everything's O.K." Fortunately, they didn't notice anything strange and drove away. We didn't finish fixing the truck but went on to the next town, where we finally repaired it. We reached Santa Clara and picked up two girls on the road who were hitchhiking to the university. We took them there and drove on.

By about one o'clock in the morning we arrived at the place we were going to leave from. We drove the truck into the bushes along the beach and walked down to the pier where the fishing boats were anchored and hid inside one. We chose a boat about sixty-four feet long that was all ready to leave the following morning. The reason we knew about the boats was that two of us were familiar with that town. We did not have to worry about being seen because at that hour no one was watching the boats. The only time they automatically check them is in the morning before the boats put out to sea. We stayed in a special hiding place in the boat, which after a while began to get very hot. I don't want to say exactly where, in case others can use the same means of escape.

At six o'clock the fishermen boarded, older men who were very strong from their years at sea. They checked the oil, started the motor, then went to the fishing cooperative to get bait. After they got that and the ice, they drove the boat to the guardhouse, where the soldiers checked it before we left. It was impossible for them to find us because of where we had chosen to hide, but twelve hours later we were almost fainting from the heat. Finally we came out and climbed quietly to the top deck where the fishermen were all together. Carrying an iron rod, we took them by surprise and said, "Hold up your hands. If not, we're going to kill you." They said, "No, no, don't kill us. We're not going to do anything. We'll take you any place you want." We told them, "No, we don't want any help at all." Then we forced them into one of the compartments and locked them inside. Two of us took turns guarding the door while the third one was at the wheel steering the boat. Although we had experience being at sea we still got lost.

At about ten the next evening we saw a key and moored there. We did not get out but just stayed several hours resting on the boat, which floated calmly. After we felt more rested we pulled up anchor and continued on our way. At two in the afternoon, one of my friends said we should return to the key because we had been traveling around for a long time without finding another one. All we saw was sea and sky and no other boats. I said we should go straight to the north until we ran out of gas, but the others insisted on going back to the key and I gave in. We started searching for it but found another one that I think we had passed during the night without being able to see it. We circled the key looking for a place to stop because the weather was getting bad. The sky was gray now and the sea was choppy. All the while we were watching to see if any boats passed. We waited just fifteen minutes and saw a ship. With a white shirt we started signalling it. The boat approached closer and stopped about 500 feet away. We put down one of our lifeboats and rowed toward the ship, which was an American fishing boat. It had an American flag, but the crew was Cuban. When we asked to go to the United States they took us on board. The place where we were was Key Damas. The fishing boat we escaped on went back to Cuba. When the boat picked us up the crew radioed the U.S. Coast Guard. Following their orders they took us to Key Perro, where we were told to wait until the next day, when the Coast Guard arrived and brought us to Key West.

MY PLAN now is to go to school until I reach a certain level and can then decide what occupation I would like. Before you go I will show you what some of us did in prison. A friend in jail tattooed this eagle on my back and other ones for me. Not all the prisoners have tattoos, only a few of us, who wore them as a form of protest. We did it to bother the guards because we knew they didn't like them. I knew I would have a fight with the guards about the tattoos and took off my shirt on purpose to show them. At the time I was surrounded by other political prisoners. The guards realized that if they hit me, they would have to hit the others, too, because the political prisoners were united. So when the guards saw my tattoos, they called me into the office. They could not do anything, though, because it was too late. All they could say to me was that since my tattoos were not done perfectly, I should not walk around without my shirt! When they said that, I answered that I do anything I want with my body and that if I had a tattoo of the eagle, it was to show what I was feeling. I said that I could just as easily have had one of the Cuban flag, because it is my flag and Cuba is my country.

Appendix

AT THE beginning of the Revolution most of the Cubans who emigrated to the United States had been associated with Batista's regime, were members of the upper class, and came from Havana and other major cities. In the following years, however, the exiles leaving by legitimate means have been, like the escapees, from all economic levels, from various occupations—not just professionals—and from the different provinces in Cuba.[1]

Over the years, the general exodus of Cubans to the United States has been marked by different patterns. An important wave of emigration, beginning in 1960, consisted of 13,000–15,000 unaccompanied children sent by their parents to be educated in the United States. *Operación Pedro Pan*, as it was later named, was arranged by Monsignor Bryan O. Walsh, Executive Director of the Catholic Welfare, with the participation of other voluntary agencies (the Cuban Refugee Program; the Children's Service Bureau of Dade County, Inc.; the Jewish Family and Children's Services, Inc.; and the United Hebrew Immigration Aid Society in New York). Cuban children ranging in age from six to eighteen years were provided with food, clothing, medical care, public schooling and foster homes until the majority were reunited with their families who came to the United States. These children were from all classes but for the most part belonged to well-to-do families. Most were in their early teens, and nearly two-thirds were boys. About 90 percent were Catholic, and the others Protestant and Jewish.

In 1961 President Kennedy assigned emergency funds from the Assistance Act to foreign countries, creating the Cuban Refugee Program, and in June 1962, Congress approved the measure.[2] The first phase of departures occurred from February 1961 to October 1962. There were regular flights between Havana and Miami, although Cuba and the United States had severed relations. During this period 153,534 Cubans registered at the Refugee Center.

The second stage began after the Missile Crisis of October 1962, when regular flights were canceled. From that time until December 1965, some 29,962 Cuban refugees were registered in the United States.

A surprise announcement by Castro initiated the third phase of the exodus—the family-reunion period. In a speech on September 28, 1965, Castro declared that all who wished to leave would be allowed to do so, beginning October 10. Exiles in the United States would be permitted to come by boat to pick up relatives. President Johnson accepted this proposal, and negotiations between the United States and Cuba began through the Swiss Embassy in Havana.

In the meantime, the Cuban fishing port of Camarioca, on the north coast of Matanzas, was opened for the possible incoming exiles, who were suspicious at first of Castro's offer. But when a few returned safely with their relatives, a huge flow of boats of all kinds headed toward Cuba. U.S. Coast Guard reports note that the first boats to leave were seaworthy, reasonably well equipped and manned by experienced boatmen, but as time went on, Cubans used almost anything that floated. The refugees included women, the very young and the elderly.

The U.S. Coast Guard's search and rescue operations to abet the trips of refugees from Cuba were based on a warning that traveling to Camarioca would be in violation of U.S. law, that the use of small boats was hazardous, and that the disorderly exit of a few could jeopardize negotiations for an organized exodus by air or ship for the others who wanted to leave. Despite these admonitions, the Coast Guard Patrol Force (consisting of thirty-foot and forty-foot utility boats at Base Miami, Base Key West, and stations at Islamorada and Marathon, and cutters in the Florida Straits off the Cay Sal Banks, aided by a helicopter) was overwhelmed by the middle of the first week. The northbound boats were constantly overcrowded. Usually the operators had no experience at sea and as a result numerous boats broke down, got lost or ran out of fuel.

The Coast Guard's initial opposition turned, in time, to cooperation and assistance for the returning boats, which carried a total of 2,979 persons to the United States. Meanwhile the attitude of the Cuban government changed. At the beginning, living quarters, provided with playgrounds for children, had been constructed at Camarioca for the emigrants. The early arrivals from Florida received special food, help in repairing their boats and fuel to return. By the end of what came to be called "The Freedom Shuttle," refugees claimed that departing boats were given low-octane Cuban gas, which they suspected was watered, thereby causing engine trouble to many. Interviews with émigrés revealed that upon the arrival of relatives from the United States, those who had asked to leave Cuba were immediately transferred to the compound at Camarioca, their property impounded by the government. There were reports that thousands of Cubans had tried to get in to the compound, many having been forced from their homes before their relatives arrived. Eventually, more than 200,000 Cubans signed agreements to emigrate. By November 15 no more boats were allowed to leave Cuba with passengers. The remaining 2,104 Cubans in the exit compound were transported to the United States on chartered boats.[3]

One concern of the U.S. government and Coast Guard had been for a more orderly, safe means of egress. Negotiations between Cuba and the United States finally culminated in a "Memorandum of Understanding" that outlined the process to reunite Cuban families in the United States by an airlift, beginning December 1, 1965. It excluded persons in critical occupations, men fifteen to twenty-six years old, since they were subject to military service, women with dependent children of school age, and political prisoners, whose release President Johnson had requested. In August 1971, the twice-daily flights that had been in progress five times a week were interrupted and sporadically resumed through April 6, 1973. In the final days, those allowed to leave were primarily the elderly. The airlift brought 260,561 Cubans to the United States on 3,049 flights. During this phase an additional 7,479 Cubans arrived in the United States by other means. When interviewed, emigrants explained that those who applied to leave were fired from their jobs and were identified as enemies of the state, subject to harassment by the CDRs. Prospective refugees were required to work in agriculture for several years and were interned in camps that were often far from their homes. Their salaries were substantially lower than the prevailing wages for agricultural workers, and their household property was confiscated at the time of their departure.

After the termination of what came to be known as the Varadero Airlift, the fourth stage began, in April 1973, and lasted until September 1978. The arrivals were mainly escapees coming on boats and rafts or Cubans leaving via third countries, principally Mexico, Spain and Jamaica. During this period 17,899 Cubans were registered with the Cuban Refugee Program. From 1975 to 1978 the number of escapees dwindled to 106. The reasons for the decline were increased surveillance and the difficulty of finding materials for fashioning any kind of escape vehicle. Those who came were primarily pairs and groups of three to five young men who managed to make rafts or stow away on commercial ships. These escapees also included a number of lifeguards who stole rental boats. More concerned about avoiding the heavy coastal patrolling than risking the sea, several of them deliberately left during storms because vigilance is less strict then. The main explanations they gave for fleeing were objection to indoctrination, unwillingness to fight in Africa, and a feeling of having few prospects for the future. Others, who had been imprisoned for previous escape attempts, said they fled because they did not trust the government's promise that families were soon going to be reunited.

ESCAPEES REGISTERED BY CUBAN REFUGEE PROGRAM						
Small-boat arrivals, June 30, 1961–December 31, 1979						11,826
Small-boat and other arrivals	*1975*	*1976*	*1977*	*1978*	*1979*	
Boat	0	12	33	19	374	
Stowaways	2	3	1	2	8	
Defectors	1	2	3	0	4	
Border Crossing	0	0	5	11	105	
Totals	3	17	42	32	491	585

The fifth phase of the general emigration from Cuba was signaled in a speech by Castro on September 6, 1978, when he announced his intention of releasing political prisoners and their families. Under the program, called Operation Cuban Reunification, 2,728 ex-prisoners and 4,421 of their relatives, a total of 7,186 Cubans, were brought to the United States between October 21, 1978, and January 18, 1980. Another 626 came as regular immigrants.[4] During 1979 there was an upsurge in the number of escapees, which totaled 491. Apart from the lapsing in 1976 of the U.S.-Cuban treaty requiring the return of hijackers, and the usual reasons of lack of freedom and increasing economic deprivation, the majority of these Cubans—which included large families and groups of ten and more[5]—mentioned the impact of the visiting Cuban exiles. They countered government propaganda that escapees would be returned to Cuba and that in the United States, Cubans were victims of extreme prejudice and poverty.

CUBAN REFUGEE PROGRAM, FEBRUARY 1961–DECEMBER 31, 1979		
Phase I	February 1961 to Missile Crisis of October 1962 (Commercial flights from Havana)	153,534
Phase II	Missile Crisis to December 1, 1965 (no direct transportation)	29,962
Phase III	Family Reunion (or U.S. Airlift) and other arrivals, December 1, 1965 to April 6, 1973	268,040
Phase IV	Third Country Arrivals and others, April, 1973 to September, 1978	17,899
Phase V	Ex-Political Prisoners and Families and other arrivals, October, 1978 to December 31, 1979	9,447
	Ex-Prisoners and Families, January 4–January 18, 1980	481
Phase VI	Peruvian Embassy & Freedom Flotilla	
		479,363
	Estimated number of arrivals, from February 1961 to July 31, 1979, who did not register in Miami, either because they arrived prior to February 1961, and had moved on, or because they arrived from Spain and did not go to Miami, or for other reasons did not register in Miami.	125,000
	Total	604,363[7]

Since the Revolution the number of immigrants to Cuba has been negligible. As a result of Cuban involvement in other countries, however, reports in 1979 stated that Africans have been forcibly transported to Cuba. More than 1,000 young Congolese, 600 of them between the ages of ten and fifteen, are reputed to have been sent from Brazzaville to Havana without the permission of their parents for training expected to last fifteen years.[6] According to other sources, nearly 4,000 young Angolans from the central areas have been sent to Cuba to be indoctrinated and to work in the sugar-cane fields. During the Cuban offensive, approximately 2,000 more Angolan boys, twelve to fifteen years old, were arrested. On August 3, 1979, Radio Havana announced that they were being brought to Cuba for political education. Another broadcast by Radio Havana, on November 13, 1979, stated that about 30,000 Cuban, African and Nicaraguan youths are studying in fifty rural schools on the Isle of Youth (formerly the Isle of Pines).

NOTES

[1] U.S. Department of Immigration, *Annual Report*, U.S. Government Printing Office, Washington, D.C., 1959 through 1977. The statistics given in these reports show that by 1968, professional and technical workers are outnumbered collectively both by members of all the other occupational groups of the Cuban émigrés and by those of particular occupational groups. In that year, for example, the total number of Cuban immigrants is given as 99,132. Of these, 5,523 were professional and technical workers; 108 were farmers and farm managers; 3,314 were managers, officials and proprietors; 7,409 were clerical and kindred workers; 2,292 were sales people; 5,113 were craftsmen, foremen and kindred workers; 12,998 were operatives and kindred workers; 613 were private-household workers; 3,979 were service workers (except private household); 103 were farm laborers and foremen; 3,847 were laborers (except farm and mine); and 54,013 were housewives and children with no occupation or occupation unreported. In the reports issued for the ensuing years this pattern remains consistent. Clerical and kindred workers; craftsmen and kindred workers; operatives and kindred workers; laborers (except farm and mine); service workers (except private household); and housewives and children with no occupation or occupation unreported are the categories that individually began to number substantially more than professionals and technical workers.

[2] From 1961 until fiscal year 1978 the funds for operating the Cuban Refugee Program amounted to $1.3 billion.

[3] See: H. R. Kaplan, "The Coast Guard and the Cuban Exodus," Public Information Division, U.S. Coast Guard (November 5, 1965); Captain William F. Gass, "Cuban Exodus," U.S. Naval Institute Proceedings (June 1966); L.C.D.R. J. A. McDonough, Jr., U.S. Coast Guard, "The Cuban Exodus, Fall 1965," Philadelphia Navy Yard (August 3, 1967).

[4] U.S. State Department Office of Refugees.

[5] Of note is the group of sixty-five Cubans who hijacked a hundred-foot dredging barge that left from the port city of Cardenas and arrived in Islamorada in the Florida Keys on February 2, 1980.

[6] "The children were selected on the basis of tests given in schools. The most gifted were told that they were to have a trip to a 'vacation camp' as a reward for their performance." Flora Lewis, "Congo Children Reportedly Sent Forcibly to Cuba." *New York Times* (October 30, 1979).

[7] Information provided by the International Rescue Committee, New York, N.Y. In November 1971 the figure given by the U.S. Coast Guard was half a million

Cuban refugees, constituting one seventh of Cuba's population, which was then 8.1 million. According to other sources, the total number of Cuban immigrants to the United States ranges from 600,000 to 750,000. The U.S. Social and Rehabilitation Service estimated that in the 1970s there were an additional 200,000 Cuban refugees outside the United States. The Cuban Affairs Section of the U.S. State Department sets the total number of Cubans who have left since 1959 at between 800,000 and 1,000,000.

ABOUT THE AUTHORS

Lorrin Philipson is a writer living in New York. She has worked for Amnesty International and the International Rescue Committee and has taught English at the Shipley School in Bryn Mawr, Pennsylvania, and at the Dalton School in Manhattan.

Born in 1941 in Cuba, Rafael Llerena is a professional photographer, who emigrated to the United States in 1961. In 1971 he helped found the Cuban Cultural Center in New York.